ORIE

Also by Pallavi Aiyar

ORIENTING

AN INDIAN IN JAPAN

PALLAVI AIYAR

HarperCollins *Publishers* India

First published by HarperCollins *Publishers* in 2021
A-75, Sector 57, Noida, Uttar Pradesh 201301, India
www.harpercollins.co.in

2 4 6 8 10 9 7 5 3 1

P-ISBN: 978-93-5422-764-6
E-ISBN: 978-93-5422-787-5

Typeset in 11/15 Linux Libertine at
Manipal Technologies Limited, Manipal

Printed and bound at
Replika Press Pvt. Ltd.

To Jean-Pierre Lehmann

Contents

Prologue

We landed in Tokyo into the thin early-morning light on an overnight flight from Jakarta. I'd never been to Japan before. A car from my husband Julio's office – the European Union Delegation in Tokyo – picked us up from the airport and drove us over suspension bridges and through densely packed streets, alongside the blur of bullet trains. Nothing felt substantial, but I recognized this feeling from my many first days in many different countries. There was a familiarity to the spongy, dreamlike dislocation, as though you could poke a finger into the air and feel it stretch like latex.

I'd spent over two decades rehearsing these emotions. Since meeting Julio in 2000, I'd lived with him in the UK, China, Belgium and Indonesia. We were practised peripatetics, but when it came to moving countries, practice rarely made perfect. What we did know was that we'd soon learn just how ignorant we were, anew.

Julio was a diplomat and I was a writer. Over the years we'd expanded our family to include two cats, Caramel and Tofu, and two boys, Ishaan and Nicolas. Between Julio and me we spoke five languages and could mangle a couple of others. Personally, I fancied myself to be somewhat of an Asianist. I had grown up in India, experiencing first-hand the early wave of economic liberalization in the 1990s. I'd gone on to live in China for most of the first decade of the new millennium, witnessing the rise of an Olympics-worthy Beijing from the razed remains of its communist past. Since 2012, I'd lived in Indonesia, where I'd written about the challenges of creating a national tapestry out of a plurality of fractured identities, a feat many former colonies, including India, had grappled with.

But when I learned in early 2016 that Julio's new posting would be taking us to Tokyo that summer, I confronted the fact that I'd been missing a critical piece of the Asian jigsaw puzzle, for there was very little of use that I knew about Japan.

I was familiar with the troughs and crests of the political topography of the region, from its democracies to its autocracies, but what all the disparate Asian countries I'd known thus far had in common was an upward thrust of people and commerce. Delhi, Beijing and Jakarta were noisy, chaotic, dynamic megalopoleis, heaving with their own contradictory promises. Their trajectories were rising; their stories suggested the promise of spring, albeit a polluted one, rather than the melancholy of autumn.

Japan was an anomaly; it's geographic location on the eastern edge of the map served as a metaphor for its seeming separateness from the rest of Asia. It was rich and quiet, old and punctual, a former colonizer rather than colony, rule-obsessed rather than loophole-hungry.

In many ways it was more inscrutable and less familiar than China had been to me before I moved there. In China, there had at least been the fried noodles and chilly chicken beloved to Indians. But encountering raw fish for breakfast was not an appetizing, or even particularly intelligible, moment for an Indian.

I only had an imprecise sense of the Japanese rampaging across the continent with bayonets and Walkmans. There were the snatches of pop songs Japan conjured up. 'Big in Japan', and also Simon and Garfunkel's 'Kodachrome' – 'I have a Nikon camera, I want to take a photograph'; The Bangles' 'Walk Like an Egyptian' – 'All the Japanese with their yen, the party boys call the Kremlin'. Someone once told me that it was possible to buy the used underwear of young women from vending machines in Tokyo. I had read a lot of Haruki Murakami, but that had hardly helped to clarify much. This was pretty much the entirety of my Japan-oriented cultural capital when Julio had announced that we'd be moving to Tokyo in the summer of 2016.

I'd reached out to the hive mind on social media for recommendations on reading and was inundated with replies like, 'Tanazaki, of course,' and 'Soseki, but Kokoro first.' I compiled a list of books and bought several of them, but dealing with the administrative minutiae of winding down life in Jakarta didn't leave me the time to actually read any of them.

I did, however, begin taking Japanese lessons. I'd learned to speak Chinese quite well, and passable Indonesian too. How hard could Japanese be, I thought? The answer, it was quickly evident, was 'very'. There seemed to be an inordinate number of long words I had to learn that didn't have any specific meaning beyond signifying politeness.

In Chinese, 'thanks' was '*xie xie*', end of matter. In Japanese, there was '*arigatou*' – informal, '*arigatou gosaimasu*' – proper form, '*domo arigatou gosaimasu*' – seriously thankful, and '*domo sumimasen arigatou gosaimasu*,' – weak-in-the-knees-with-gratitude-thankful. Then I came across, '*yoroshiku onegaishimasu*'. 'What does that mean?' I asked my teacher. 'It means, thank you,' she replied. Basically, it was possible to learn Japanese for a month and only end up being able to say thank you.

I ranted about the fussiness of Japanese grammar over lunch with Koyama-san, the Jakarta-based Japanese mother of a friend of my older son. 'Not sure how I'm ever going to manage to learn all those conjugations,' I groaned. Koyama-san looked at me unblinkingly and replied, 'I think Pallavi, for you the bigger problem is going to be to learn how to talk softly.'

I was going to have plenty of opportunities to learn the painful truth of her words in the coming years.

1

Lost and Found

Every move has its particular set of challenges that have as much to do with the country being moved to, as with the person moving. Is the movee single or en famille? Linguistically polyamorous or committedly monolingual? In a good mood or resentful? Is the country in question polluted? Cold? Home to competent dentists?

Somewhere at the intersection of the answers to these questions, the initial response to each new 'home' springs forth. In London, as a student, I had found the light-deprivation of the long winter to be the hardest adjustment. In Los Angeles, I'd struggled with the lack of public transport, while in Beijing my terrible Chinese had me constantly ordering soup (pronounced '*tang*') when I wanted sugar (also pronounced '*tang*' but in a different tone). Jakarta's epic traffic jams had never ceased to be frustrating, and the size of the city's sewer rats gave me constant cause for pause.

What of Tokyo? In Japan, the first big and rather unexpected challenge I encountered was getting a mobile phone. Being phoneless is to feel adrift in a torturous limbo of missed calls and Facebook likes that one remains un-notified of. Never before had Descartes been in greater need of an update than in the twenty-first century. Over the last two decades, between first Nokia and then Apple, *cogito ergo sum* had surely been pushed aside by *habeo a phone, ergo sum*. But if 'I have a phone, therefore I am' were true, what of the phoneless?

Clearly, I needed a mobile before I could process any kinds of thoughts about Japan, but this did not prove easy, or cheap. I discovered that there was an oligopoly of services that forced you into buying both a phone instrument and a two-year-minimum contract that cost a base amount of about 70 USD a month (I came from India, a country with a 0.02 USD mobile data plan, the cheapest in the world[1]).

It was almost ten days before I finally found a service offering a more affordable, less constrictive plan, but they needed a driving license as a non-negotiable perquisite. I didn't drive.

And getting a mobile proved to be a stroll through a Japanese ornamental garden compared with opening a bank account. We were instructed by Julio's office to open an account with Prestia, part of Sumitomo Mitsui Banking Corporation, since they offered an English-language service and specialized in servicing 'foreigners'. The process took about three hours, a length of time for which there seemed no decipherable reason. We endured a lot of sitting in front of an official while he clucked, stared at documents we had filled out, including a pledge that we were not members of any 'anti-social force', an allusion to the *yakuza*, the Japanese mafia. Occasionally, we were moved outside the office to a waiting room.

At one point we inquired about the possibility of getting a credit card, figuring that we might as well optimize the opportunity cost of the time spent at the bank that day. 'I do not recommend getting a credit card with us,' answered the stilettoed lady who answered our query. 'It will be very difficult for you to manage. Better to get foreign one.' When put like that, who could argue?

Finally, just as the bank-account light at the end of the form-filling tunnel was dangling into view, we were informed that joint accounts did not exist in Japan. Ergo: after all this we had only managed to open a single bank account for my husband. They offered to restart the process for a separate account for me, which I declined, saying I would come back another day. In the event, I never returned. The prospect of repeating those three hours was about as appetizing as eating very stale sushi, making Japan the only country in the world I have ever lived in without opening a bank account.

It was startling to find that the hardest parts of starting a new life in Japan had been amongst the easiest in others, including Indonesia, the developing country that we had moved from. Jakarta was a heaving, traffic-clogged, open sewer-lined conurbation, but it had also been dynamic and technologically innovative. New apps had sprouted from its loamy start-up soil almost daily, allowing for everything from ride-hailing motor bike services to mobile payments.

Japan by contrast felt dated, as if it still existed in the pop hits of the 1980s. My admittedly uninformed preconceptions of the country had been imbued with cutting-edge cool: neon, robots, fast trains, consoles. But while the Japan I encountered in 2016 certainly had its share of neon, it was anachronistic in many other ways.

In neighbouring China, even beggars had begun accepting e-payments,[2] but in Japan I regularly found myself dining at restaurants only to discover that they didn't accept credit cards. Waiters were often dressed in full livery, coat tails and all, but when confronted with a malfunctioning card payment terminal (in the instances these were available), they gawped and gasped as though beholding complex satellite machinery. Taxi drivers wore white gloves and thanked passengers for their custom with the finest rhetorical flourishes, but the Japan Taxi app remained the world's most byzantine and least economical.

The country came across like an upper-class spinster from a historical novel with impeccable manners who spent her days dabbing the edges of her mouth with a linen napkin while internally tutting at the uncouth dining etiquette of today's upstarts, id est: the Chinese.

There were few ills that the Japanese did not ascribe to the Chinese: pollution in the oceans, talking loudly, eating ice-cream while walking, dumping plastic in the paper recycling bins. In short, the Chinese were lacking in good manners, which was a very serious accusation in Japan.

Over the four years I lived in Tokyo, I was handed 'manner guides' to everything, from how to view cherry blossoms to how to prepare oneself before taking a dip in a hot spring. Posters in the metro sternly queried readers, 'How are your manners?' The consensus was that those of the Chinese were not up to scratch.

(All I could think was that the Japanese were obviously underexposed to Indians.[3] It was sort of sweet, their innocence of dirt and the depths to which lack of civic consciousness could plunge: think empty packets of potato chips thrown out of car windows as a means of garbage disposal, men urinating right *outside* public toilets, temples blasting religious music on loudspeakers in residential neighbourhoods *all night.*)

But although people here tended to become un-Japanishly animated were the topic at hand the bad behaviour of Chinese tourists, they displayed an odd reticence in discussing more substantive issues related to that country's rise. When I told people I'd lived in Beijing for seven years, the likeliest response was a blank stare, or at most a soft sigh suggesting commiseration.

In every other country I'd been to, people couldn't ask me enough about China. Was its economic growth sustainable? Did the Chinese really eat dogs? What were the implications of Beijing's investments in Africa? But the average Japanese seemed more interested in India – yoga, Bollywood, sarees, curry – and even Belgium – waffles, chocolate, the Eurostar – than the rising star in the international firmament, China.

And yet, few countries were as intertwined as China and Japan. They traded in the hundreds of billions of US dollars. They had a tense maritime border dispute. They were strategic rivals and geographic neighbours.

Shin Kawajima, a professor of Chinese Studies at Tokyo University, someone I had occasion to interview several times as I followed the ups and downs of the Sino-Japanese relationship, said the Japanese attitude to China was split along demographic lines. Millennials who had grown up with a powerful China as fact were more positively disposed towards their giant neighbour. For others, China's growth could be an awkward reminder of Japan's stagnation. Those who recalled a time when Japan was soaking in a bubble bath of yen while China struggled as an agricultural backwater, often felt unmoored by the new normal of a rich, ascendant China, capable of dictating geostrategic terms. Rather than face up to this discomfort, they tended to resort, ostrich-like, to what was often the Japanese default to disagreeable situations: ignore and carry on.

But this explanation did not cover what – to anyone who knew both Japan and China – was as hard to miss as the Great Wall of China itself: Japan was a culture profoundly indebted to China. Its language, religion, aesthetics, architecture, literature and many of its social norms could be traced back across the Sea of Japan to the Chinese mainland. Japan had certainly adapted, honed and elaborated different aspects of all that it had received from China, but the bedrock of its culture remained Chinese.

These musings lay in the future, being too coherent for anyone in the throes of adjusting to life in a new country. A selection of observations I posted on Facebook in 2016 from that period tracks better the somewhat random process of making sense of the kaleidoscopic impressions, serendipitous conversations and purposeful reading – which constitute the recipe for finding one's bearings in a new land.

August 28:

> Four different Japanese onomatopoeia to describe rainfall.
>
> When the rain falls 'shito shito', it's constant and enveloping.
>
> When it rains 'zaa-zaa', it's a sudden downpour, typhoon-strong.
>
> At the very outset of a shower, it rains 'potsu-potsu': a few early drops and a darkening sky. At this stage it can also be 'para para', a bit random as though someone were spraying occasional moisture on plants out of a watering can.

(This post was written three days after we'd arrived to very rainy weather.)

August 30:

> OK, so more fascinating discoveries. This one thanks to Yujiro Hashi. There was a time when the Japanese equivalent for 'the whole world' was 'the three

countries.' So, instead of saying 'You are the most beautiful person in the whole world,' they would have said, 'You are the most beautiful person in the three countries,' although the import would be the same. The fascinating part is that the three countries referred to are Japan itself, China and India. That was the whole world according to the Japanese mental map of the time. The phrase (now antiquated) is: san goku ichi no xxx, i.e. 'the best xxx in the three countries (whole world). San goku ichi no hana-yom or the most beautiful bride in the world, is an expression still used at weddings.[4]

September 2

A photograph of a sign at the Omotosendo metro station in Tokyo that read: '*Please yield to each other when passing through here,*' with the comment: *A formula for world peace.*

September 14

A photograph of an item on the menu at a French restaurant advertising: '*Salad (Backet+drink) 1,500 Yen,*' with the comment: *It took me a while to figure out the 'backet'* (baguette).

September 19

Late night haiku reading:
Late autumn –

A single chair waiting
For someone yet to come.
Arima Akito

September 21

A photograph of a bottle of air freshener I had just purchased with the comment: *Google translate app is translating this room freshener as having a 'mist of refreshing Nazi' smell. Surely not!*

September 25

> Neighborhoods in Japan have public centres for kids to play in. Crafts activities, library, sports and music facilities. All free. We just signed up at ours, right behind our apartment.

I knew from past experience that there would be an approximately six-month window in Japan when I would *see* everything. On the subway, I'd actually read all the text on posters and advertisements. I'd eavesdrop on conversations, sometimes just for the inflections if I couldn't decipher the words. I'd notice body language, how someone held a hand over their mouth before laughing, how they slurped on noodles or used pickled ginger to brush soy sauce onto their sushi. I'd look at manhole covers.

But being a mom to young (five and eight at the time), rambunctious boys left me battling for slivers of time to achieve anything substantial other than unpack boxes and make the school run. I fulminated about the lack of a school bus as I ferried the children back and forth. On inquiring about why our expensive international school didn't provide a bus service, I'd received a reply stating, 'Most of our pupils walk, bicycle or take public transport.'

On only my second day in Tokyo, I had seen a little kid of about six, heaving a school bag that was nearly as big as himself, wandering alone down a busy Tokyo road. Naturally, I'd run after him to offer help, imagining that the boy had somehow lost his parents. But before I could catch up, he'd pulled out a metro pass from his pocket and disappeared with cheery unconcern into the bowels of one of the capital's busiest subway stations.

Still, it took me months to become inured to the sight – unthinkable in every other big city that I'd lived in (New

Delhi, London, Los Angeles, Beijing and Jakarta) – of elementary school children, sometimes in groups, but often singly, hopping onto buses, changing trains in subway stations and walking along thoroughfares on their way to, or from, school. In Japan, this was as unremarkable as, well, clean public toilets.

I posted a picture on Facebook of a cherubic schoolgirl, barely waist-high, waiting for a metro by herself. Within hours I was inundated by messages from friends who were both amazed and envious. 'In Delhi, even my thirteen-year-old is walked to the bus stop about seven minutes away,' someone commented. 'We don't let our six-year-old go out to the park without a posse of "guards",' another friend wrote, to which yet another added, 'Actually we don't even send them to the park anymore. Sad and so unfair when you see how life should be lived.'

I discovered Japanese children begin travelling to school by themselves from grade one of primary school, when they are about six years old. Those who attend public schools in the neighbourhood they live in walk to school. Those enrolled in private schools – often located in distant parts of the city – take the metro or bus, or a combination of the two.

The training for this journey begins when children are in kindergarten. They are encouraged to observe their older siblings going about on their own. Parents show them how to safely cross roads and point out places where they could go for help if they were ever in trouble. The 'safe spot' of choice is the convenience store, or *konbini*, as the term is abbreviated in Japan.

More than 55,000 7-Elevens, Family Marts and other *konbinis* punctuated Japan, with the frequency of commas in a run-on sentence.[5] Any lost or distressed child could ask to use the phone at one of these stores and wait there until her parents arrived to collect her.

Japan regularly came out on top of the list of the world's safest countries.[6] According to its National Police Agency, in 2016, the number of crimes reported hit the lowest level since the end of the Second World War. Despite having a substantial population of about 127 million, only 950 murders and 1,511 cases of robbery were reported in 2019.[7]

In addition, public infrastructure was excellent. Trains were regular and preternaturally on time, with railway companies publicly flagellating themselves for – wait for this – their trains departing a few seconds early. (In November 2017, the media was filled with stories about an express line between Tokyo and the city of Tsukuba that departed twenty seconds early, at 9:44:20 a.m. instead of 9:44:40 a.m. The line's management issued a 'sincere' apology 'confessing' that the crew had not 'sufficiently checked the departure time and performed the departure operation'.[8])

But perhaps the most crucial ingredient in the recipe that allowed Japanese children such independence was an accepted reliance on community, more reminiscent of a village than of big-city culture. While researching a story on the subject, I came across an article in the *Atlantic* magazine that quoted Dwayne Dixon, a cultural anthropologist, as saying, '[Japanese] kids learn early on that, ideally, any member of the community can be called on to serve or help others.'[9]

Schools also distributed a special yellow patch that first graders wore on their uniforms, identifying them as newbies to the art of navigating in the city. Adults kept a special eye out for these patch-wearers. Retirees sometimes volunteered to usher children across roads safely as they walked to school. Households could also volunteer to display signs outside their homes indicating their willingness, *konbini*-like, to provide refuge to any child in need.

After a few weeks of witnessing the practised navigational skills of kids younger than him, my older son began clamouring to be allowed to travel to school alone. I was reluctant; he didn't speak any Japanese at the time. Two years into our stay, however, I relented. By the time my son turned ten I not only allowed him to travel back home unaccompanied on public transport, I also had him chaperone his younger, seven-year-old brother. If this scenario had been described to me when I still lived in Indonesia, I'd have thought it likelier for my children to sprout wings and fly home rather than travel alone in a city of 30 million. Life in Japan was often like that: stranger than fiction.

The worst, albeit fairly frequent, mishap to befall the boys on their solo bus journeys home was a left-behind lunchbox. In any other country this would have implied a steady stream of cash flowing from the parental wallet to a replacement-lunchbox retailer. But Japan was the country where What is Lost was Always Found.

Every time a lunchbox was left on the bus, I would get a phone call from the bus company's lost-and-found office where someone would explain to me that I needed to collect the lost item from their office at my convenience. (I'd had the foresight to scribble my number onto a label affixed to the inside of the boxes.) When I went to collect it, I was usually greeted by a bevy of officials exclaiming in delight at the mere sight of me.

'Oh good, you're here,' they'd coo before offering up the lunchbox, all the while apologizing for having washed it out after throwing away the half-eaten jam sandwiches that had been squished inside. We would then proceed to bow at each other many, many times, while I used up my extensive 'thank you' vocabulary. I would thank them. They would thank me for thanking them. I would thank them for the sentiment. And so it would go.

Over the years, my husband left his iPhone in a taxi in Kyoto; my brother forgot his passport in a hotel lobby in Hokkaido; I left my unbacked-up laptop on the monorail to Haneda airport. Between all of us we regularly 'lost' umbrellas, jackets and hats.

Every single item was retrieved. I found the aforementioned jacket, which had fallen out of my bicycle basket while I was riding home from the supermarket, neatly folded and placed on the side of the road by an anonymous passerby. Walking around our (admittedly well-heeled) neighbourhood, I often spotted assorted items: a child's stuffed toy, a piece of jewellery, a bag, all thoughtfully, occasionally even artfully, arranged to the side of the pavement, safe from trampling feet or flattening bicycle wheels, calmly awaiting retrieval by their rightful owners whenever they realized they had lost something and retraced their steps.

According to the Tokyo Metropolitan Police Department's 'Acceptance Status of Notification of Found Items and Notifications of Lost Items', conscientious finders handed over more than 4.1 million lost items to the city police in 2018. The number of found items handed in was about four times the number of missing item complaints filed.[10]

And it wasn't just umbrellas being handed in, although there were an awful lot of these (the Tokyo police handled a total of 3,43,725 umbrellas in 2018).[11] The amount of hard cash turned in to the police was astonishing. In 2018, 3.8 billion Yen or around 35 million USD was found and handed in, in Tokyo alone. Across Japan there was an 87.5 per cent chance of finding lost money, the percentage calculated on the basis of complaints received by the police against found hand-ins.[12]

On the second Monday after we'd arrived in Japan, I'd woken up alarm-clock-buzzed. It was the first day of the school term, and I wanted to take my children in early to help them settle in. We wolfed down breakfast, made sure the school uniforms were wrinkle-free, and then I grabbed my handbag, rummaging inside for my wallet to make sure I had enough change for metro tickets.

I reached down and searched inside the bag's roomy interiors, encountering a bottle of hand sanitizer, some tissue paper, assorted pens, ibuprofen, a lip pencil, dark glasses,

stain remover, a tube of antiseptic lotion for cuts, a hairbrush
and a business card holder. But, no wallet. There needs to
be a word for that cold moment of pre-conscious awareness
of a lost wallet.

Japanese had all sorts of other words. *Tsundoku*, for piling
up unread books by your bedside; *shinrinyoku*, literally forest
bathing, for immersing yourself in the woods; *mono no aware*
for the sense of beauty and pathos in the fleeting nature of
existence; *soine* for the unique sensuality of sleeping together
with an infant. The lost-wallet moment was crying out for
a moniker, although I'm not sure naming the feeling would
have helped in alleviating its trauma.

My wallet had some cash in US dollars and yen. I could
shrug that off. But it had credit cards from banks in three
different countries, and once I cancelled these I would be
unable to activate replacement cards without inputting new
starter pin codes in ATMs located in those countries. This
was not something I could do from Tokyo. Worst of all,
the wallet had my new residence card for Japan, a prized
item I had been warned never to lose, given the amount of
bureaucratic paperwork it would take to replace.

My husband took the children to school, while I turned
the house upside down looking for the wallet. I was in tears.
Starting life in a brand-new country was hard enough. Now
I was contemplating a desolate future, marginalized as a
consumer and literally without identity.

I racked my brains about when I'd last seen the wallet and
came to the grim conclusion that it had been two days earlier,
on Saturday, when we'd travelled across town to visit friends.

I retraced my steps and asked at the lost-and-found offices of the two metro stations we'd passed through, to no avail. I walked about my neighborhood aimlessly, looking at the floor as though intensity of staring could conjure up wallets.

Finally, I returned home and lay defeated, sniffling on the couch, when the phone rang. It was Preeti, an Indian who had lived in Tokyo for close to two decades. Her sister, who had been a friend back in Indonesia, had introduced us. She was calling to check up on me, a kindness I wouldn't have blamed her for regretting. Instead of a tete-a-tete she received an earful of misery as I spluttered and panicked and recounted my tale of woe.

She suggested I report the loss at the local police box. At the time I thought this a rather bizarre proposition. Go to the police when you'd lost something? Why? In India the police were people to be bribed to leave you alone. In China they'd been poker-faced apparatchik-types, whom I associated with having to fill out self-criticisms for violating obscure rules: not registering my cats, failing to carry my journalist pass at all times, travelling outside Beijing without seeking official permission.

In Brussels, a useless meeting with the police had been amongst my first acts on city soil.[13] We'd arrived in the 'capital of Europe', jet lagged after a red-eye flight from China, and been robbed of our laptops, handbag and other valuables in the arrivals hall, as we stood *directly opposite* a police booth.

Consequently, I'd spent the first two hours of my life in Belgium filing a theft report at the airport police station, sitting across from a paunchy officer who'd seemed ghoulishly amused by my predicament and spent more time talking about how Indian food did not agree with him (too spicy) than in the details of my story. When he'd finally handed me a typed-up copy of the police report, I'd noticed that at no point had he asked me for my contact details. 'Um, should I give you my phone number?' I'd asked. 'Why?' he'd replied, looking genuinely befuddled. 'So that you can let me know if you find our things,' I'd answered, making sure to enunciate deliberately (by this time I wasn't sure that he was over-bright). He'd looked at me as though I were a particularly exotic Indian insect and equally slowly said, 'You can phone the airport's lost-and-found department in a few days. If we find anything, we'll deposit it there.'

Back in Tokyo, my husband and I decided to heed Preeti's advice and visit the closest *koban*, as police boxes in Japan are called. This wasn't because I thought it to be a useful exercise, but because it was something to do, and anything beat doing nothing but wallowing in my wallet-losing stupidity.

The koban was a 200-metre walk from our apartment, past the local park on one side and a posh tennis club on the other. It was tiny, about 10 metres across, and housed two chairs, a table and a phone. In charge of this territory were two young and disconcertingly alike policemen, sweating in their formal navy-blue uniforms. They looked somewhere between pleased and alarmed to see us approaching. I guessed pleased because it didn't look like there was much other action in their day, and alarmed because we were foreigners. The reaction of many Japanese to a foreigner was to spasm away in terror at the prospect of having to communicate with someone likely to speak in English.

But Julio had studied Japanese for a semester at university more than twenty years ago and he gamely made a stab at explaining the situation in pidgin. The policemen listened to his gobbledygook with politely blank expressions until they caught the word, 'walleto'. This they obviously recognized. And lost and found was their super power. It was as if they'd grown capes. In moments they had us seated and filling out a long form that asked me to detail the last time I'd seen the wallet, what I thought might have happened to it, and (unlike in Belgium) put down all my contact details.

One of the cops took the form from me and, without further explanation, began to make a series of phone calls. I was ready to leave, but it was so humid that I felt stuck to the chair. Overcome by misery and enervation, I blanked out to the audioscape of the policeman's 'ah soooooos'. I had no idea whom he was talking to or even about what, but the sounds he made were as soporific as the susurrations of the cicadas that blanketed the whole city in August.

I'm not sure therefore how long had passed before I noticed that the 'ah soooooos' had changed to more perky 'neeeeees' and that Julio was listening to the conversation with some excitement. 'What is it?' I asked, to which my husband shushed me (quite rudely).

I closed my mouth and tried to tune in to the policeman's natter, but was unable to pick out a single word that made sense to me. After a long time, the cop hung up, turned to

Julio and spoke to him in Japanese. I tried to glean something from his expression, but it remained deadpan.

Julio looked at me. 'What?' I said, resisting the urge to scream. I hated not being able to follow anything. 'I think,' Julio said slowly, 'I think they might have found your wallet.' I gasped with laughter. My poor husband! His Japanese must be even worse than I'd imagined. 'Darling, I think he meant to tell you that *if* they found my wallet, they would let us know. You really need to start some Japanese classes soon.' I shot my other half a fond glance.

'No,' said Julio firmly. 'We need to go to this other police station.' The koban cop had handed Julio a map and was pointing at a spot that looked about a kilometre away from where we were. In a daze, not quite believing what was unfolding, we walked towards where we'd been instructed to go.

Twenty minutes later we found ourselves in front of a large police station in the Roppongi area, a schizophrenic Tokyo neighbourhood that was a mix of disreputable watering halls and tony malls. We walked up the stairs to a large office area where we handed the report our koban policeman had made out to a brisk woman officer. She glanced at our document and turned on her heels, marching up to an array of steel lockers, one of which she unlocked to slide a tray out, upon which my burnt-orange wallet emerged, miraculously unscathed. We were asked to check its contents. Everything was in there from cash to cards.

Five minutes later I was back out in the afternoon glare, blinking at the glorious abnormality of what had happened:

the recovery of a wallet lost two days earlier within an hour of reporting it to the police. How exactly the wallet had been located was lost in translation, but we gathered someone had found it on the street and turned it in.

So, what accounted for this marvel? Did the Japanese just have morally superior DNA compared to the rest of the world? Although there were enough Japanese who trotted out more-or-less provocatively phrased variants of this reasoning, I remained unconvinced, as always, by genetically determinist logic. I cast about for other explanations. Did eating a lot of sushi make you a better person? Was it the cultural influence of Zen Buddhism? Were the lost-property return rates higher simply because it was always so easy to locate a koban to hand in found items to?[14]

Over the years I came to the conclusion that trust bred trust; good deeds encouraged good deeds. If someone had taken the trouble to turn in your valuables to the police, you were much more likely to do the same for someone else in the future. It was the result of the normalization of civic behaviour.

This normalization accounted for the village-like levels of public faith in the urban jungle of one of the world's biggest cities. From a young age the Japanese had a hierarchy of values drilled into them, in school and at home, wherein the comfort and needs of others were placed on par, or above, their own. It was why people were discouraged from talking loudly in public. It might disturb others who shared the same space. It was why Japanese football fans famously cleaned up after themselves, and even after others, following a big game.

It was why people were always on time to appointments. To be late was to be disrespectful of the time of others.

In school, children took turns cleaning classrooms and toilets instead of relying on staff for these services. At construction sites, workers joined in communal calisthenics before beginning the day's labour. The collective performance of these activities fostered a sense of interdependence, of a joined ownership of public space, of the value of civic conduct.

The rules governing social behaviour in public were numerous, and policed both organically and institutionally. Everybody minded everybody else's manners. There was a particularly deathly blackness to the stare that transgressors received from the virtuous. Transgressions included a very long list, from eating on public transport to standing on the right side of an escalator. Social enforcement was backed up with explicit signage forbidding people from various behaviours: Don't run, Don't jump, Don't talk, Don't touch, Don't climb.

There were utopian aspects to Japanese social norms: safety, trust, cleanliness and punctuality. But the dystopian other side of the coin included the suppression of idiosyncrasy and spontaneity. People even tended to hide their laughter by clasping a hand to their mouth, as though stuffing the joy back into themselves.

As a foreigner, I was able to enjoy the benefits of the former and avoid the strictures of the latter. *Gaijin* were forgiven their oddities. But I was a particularly privileged foreigner, with a European husband and a fancy address.

For the immigrants who worked lower down the social order in blue-collar jobs, racism was rampant. I'll address this in later chapters, but it suffices to say that for an advanced economy, Japan had very few immigrants to begin with.

In 2019, the country accepted forty-four asylum applications (it received 10,375). The number of foreign residents was about 2.5 million, or 2 per cent of the total population.[15] Even India had a higher corresponding number, with about 5.2 million resident immigrants as of 2015.[16] The foreign-born population of the United States, Germany and Russia stood at 46.7 million (about 14 per cent of the total population), 12 million (15 per cent of the total population), and 11.6 million (8 per cent of the total population), respectively. Over the course of the years I lived in Tokyo, the government gradually relaxed its immigration policy, caught as it was in the demographic pincers of a declining birth rate and an ageing population.[17] But immigrant numbers remained low and policy-fraught.

One reason many Japanese opposed more immigration was because they feared losing the social cohesion and trust that made their cities safe and clean. The racism implied in the idea that foreigners were somehow criminal and dirty was rarely challenged in the domestic discourse. My liberal instincts were appalled, but over time I found myself telling my kids things like, 'Be careful in Ginza (a busy commercial district), there are many foreigners around.' The fact that we were foreigners ourselves was an irony not entirely lost on me, but my children were used to leaving bicycles unlocked, bags unattended, and had long ago forgotten the fact that it was possible for 'lost' lunchboxes to stay that way. I needed to remind them to be more careful around tourists.

Prejudice aside, the relative homogeneity of class and race in Japan was one piece of the complex puzzle that explained the country's highly evolved civic conduct. The fault lines of caste, class, ethnicity, region and religion that were so acute in the other countries I knew well – India, Indonesia, Belgium and China – were only faintly etched in Japan. This is not to say that they did not exist. Homeless tramps stared blankly out of makeshift shacks in the corners of certain parks in Tokyo, even third-generation ethnic Koreans and Chinese faced systematic social and professional discrimination, and women continued to struggle in a myriad ways.

While crime rates were low relative to most other parts of the world, serial killers and crazed rapists did hit the headlines ever so often. Over a million people were designated as social recluses or *hikikomori,* not leaving their rooms or homes for years on end.[18] People were literally dying from overwork, with Japan having a special word – *karoshi* – for these deaths.[19] For all their highly evolved social conduct, many Japanese drank themselves sick every night. The very first time I visited an *izakaya,* as Japanese pubs were called, an ambulance came by to pick up a young office worker who had blacked out, drunk, at the table next to me.

Clearly, there were layers to Japan, and unearthing them all would probably take a lifetime. But I knew right off the bat that I'd landed somewhere special. Nowhere else I knew blended the comfort of the first world with the anthropologically beguiling complexity of less westernized societies. Japan was not-Europe and not-quite-Asia. It was both reassuringly recognizable and utterly befuddling. Many 'experts', including many Japanese, have written tomes on the ostensible uniqueness of Japan.[20] I wanted to avoid that trap, and the chauvinistic nationalism it encouraged. Everywhere is unique, which is to say that nowhere truly is. But although Japan might not be entirely exceptional, it was tantalizingly close to it. And to be able to call it home for four years was certainly an exceptional privilege.

2

Breaking and Healing

'The wound is the place where the light enters you,' the thirteenth-century Persian poet Rumi sang in my head, as I examined a ceramic bowl in a tiny café in western Tokyo. The simple bowl had been elevated to a luminous objet d'art by the gold-filled cobweb of cracks spread across it.

I'd first heard of *kintsugi*, the Japanese art of repairing ceramics, a few years before moving to Tokyo. A meme had been doing the rounds on Facebook with the picture of a grey bowl rent by snaking golden tributaries, and the words: *Japanese repair broken pottery with powder gold lacquer to highlight imperfections, not hide them.*

I'd been feeling somewhat cracked myself at the time, recently diagnosed with an anxiety disorder. Battered by waves of illogical, terrifying panic, I was put on medication, possibly for life. The kintsugi meme stayed with me through the long nights that I struggled to fall asleep. I imagined being luminescent, lit through all the holes in my mind. I rolled the word 'kintsugi' around in my mouth, even as my tongue felt swollen with the dread of being beyond repair.

By the time we moved to Tokyo, I'd been better for a while and hadn't thought of kintsugi for months. But a day came when I realized that our apartment was 'done', the kids were settled in their new school, and I'd finished the manuscript for the book I'd been working on for the last couple of years. It was time to begin writing about Japan. But what about it? The dynamism of Beijing and Jakarta was absent here. There was no equivalent of the Euro crisis that had been journalistic fodder for me in Brussels. It was then that the broken bowl stumbled back into my consciousness. Of course, I thought, kintsugi.

I began searching for a craftsman to interview on the subject, but it proved difficult. The centre of traditional crafts in Japan was in the west, the region called Kansai, with Kyoto as its fulcrum. Tokyo was in the east, in the area called Kanto. Eventually I found an online story about Kunio Nakamura, a former TV producer who held regular workshops teaching kintsugi at a café in a western suburb of the capital. I tracked down his Twitter handle, and after a short exchange, arranged to meet him.

I was late for the meeting, having become hopelessly lost while changing trains at Shinjuku. In retrospect, this was only to have been expected, given that Shinjuku is in the Guinness Book of World Records as the busiest station in the world (over 3.5 million people pass through it daily).[21] I had been buffeted by gales of commuters, tossed down erroneous passageways and had my charades skills put to test as I sought assistance in locating the right platform. But nonetheless, I'd been acutely guilty at my tardiness, aware that I was living up to an Indian stereotype.

The cafe was up a narrow flight of stairs and I was out of breath by the time I knocked on the door. The man who responded had untidy hair, and lips that hinted at a smile even when at rest. It was Nakamura-san. He calmly handed me a bowl of tea as I babbled apologies and watched me sip it until my breath lengthened.

Then he gestured for me to sit by a long wooden table with a smorgasbord of earthenware laid out on it. I realized he'd hardly spoken a word even as I'd been talking up a storm, in yet another stereotype of Indian verbal diarrhoea meeting Japanese reticence.

But once he got started on kintsugi, Nakamura-san found his voice. He stroked a misshapen pot as if it were a favourite pet as he explained how the sap of the urushi tree, a powerful natural adhesive, is mixed with powdered gold. Unlike other methods of repair, like welding or glueing, kintsugi's power was in its refusal to disguise the brokenness of an object, he said. It did not aim to make what was broken as good as new, but to use the cracks to transform the object into something different, and arguably even more valuable.

I was offered, and accepted, another bowl of steaming tea as we examined all the different pieces, one by one. Some had shards of ancient pottery or coloured glass inserted to make them whole again. Others were examples of the more classical technique of gold-dusted lacquer filling in the fractures.

Kin meant 'gold' and *tsugi* 'to join.' But for Nakamura-san, kintsugi was not just a practical craft, although it undoubtedly prolonged the utility of things. Rather, it was a philosophy that spoke at a visceral level to the human condition. It was the idea of *wabi sabi* made tangible.

Wabi sabi was one of those confounding terms that you couldn't get very far exploring Japan without bumping into. Foundational to the country's understanding of itself, the concept was inextricably entwined with Zen Buddhism, which accounted perhaps for its ineffability. Zen truths were always cryptic: intuitive rather than rational, sensed rather than understood.

Many a foreigner came to Japanese Zen via Dr Daisetsu T Suzuki's seminal work, first published in 1938, *Zen and Japanese Culture*. I was no exception. The book had sat on my shelves in many different countries, but it was only after moving to Tokyo that I began dipping into it. Reading it proved exciting, but also frustrating. I would feel a great stabbing moment of clarity, only to have it float away the moment I tried to pin it down. On page 12:

What is Zen?
I do not understand.
What is Zen?
The silk fan gives me enough of a cooling breeze.
What is Zen?
Zen.[22]

At the outset, Suzuki describes Zen as: 'The product of the Chinese mind when it came into contact with Indian Buddhist teachings in the first century AD.' Zen was a more practical, less metaphysical version of Indian Buddhism, in keeping with the 'practical' Chinese temperament.[23]

I'd long argued that stressing Buddhism as evidence of the commonalities between India and China obfuscated the fundamental differences between the two civilizations.[24] Indian religions, including Buddhism, were steeped in metaphysics, with questions of an ontological and epistemological nature at their hearts. What is the soul? How do we know what is real? How does inductive reasoning stack up against deductive reasoning? The search for answers to these questions had created a lively debate between the schools of thought in India, firmly implanting a tradition of argumentation in the culture. Territorial integrity and notions of empire were not as central to India's self-image as much as metaphysical beliefs. As a result, its civilization was more a conceptual than geographic entity.

In contrast, China was more coherent territorially. Its empire was underpinned by philosophies like Confucianism that tended less to the metaphysical and more to the practical, legalistic and political. In China, Buddhism's otherworldliness, its emphasis on renunciation, was reconciled with the Confucian preoccupation with the here and now, to give birth to what became Zen (Chan, in Chinese) Buddhism.

In the late twelfth century, Zen travelled further east and took root in the Japanese archipelago. In Japan, the practical aspects of the religion became even more pronounced. All Zen monks had to do manual, and menial, labour, including gathering fuel, picking tea leaves, cultivating the land and cleaning the temple. Suzuki recalled a koan (parable) in which a Zen master, asked about his future life, answers:

'Let me be a horse or donkey and work for the villagers.'[25] This was in stark contrast to the Indian Sangha, where for centuries monks had been prohibited from working, supported in their material needs by the generosity of their neighborhood lay community.

The democratization of labour in eastern Buddhism had long-lasting social effects. In *Smoke and Mirrors,* my China memoir, I'd made the case that this crucial difference between India and China explained much about their divergent trajectories.[26] When I was growing up in India, a special 'toilet-cleaning lady' had been employed in our home to scrub our commodes, a job no one else was willing to perform outside her caste. In contrast, in China, my newly wealthy but old-fashioned landlord used to come around and fix our frequently malfunctioning toilet himself. As for Japan, our toilet in Tokyo not only never needed any fixing, it was a veritable objet d'art.

It was as if India-China-Japan formed a great Asiatic triangle of the metaphysical-political-aesthetic. This argument was reinforced by examining the kinds of philosophers prized by each culture. India was the home of the Buddha and China of Confucius, while Japan's most quoted thinker was probably Sen no Rikyu, the sixteenth-century master of tea ceremony.

Wrapping one's head around tea ceremony was as important to understanding Japan as reading the Analects was to China, for it was in *chado* – the way of the tea – that Japan's philosophical heartbeat pulsed. There was an elaborate set of rules to the ceremony, many so subtle as to be invisible to the untrained eye: tiny gestures used in scooping out the tea and holding the bowl properly; casual allusions to literary classics and season-appropriate poetry that enhanced the experience of sipping the beverage; knowledge of ceramics so as to be able to comment with authority on the texture of the tea bowl and the quality of other utensils. All of these were important components of the ritual of tea.

And yet the great tea masters, in the spirit of Zen, dismissed the notion that tea ceremony was about anything but the drinking of tea: smelling it, tasting it, swallowing it. It was the tea*ness* of tea, not the ceremony surrounding it, that was the entirety of its metaphysics. But you nonetheless had to spend years learning the associated rituals, to work towards that moment when all the training fell away, unlearned. It put me in mind of the French art critic Georges Duthuit's observation of Zen-inspired painting: 'Draw bamboos for ten years, become a bamboo and then forget all about bamboo when painting.'[27]

While the Zen masters may not have made the best philosophers, being both esoteric and irrational, they were always fine artists, which perhaps helped explain the aesthetic underpinnings of Japanese thought. Tea ceremony was both an art and a philosophy. The same could be said about other classical Japanese arts: calligraphy, painting, poetry, flower arrangement, incense appreciation, as well as the martial arts. These pursuits were called paths or '*do*' (from the Chinese Tao). So you had *chado* (the way/path of the tea), *shodo* (the way/path of handwriting), *kado* (the way/

path of flowers), *kodo* (the way/path of incenses), *kendo* (the way/path of the sword) and so on.

What these '*dos*' had in common was their Zen centre, the importance they placed on repetition, their focus on the moment rather than on the end, their belief in simplicity. By the fifteenth and sixteenth centuries, Zen had permeated deep into Japanese society and culture.[28] The problem, however, was that this was a culture with an identity problem.

For centuries, Japan had been discomfited by a sense of insecurity about its place in the cultural universe. China was *Zhongguo*, the 'middle kingdom', central, powerful, the font of all things sophisticated, technically polished and grand. Everything Japanese seemed to have come from China, from Zen itself to the Japanese writing system, ceramics, paper and literature. The only thing against the current of this cultural flow was the folding fan.[29]

When tea masters in Japan began casting about for what was truly Japanese, they found only the rough and primitive: Shinto shrines with thatched roofs, earthenware rather than porcelain. Japan was the rustic margin to China's polished centrality. In a shift of perception, with long-lasting consequences, tea masters began to declare the crude, misshapen pottery that the Japanese produced to be wabi sabi, and for wabi sabi to become the basis of refined aesthetics.[30]

Suzuki explains *wabi* as meaning 'poverty', or negatively, as 'not to be in the fashionable society of time'.[31] It refers to an artistic style where beauty is embodied 'in a form of imperfection, or even ugliness'. *Sabi* is 'when the beauty of imperfection is accompanied by antiquity or primitive uncouthness ... apparent simplicity or effortlessness in execution ... and lastly, inexplicable elements that raise the object in question to the rank of art'.[32]

Tea masters like Sen no Rikyu (1522–1591) rejected Chinese ostentation and made tearooms like tiny country cottages, just a few *tatami* mats-wide, with a hearth cut into the floor. They began to use lumpy and unadorned tea bowls, which, if broken, were repaired and reused.[33]

Back at Nakamura-san's café, the conversation remained focused on wabi sabi and its emphasis on finding beauty in the weathered and the aged. Nature's cycles of growth, decay and erosion were embodied in frayed edges, cracks and rust. A wabi sabi way of seeing embraced these markers of passing time. A brand-new tea bowl, no matter how glistening, could never compare to an old kintsugi-repaired one, Nakamura-san opined. 'Do you understand?' he asked. 'It is difficult with my English.' I understood so intensely that I had to stop myself from hugging the man and possibly shocking him beyond even the repair of kintsugi. I contented myself with a nod.

The café owner had long had an interest in old things, having started his career as a TV director for an Antiques Roadshow-type of programme. He collected pottery and taught himself kintsugi. But then in March 2011, an earthquake, the most powerful in Japan's history, shattered much of the country. Thousands of people were killed and hundreds of thousands of homes destroyed.

It was a seminal event for Nakamura-san. 'I realized we needed to repair ourselves, to remake things,' he said. He quit his job and started holding workshops in some of the country's most devastated areas, encouraging people to bring in treasured ceramics that had broken in the earthquake and teaching them how to mend these.

As the afternoon wore on and we began sipping a third cup of tea, Nakamura-san sank into a long silence. A few months ago this would have caused me acute discomfort. Until moving to Japan, I'd tended to feel that if my interlocutor didn't talk, she was expressing her boredom. But I was coming around to becoming cautiously appreciative of what, to a talkative Indian like me, was the 'peculiar' Japanese ease with silence.

I would hand my business card to someone, expecting them to make a quick comment in response. Instead, they would stare at it for an inordinately long time before carefully putting it away, often without any verbal accompaniment.

Silences inhabited much social behaviour in Japan. At the end of my weekly yoga class, for example, run-of-the-mill chatter about weekend plans or Netflix series was glaringly absent. Instead, students spent several minutes painstakingly wiping their yoga mats clean for subsequent use by others, in silence. At restaurants it was not unusual to see groups of friends sitting together and eating silently, save for the slurp of noodles and splash of soup. I once saw a toddler fall off a swing at a public park and scream, silently. He screwed up his eyes and pulled back his lips into a grimace, but not a sound came out of his mouth.

Hanging out with Japanese friends could feel awkward to someone used to chatter. Conversation rarely flowed. I would ask a question, nothing too difficult to answer, something like, 'Do you like reading?' And then I'd have to wait, and wait, and perhaps wait even longer for the answer, which after all that contemplation could well be a monosyllabic 'no'.

The silences, I came to realize, were not hostile. They were just not perceived as something problematic. There were so many times when people had nothing to say, but in many cultures we said something anyway. Not so in Japan. Some Japanologists attributed this trait to – you guessed it – Zen. Roger Davies, Professor of Applied Linguistics at Ehime University in Matsuyama, for example, claimed that since, in Zen, 'wisdom and eloquence are to be found in silences rather than the verbalization of human concepts, the Japanese privilege silence over words'.[34] Suzuki concurred, positing that Japan's particular character in intellectual life did not lie in 'the richness of ideas, or brilliance in articulation', but in staying 'quietly content', feeling 'at home in the world'.[35]

Silence, pauses, space, shadows, emptiness, were prized across Japanese aesthetics, from painting and architecture to appreciation of rice wine, *sake*. The principle of less being more was perhaps nowhere more evident than in ink brush paintings called *hoboku* (literally broken/splashed ink) where a miniscule number of lines and blotches could conjure up entire landscapes. As though by sorcery, a few triangles next to some squiggles evoked mountains and sea and a tiny human-sized ship adrift amidst the immensity of nature.[36]

A former Japan correspondent for the *Financial Times* mused about sake along similar lines. In *Bending Adversity*, a wonderfully readable introduction to contemporary Japan, he wrote:

> A master of wine who is also an expert in sake once told me that the most elegant Japanese rice wines are defined by the absence of taste, the reverse of what one looks for in a claret ... 'Sake is about what's not there. With wine it's about what's here. It's like in speech. The pauses and the silences, the things that aren't there give a hint of the meaning. The most elegant sakes are barely there at all.'

This was a truth that many who visited Japan discovered at their own peril, finding themselves fall-down drunk after only a few glasses of sake, a wine that tasted barely stronger than water. But with an average alcohol content of 15-16 per cent, it packed quite a wallop.

No one argued quite as eloquently for the place of emptiness and shadow in Japanese culture than Junichiro Tanazaki (1886–1965), the novelist whose name had cropped up in almost every suggestion I'd received from friends-in-the-know on what to be reading on Japan. In his extended essay, 'In Praise of Shadows', Tanazaki made the case for the nuance of shade being at the heart of Japanese culture. According to him, the interplay of light and shadow, underlain by a deep recognition of the illuminating qualities of darkness, was central to an appreciation of everything

Japanese, from ceramics to traditional performance arts like Noh, as well as the architecture of the home.[37]

Tokonoma, or recessed alcoves, were a typical feature of reception rooms in the traditional Japanese home. These were usually decorated with a hanging scroll and a flower arrangement, both reflective of the season. Tanazaki wrote of them:

> In recessed alcoves lie a scroll and flower arrangements, but these serve not as ornament but rather to give depth to the shadows ... they are empty spaces marked off with plain walls and wood so that the light drawn into them forms dim shadows within emptiness and yet when we gaze into the darkness that gathers behind the cross beams and around the flower vases, though we know it is mere shadow we are overcome with the feeling that in this small corner there reigns complete and utter silence; that here in the darkness immutable tranquility holds sway.[38]

Back at the café, Nakamura-san sighed, inflating the silence that had descended on us. At length, he pointed at a teacup. 'That's my favourite. You know, for us (Japanese) particular pieces of pottery are like family members. We cannot just throw them away.' Four tiny sparkles of gold glinted from the teacup's otherwise dull earthen rim, where chips had been filled in. He picked it up and turned it over in his hands. 'Maybe this cup is nothing special, but I want to use it forever.'

Nakamura-san claimed that kintsugi's emphasis on reuse was attuned to a 'special' Japanese sensibility that tilted towards minimalism and long-term use of a few prized objects. It was a line of reasoning that fitted in nicely with the Marie Kondo version of Japan that was the archipelago's international image *du jour*. Minimalism, thriftiness, reuse, small spaces were what Japan conjured up in the global imagination, in contradiction to the associations centred on consumerism, pollution, and excess that China conjured up.

And yet, I'd noticed more casual use of plastic in Japan than in any other country I'd lived in. Beijing had banned the use of single-use plastic bags in stores as far back as in 2008. My supermarket in Jakarta had begun levying charges for plastic bags in 2016. In Tokyo, on the other hand, our neighborhood grocery store shrink-wrapped individual bananas, while the local bakery sent me home with each of the several croissants I bought on Saturday mornings encased in separate plastic wrapping.[39] It was common for fruit and vegetables already packaged in plastic to be re-wrapped in more plastic at the checkout counter before being put into their final carry-home plastic bags. Japan was in fact the world's second-highest user per capita of plastic packaging, according to the United Nations Environment Program.[40]

And the Japanese homes I visited were a far cry from the lightly scented temples to neutral colours and tidiness that Muji catalogues would have us believe the average person in the country inhabited. They were so tiny (it wasn't uncommon for a middle-class family of four to live and cook in a space of about 50 square metres), that toys, bedding, utensils, cleaning equipment overflowed from shelves and onto the floor in a flood of clutter. The problem of *gomi yashiki* (houses overflowing with junk) and *gomi-beya*, (apartments crammed with junk from floor to ceiling) were the staple of reality TV shows and newspaper features.[41]

There were many reasons for the extreme messiness of many Japanese homes. The space crunch and consumerism (to which Zen spirit notwithstanding, Japanese were as much susceptible as anyone else) were the obvious culprits. Another uniquely Japanese factor was the complexity of mandatory recycling rules, which could feel like they required an advanced degree to master. Legislation dating to the late 1990s mandated that every household had to separate waste into burnable and non-burnable categories. But this was just the tip of the recycling iceberg. There was a vertiginous array of categories to further sort non-burnables into: plastic and PET (polyethylene terephthalate), cardboard and glass, spray cans and old cloth. For instance, in Japan's second-largest city, Yokohama, citizens were handed a twenty-seven-page manual on how to sort about 500 different items. Example: lipstick was usually 'burnable', but an empty tube could go into 'small metals'.[42] Milk cartons had to be rinsed with water, cut open and dried, then bundled together with items of the same size with a paper string – unless the interior was processed with an aluminum or wax coating, in which case they went in the non-burnable garbage. Small wonder that some people hoarded rather than made the effort to dispose at regular intervals.

A significant number of hoarders was also mentally ill. Some overlapped with a category of people who had turned into extreme recluses, choosing to end all social contact and often refusing to leave their homes for years on end. These latter were known as *hikikomori* and numbered over a million. Coined in the late 1990s by psychologist Tamaki Saito, hikikomori was a term used interchangeably for the condition and its sufferers. Since then, it had become a widely acknowledged social condition in Japan. However, its precise contours remained debated, including whether it was primarily a medical illness, a social disease, or even a cultural condition.[43]

The fact was that when it came to mental health, Japan was far more Asian than Western. Mental illnesses were stigmatized and often undiagnosed. Emotional expression was discouraged. Suicide rates were high, the highest amongst OECD members. In 2019, 20,169 people committed suicide in Japan, bringing the country's suicide rate to about 16 per 100,000 people. By contrast, in 2018 the suicide rate for the United States, which has more than twice Japan's population, was 14.2 per 100,000, for Canada 13.8, and for the UK 11.2.[44]

Suicide had a strange cultural cache in Japan, with a number of famous figures having chosen to end their own lives, on occasion through ritualized disembowelment called *seppuku*. In 1970, celebrated writer Yukio Mishima had sliced open his belly with a sword and then ordered his followers to decapitate him. Even the prime originator of wabi sabi, the tea master Sen no Rikyu, committed seppeku in 1591 (his last act had been to hold an exquisite tea ceremony). In killing himself, Rikyū was following orders from the formidable *daimyo* Toyotomi Hideyoshi. Before cutting himself he wrote a verse, addressed to the dagger with which he would take his life:

> *Gratitude to thee,*
> *O sword of eternity!*
> *Cutting through Buddha*
> *And through Bodhidharma too –*
> *Thou hast prepared the way for me.*

But I was not thinking of any of this as I sat late into the crepuscular afternoon with Nakamura-san, exploring kintsugi and its poetry. I was very taken by its underlying philosophy and got positively mawkish in the article I went on to write about it for a magazine:

> Kintsugi inscribes an object's story into its body: the moment of the breakage, the fact that it was loved enough to be repaired, that it is likely to be handled with care in the future...We have all been broken at some point. And the essence of who we are is not located in some flawless image we might present, but along the fault lines of our biographies. Kintsugi

encourages us to embrace our past along with its
scars; to realize that our cracks make us even more
beautiful.[45]

I'm not sure Mishima or any of the others who committed
suicide in Japan with such worrying frequency would have
been healed by contemplating kintsugi. I doubt that reclusive
hikikimori would agree that their cracks made them more
beautiful. What Japan really needed was better awareness of
mental illness and more professional care for the sick. And
yet it was difficult to dismiss the importance of the aesthetic
ideal encapsulated in repairing ceramics with gold dust too.
Japan was both deeply Zen and deeply troubled. Only naïve
observers felt discomfort with contradiction. I had long
come to the conclusion that the truth was rarely singular
and always messy.

And so I was at ease knowing that China was both
a chaotic and controlled society, or that India could be
simultaneously compassionate and cruel. Japan, I realized,
was both profoundly healing and deeply broken. It was
this contradiction that made it real; not the orientalist's
stereotype of a land full of people gazing at the moon, or a
humourless dystopia of overworked salarymen, neglected
wives and cluttered apartments. It was sometimes both and
at other times neither. Mostly it was in-between.

By the time I finally left the Rokujigen café, it was already
early evening and I realized I was starving. In my anxiety
about being late for my meeting with Nakamura-san, I'd
skipped lunch. At the metro stop, I found myself looking at

the familiar golden arches of a fast-food chain I would not usually admit to eating at. But in my defence, and true to the country's reputation for culinary excellence, the chicken and cheese burger at McDonald's in Japan somehow managed to taste like food rather than plastic.

As I chomped my way through a set of rather un-wabi sabi burger and fries, I thought about what my choice of first stories about different countries said of them. In China, my first reports had been about the 2003 SARS epidemic and the government cover-up that minimized the numbers of those affected. It was essentially a political story aimed at understanding the challenges an authoritarian system had in dealing with public health crises. In Brussels, my first piece had been on the long-negotiated-but-going-nowhere India-EU trade agreement. In Japan, it was on ceramic repair.

Alex Kerr, an American Japanologist who is also, uncommonly, a Sinologist, posits that lovers of China are adventurous thinkers, with critical minds. Lovers of Japan, on the other hand, tend to be sensuous and intuitive. Kerr, who had studied Chinese at Oxford, described his China studies friends from university as politically charged, endlessly talking about the ramifications of Chairman Mao's mass campaigns and later the Tiananmen Square massacre. In contrast, if asked about the most exciting moment of their lives, his Japan-loving friends responded along the lines of 'I was meditating in a Zen temple and I heard the swish of silk robes of the monks as they walked by.'[46]

China's modern history had been volcanic, featuring civil war, colonial occupation, a communist revolution and an audacious experiment in state-led capitalism. Changes that in most nations had taken place over centuries had been compressed into a few decades in China, so that change had been its only constant. But in Japan, ever since the Second World War, uninterrupted peace and settled social systems had created a land of stasis, where it was possible to argue that repairing broken tea bowls was the most exciting event one was likely to encounter.

As for the swish of monk's robes, I was about to find out how exciting these were at first-hand. An important part of my recovery from mental illness had involved meditation. In Indonesia, where I'd first been diagnosed, I'd had no access to professionally organized sessions and had relied on a downloaded app on my phone, where a calming voice directed me to focus on my breath. In the months leading up to the move to Japan, I'd grown lax in my practice as I'd felt increasingly well and less in need of help. I was aware, however, that I should not take my mental well-being for granted. And I was in Japan, the incubator of Zen.

It was thus that I became a student of Zazen or Zen meditation. About once a week, I'd wake at 6 a.m. and walk from my home in the city's embassy enclave, past the turtles floating in the neighbourhood park's pond, through a busy traffic intersection and into a local temple complex. Entering through the slate-tiled archway of Kourin-in temple was like passing between worlds. On one side there were jam-packed trains to catch. On the other there was refuge, and daily hour-long Zazen meditation sessions.

Zazen was the source of all the fashionable mindfulness workshops and apps creating a stir amongst the international jet set. Yet it was as simple as sitting still and listening to the breath. At the meditation hall in Kourin-in, there were usually between twenty and forty people. We sat in half-lotus position on two layers of cushions, the upper layer folded back to raise the pelvis. Our hands rested in our laps, with the tips of the thumbs touching each other to form an oval.

At 7 a.m., a gong was sounded and all body adjustments and throat clearings hushed. We concentrated our attention on that moment, moment to moment. At the outset, the surrounding sounds impinged forcefully on the consciousness – the muted chanting of monks, the occasional twitter of birdsong and the distant hum of traffic. But after a while, perhaps ten minutes, maybe fifteen, the mind stilled and was able to focus on the breath. Then there was nothing but the inhale and the exhale, repeated again and again.

Zazen meditation was one of those deceptively simple rituals that the Japanese had perfected. Like tea ceremony, its disarming simplicity hid an ineffable complexity that eventually caved in on nothing but itself.

At some point the sharp thwack of wood hitting bones sounded out. The *jikijitsu* or monk in charge of the session was afoot. As was the norm in Zazen practice, he used a *keisaku*, a long wooden stick, to strike the shoulders of mediators. The blow was meant to alleviate drowsiness and to sharpen the focus. It felt surprisingly light, given the sound it generated. One had to invite the blow by folding the hands into a namaste and bowing slightly as the jikijitsu passed by. I usually avoided inviting the keisaku upon me, but there were times that I was guilty of sneaking a peak at other meditators while they were being struck.

One time, an elderly man in a rather dishevelled suit keeled right over as the stick hit his shoulder. The jikijitsu looked stricken; the room erupted with concern. Had the monk just knocked someone out cold? It turned out the man was punch drunk, having turned up to the temple after what must have been an eventful night. An ambulance was called to take him away and the meditators returned to their breath soon after.

On most days, I joined the jikijitsu and a handful of others for a cup of freshly made green tea after the hour-long session. The meditators were typically a mix of professionals and housewives in their thirties or forties. Some of them commuted up to an hour to make it to the session. There was rarely much chitchat during the tea drinking, although murmured comments about the flowers in season were acceptable, especially in spring. 'Did you see the cherry blossoms lit up along the Meguro River yet?' 'The wisterias are late this year.'

In the summer, the favoured topic shifted to insects, in particular the choral chirping of cicadas that dominated the city's auralscape. A young lady was very incensed about the mosquitoes that had infested her local park. As she showed off her angrily welling bites, I thought of a haiku I had just read about mosquitoes, by the great master Kobayashi Issa (1763–1828):

> *Mosquito at my ear –*
> *does he think*
> *I'm deaf?*

I was almost about to recite it for the tea-drinkers but then thought I'd come across as unbearably pretentious, for I'd (admittedly pretentiously) also been reading 'Essays in Idleness' by Yoshida Kenko, a fourteenth-century Buddhist monk and poet, over breakfast. Kenko was forever admonishing the reader to be modest, being of the opinion that, 'To parade your own knowledge and pit it against others is like a horned beast lowering its head at an opponent, or a fanged animal baring its teeth.'[47] So I kept my haiku to myself and instead joined the others in a communal symphony of sympathetic noises. Despite my natural instincts, I was adapting to the Japanese adage, 'The nail that sticks out, gets hammered down.'

3

Seasonal Flavours

Ireeled into the cherry blossom-fringed entrance of the Zen temple, Tenryuji, one more of Kyoto's endless UNESCO World Heritage sites, inebriated on the moment. The capital of Japan for much of the country's history (794 to 1868), Kyoto was a place to be yearned for. I'd been reading so much about Japanese aesthetics in the months after moving to Tokyo that I had begun to miss the city even before visiting it. I think the haiku master Matsuo Basho (1644–1694) was somewhat to blame for this non-linear state of affairs. Of Kyoto, he wrote:

Even in Kyoto –
hearing the cuckoo's cry –
I long for Kyoto.

Soon after chancing on this poem I booked a family trip to the city for the second week of April to coincide with the children's spring vacation. When I announced our plans to friends, everyone was in agreement that we'd love it, but that it was a pity we'd be missing the sakura (cherry blossoms). That year the flowers were expected in late March. Sakura were in full bloom for a few days at most, and the 'season' lasted for about a week to ten days. The brevity of their bloom and the pathos they evoked at the profound impermanence of things had launched a thousand haikus and philosophical treatises.

As tea ceremony bowls embodied wabi sabi, so the sakura represented another of Japan's difficult-to-translate cultural philosophies, mono no aware – which, roughly speaking, was the pain of the finiteness of things, laced with the knowledge that transience was an essential part of their beauty. Basho put it best, again:

Between our two lives
there is also the life of
the cherry blossom.

But cut to modern-day Japan, and sakura was not only setting the hearts of swooning poets afire but the cash registers of retailers too. For weeks before full bloom, the shops in Japan had switched to saccharine sakura mode, with cherry blossom Kit Kats, cherry blossom cookie cutters, cherry blossom-decorated chopsticks, plastic cherry blossoms, cherry blossom cocktails, *sakuramochi* or rice cakes wrapped in cherry tree leaves, and so on and on, on offer.

The frenzy had begun in late January, when Tokyo was still shivering in the hard grip of winter and talk of flowers seemed about as relevant as contact lenses for a blind woman. But on TV a 'blossom forecast' was on air, offering a petal-by-petal analysis of the advance of the blooms as they rippled from the deep south to the north of the archipelago, like a pink-and-white Mexican wave. The season in the southern island of Okinawa did in fact begin in January, although it took about two months or more to travel up to Tokyo.

And because this was Japan, where accuracy is not an option as much as an axiom, the sakura season wasn't official until a specially appointed civil servant, one amongst an army of whom spent weeks examining 'barometer' trees in locations that were kept secret to protect them from blossom saboteurs, gave the signal that yes, indeed, the trees were in bloom. Over 600 different varieties of cherry trees exist, but it was the pale pink blossoms of the *yoshino* – Japan's most common type – that were used by the bloom-investigating bureaucrats as the yardstick by which to declare the season open. The green light was usually given after more than five blossoms had unfurled on a yoshino tree at Tokyo's Yasukuni shrine.

This could be anywhere between mid-March and early April, and all the predictions for 2017 (my first spring) were for late March. As it happened, March came and went with everyone staring at trees whose blossoms remained as tightly closed as a newborn's fist. It was a tense time, like when your period is late and you feel on edge, delayed, alert.

And then one morning I woke up to a world transformed. The streets were blushing shades of pink. The very air felt aglow. As we drove the children to school that morning, people seemed to be walking about in slow motion, rubbing their eyes in wonder at this miracle of nature. But the meditative contemplation didn't last too long. By the afternoon, it was party time.

The Japanese may have tackled sakura appreciation with the kind of ardour that other countries reserve for sporting events or religious festivals, but this was a passion fuelled with copious quantities of alcohol. The blooming of the cherry trees went hand in hand with *hanami*, i.e., wild boozing sessions held under the blossoms. Although hanami literally means 'looking at flowers', in practice it meant getting shit-faced.

During sakura week, Tokyo's usually staid public parks, (filled with all the standard signs of 'no running', 'no shouting' – everything just short of 'no happiness') were transformed into venues for rowdy celebrations, with everyone from grandmas to pet dogs in prams (for which the Japanese had a penchant) in the mood to let down their hair.

Over the week, I attended several hanamis with family and friends, including quite a spectacular one at the Aoyama cemetery, where thousands of headstones sheltered under a floral parasol. Initially, I'd felt a bit awkward to be merry-making in such sombre surroundings, but then I'd reminded myself that in Japan Shinto deities were partial to offerings of sake, as was the average ancestor. It was common to spy beer cans and cups of sake amongst the flowers and incense that were standard offerings at gravesites.

But the largest, most rambunctious, hanami I attended was at Yoyogi, Tokyo's equivalent of New York's Central Park. The entire scene was liminal: usual social conventions turned topsy-turvy by the sheer force of the sakura's beauty. Raucous revellers took up space under every available tree. There were students playing hooky from classes and neighbourhood groups who'd organized their own sake-soaked viewings for senior citizens. There were canoodling lovers and assemblies of office workers dispensing, for once, with the strict hierarchies of the workplace. Usually reticent families spontaneously invited our boys to join in games that ran the gamut from skipping rope to dribbling football. Everyone smiled and looked happy. It was as if haiku great (and my personal favourite) Kobayashi Issa's poem had come to life:

Under the cherry-blossoms
there's no such thing
as a stranger.

If this had been a Hindi movie, it would have been a scene in which a peacock suddenly appeared with unfurled tail and danced in choreographed unison with the picnickers. There was none of the passive aggression that was so common in Japan. The hordes of social-rules-in-public enforcers had either stayed at home, or were too inebriated on alcohol and flowers to give dirty looks. But this *was* Japan, and to call the picnicking 'freewheeling' was an adjective too far.

First off, every group brought along their own *gomi* (rubbish) bags into which they constantly recycled empty bottles and food packaging. Even the drunkest of bacchants staggered home only after ensuring that not a paper napkin had been left in their wake. And then there were the sakura-viewing etiquette guides. At one of the parks I visited, I was actually handed a sheet of paper with 'Mind Your Manners' headlined in English. The leaflet had been produced by the local municipality and warned bloom-gazers not to start fires, stand on the roots of the trees, be annoying to others, touch the trees, pluck the blossoms or to litter.

The need for such a document became clearer after my first encounter with a star tree – these were usually old and storied, with the girth and beauty to warrant them the kind of attention that in India was reserved for cricketers. By Japanese standards, the picture-clicking crowds surrounding these arboreal celebrities could almost be described as a scrum.

The upshot of the late blossoming that first spring in Japan was that we unexpectedly found ourselves in Kyoto, in full bloom. Even Tokyo's sakura-soaked glory had not prepared us for the off-the-charts beauty of Japan's old capital lit up with flowers. I actually wept, and this is not literary exaggeration, when at the entrance of Tenryuji, a heron perched, held breath-still, under the fronds of a weeping cherry tree. Its grey and white silhouette was so easily mistaken for an ink-wash painting that I began to think the Japanese aesthetic was more about realism than Zen. Exploring the city's temples and shrines was like having wandered into an ethereal image on a nineteenth-century folding screen.

Later, we walked down the 'Philosopher's Path' that ran from the Silver Pavillion temple[48] in the city's north along a sakura-lined creek, and I felt I was literally bathing in mono no aware. I ooohd and aaahd so often that my husband threatened me with divorce if I didn't desist, and my children covered their ears and rolled their eyes. 'Mama's gone crazy,' I overheard the little one whispering to his brother. I called a snack break and treated everyone to sakura-flavoured ice cream, which temporarily restored my popularity.

The next day we visited the bamboo grove at Arashiyama in the far west of Kyoto. Walking through the bower formed by the soaring stalks of bamboo was travel-article-worthy, but I had to confess a growing irritation with the platoons of Chinese tourists, one of whom I caught spitting in the corner. 'Come on man!' I felt like telling him, 'There are enough stereotypes about you guys here already. Did you really have to do that?'

Japanese tourists seemed to shrink when you brushed past them in tight spaces, to give you more room. The Chinese, on the other hand, expanded and occupied. I felt a tad guilty feeling these feelings, as if now because I lived in refined Japan, I was suddenly too good for the boorish Chinese. But then a particularly pot-bellied Beijinger (I could tell from his accent) with the face of a blowfish, began yelling to someone a few metres away, '*Cesuo zai nar? Wo yao lashir.*' How I wished in that moment that I did not understand Mandarin. The man had just shouted out: 'Where's the toilet? I need to take a shit.' My ears!

Luckily, my auditory organs were well recovered by the afternoon, having been healed by a singing bus driver. The bus in question was headed back to central Tokyo and the driver had been singing a most bewitching melody.

Sakura, sakura
Uayoi no sora wa
Mi watasu kagiri
Kasumi ka kumo ka
Nioi zo izuru
Izaya izaya
Mini yukan

The tune stuck in my head and became my mental soundtrack for the rest of spring that year. I googled the lyrics, which translated into English thus:

Cherry blossoms, cherry blossoms,
Across the spring sky,
As far as the eye can see.
Is it mist, or clouds?
Fragrance in the air.
Come now, come,
Let's look at them, at last!

Over the years, whenever I heard this song – which was often, because it was as common in spring in Japan as '*Jingle Bells*' in December in the US – it made me happily melancholic. I knew I would never again capture that intoxication of being in Kyoto for the first time, but I was happy I'd had the chance, once.

The evening of our last day in Kyoto, we'd gone to what is often described as the most beautiful street in Asia: Shimbashi. A willow-and-blossom-threaded stream ran along one end, with teahouses, art galleries and antiquarians connected to the street by the half moon of a stone bridge. Shimbashi was in Gion, the city's traditional pleasure district. Once the playground of geisha, it was now the lair of tourists desperate to catch a glimpse of geisha.

As dusk gathered and the yellow street lamps started coming on, I spotted the white-faced, slightly bowed figure of a *maiko* (apprentice geisha) hurrying by. But with a swish of a richly decorated kimono she had disappeared, leaving only the flutter of a restaurant entrance's curtain in her wake.

The next day we returned to Tokyo, where the blossoms had already turned to petal snow and lay in great drifts on the streets. In the weeks that followed, I embraced floral tourism and hunted for the best spots to view wisteria, then azaleas and hydrangeas, and finally, lilies. Before I knew it, it was June and the season was about to flip a page. Summer's time was nigh.

Summer in Tokyo was evisceratingly hot (and I say that as an Indian). The humidity rendered me almost catatonic, revivable only if allowed to gorge on watermelon and peach. The fruit in Japan were as sweet as it was hot in August. But with the fruit came the insects, particularly cicadas, who emerged from their eggs for a week of frenzied love-making, during which they made the racket that formed Tokyo's aural summerscape, from July through early September. They weren't the most attractive creatures (like cockroaches, although with gossamer wings), yet the pithiness of their existence was as mono no aware as sakura, and therefore fertile soil for haikus. Basho wrote:

Nothing in the cry
of cicadas suggests they
are about to die.

And also:

Lonely silence,
a single cicada's cry
sinking into stone.

But it was only after reading Junichiro Tanizaki's masterpiece, *The Makioka Sisters*, that I began to associate summer with another, more ornamental, arthropod: the firefly. Amongst the genteel pastimes of the four Makioka sisters from the novel, catching fireflies caught my imagination. *Hotaru-gari* (firefly hunting) turned out to have been a popular summer activity of the Japanese bourgeoisie, before industrialization and pollution made cities inhospitable for the jewel-like flies.

The imagery of this Basho haiku was almost unbearably evocative to me, ephemeral, simple, visceral:

Blade of grass
a firefly lands
takes off again.

And for a change from Basho there was also this, by renowned female poet Fukuda Chiyo-ni (1703–1775):

Cool clear water
and fireflies that vanish
that is all there is ...

But for when I needed a laugh, or just a break from an excess of mono no aware, there was always Issa and his clever, witty verses:

Call it a refuge
for all the fireflies in town
– my house!

Urban development had long wiped out these once-numerous harbingers of summer from Japan's cities. But the nostalgia evoked by them was a business opportunity. Today, a few companies bred and sold fireflies for the private gardens of hotels and restaurants so they could still be admired, for a price. It took me until our third summer in Japan to be able to persuade Julio that it was worth coughing up the large amount of money for a rather poor buffet dinner that a fancy Tokyo hotel charged as the price of entrance to their 'firefly garden'.

This was a sprawling classically designed space, within which a few dozen hotaru flitted about like the sparks from stars. The whole experience was fake, but with only a minor suspension of belief it was possible to imagine we were back in Edo times, tracking the magic of the fireflies under the moon. Many of our fellow diners had come clad in *yukatas* (summer kimonos made of brightly coloured cotton). Some carried lanterns that glowed as golden as the hotaru themselves. There were rustlings and giggles and sighs of excitement whenever a firefly landed somewhere close by; the heat was leavened by the occasional breeze.

The summer in Japan was not without its charms, but what I liked best of all was that it signalled my favourite season, autumn, was round the corner. By late September and almost all the way till early December, much of Honshu was set ablaze in crimson and gold. It was as if all the country's gingkos and maples wanted to live their best life before bowing to the inevitability of winter. The evenings lengthened, the air crispened, the crackle of cotton gave way to the rustle of silk. There was freedom from the heaviness of summer and a glaze of melancholy at the realization that this freedom had only one outcome: the leaves would wither and fall. One just had to learn to embrace that ending.

The writer Pico Iyer and I have never met, but we share a few things in common: our surnames, the fact that we live in Japan for large parts of the year, and that we have written about the peripatetic lives of global types. As I was struggling to shape this chapter, he happened to publish a meditation on autumn in Tokyo. He called it the season of 'fire and farewells ... of subtractions, the Japanese art of taking more and more away to charge the few things that remain'. (In Marie Kondo-speak this translated as only hanging on to stuff that 'sparks joy'.)[49] He also mentioned that more than four times as many classical poems were set in autumn and spring than in summer and winter.

I think that Basho was the master of the autumn verse, capturing its pathos and pulchritude with gnomic perfection:

With what kind of voice
would the spider cry
in the autumn wind?

And:

I go
and you remain
two autumns.

And:

On a leafless branch
A crow comes to rest –
Autumn nightfall.

And:

> *First day of Autumn*
> *My heart is pounding wild*
> *Ah! The full moon.*

And because there *are* other poets, here's one from Issa:

> *In September*
> *The sky wears*
> *A lined kimono.*

I have to stop myself now, or this book will turn into a compendium of haiku, something I imagine all books on Japan tempt their authors towards. Talking about the seasons in Japan without poetry is especially hard. In the autumn, there was an actual day (*tsukimi*) dedicated to preparing to look at the full moon. And because the word for moon, *tsuki*, was a homonym of the word for wine cup, *zuki*, drinking sake on an autumn evening while gazing up at the moon was the done thing.

In late fall, we always went to *momojigari* (admire autumn leaves). The boys, spouse and I tramped up and down hills, walked through magnificent temple gardens and ate chestnut ice cream and persimmons. I tended to catch religion on these outings, imagining God going around with a giant palette of paint, splashing colours across the landscape. I suppose everyone has their own idea of what heaven looks like. Mine is a Japanese garden in fall, and a Japanese fall is exactly how I want to exit this world: with almost obscene flair, a loud look-at-how-gorgeous-I-am bang.

And thus we came to winter, a season that I had a complicated relationship with. In Beijing, winter had brought howling winds from Siberia that would coat the city lakes in ice and leave me convinced that happiness was an emotion forever lost. In Brussels, winter had been about fifty shades of grey. The morning's ash grey would give way to a lighter one at noon, before turning to a glowering charcoal by mid-afternoon. But in Tokyo, the winter skies were bright and clear; the temperature rarely fell below zero.

Elsewhere in Japan, in the north, and up in the mountains, the year's work and weariness were washed clean by heavy, powdery snow, prompting musings about whether the cherry blossoms would be early next spring. Modern haiku master Mizuhara Shuoshi's (1892–1981) work evoked Basho when he wrote:

A new year begins –
with the blooming
of a single frosty rose.

And Basho was almost Issa-like in his humour in this one:

When the winter chrysanthemums go,
there's nothing to write about
but radishes.

This particular haiku spoke to me because I was running out of things to write about for my column for *The Hindu* newspaper. The chill made me sticky for home. I was loath to leave the hum of my artificial fireplace to go exploring. The kids, on the other hand, couldn't wait to range. After four years of living in Indonesia, where it had been either hot and humid, or rainy *and* hot and humid, the cold sparked their imagination and reserves of youthful energy. When it snowed they screamed in excitement and lay down in the drifts, shaping snow angels with the hollows of their soft bodies.

And there was skiing. The children wanted to ski and I wanted them to ski, except that they also wanted me to ski and I did not want to at all. I was convinced that in snowy conditions Indians were made to drink chai and eat samosas, indoors. Lumbering about on awkward podal appendages in blizzards was best left to Europeans.

We ended up spending two winters visiting ski resorts, where the boys and Julio took off for the slopes while I read novels, soaked in hot water springs and contemplated haiku. I even tried out snowshoeing, but skis and I remained at a comfortable distance.

Then came a day when we'd been in the world-famous ski resort town of Niseko, in Hokkaido, for almost a week. The setting was exquisite, with giant trees in snowy overcoats – a veritable winter wonderland. I should have been tingling with sensory pleasure, but I felt a bit lonely. I was abandoned all day as the rest of my family spent hours on the slopes. When they finally returned, the children whined at me for not joining them. 'Come on, Mama, give it a try.' My younger one, who was prone to pious one-liners he'd picked up from Cartoon Network shows, said, 'The hardest part of life is being brave enough to try.'

What could I do? I ignored my misgivings and trudged down to the ski school to sign up for a private class the following day. The only spot available was towards the evening, when it was especially frigid, but I was now into the spirit of giving things a shot. Who said you couldn't teach an old dog new tricks? This youthful-at-heart mutt was about to show the world her moves.

The lesson got off to a spanking start. My instructor was sympathetic and encouraging. As advised by him, I made pizza-wedge shapes with my knees and within minutes I was making it down baby slopes without keeling over. Soon we tried out a longer slope, and by the time the session was drawing to an end I was imagining a glorious future as an Alpine skier, my kids looking at me proudly as I whizzed by. 'That's *my* mom!' they'd tell their friends.

The sky grew darker and the instructor said we had time for one last run. 'Want to try simple turns?' he asked. 'Sure,' I replied, when I should have screamed, 'Nooooooo!' Hindsight is so very useless. We set off. Slowly, I turned right, and then left and then, ow, crack, shit!

I'd fallen so badly, my boots had automatically unlocked themselves from the skis. And I knew, I just knew in my gut, that my knee was all wrong. Eventually, I made it back on my feet and refused the instructor's offer to call for the emergency snowmobile to help me off the slopes. Instead, I strapped my skis back on and skied all the way down. What kind of a masochist was I, you might ask? The kind who was in denial.

I hobbled over to the hotel's hot springs, hoping it would help matters. But that night I was in so much pain that all I could do was cry, quietly, so as not to disturb the children. The physiotherapist I consulted the next day told me that heating my knee in the springs had been the worst thing I could have done for it. What I'd really needed was an ice pack. I bit my tongue and didn't say what I was thinking, which was that what my knee had *really* needed was for me to have stayed far away from anything related to skiing.

I was told to get an MRI as soon as I returned to Tokyo. The worry was that I'd torn my ACL (anterior cruciate ligament), an injury that would require surgery and months of rehabilitation. The thought of trying to cope with two young children, a job, and a duplex apartment where I needed to climb up a flight of stairs to get to my bedroom, all with a busted knee, was devastating. I googled ski-related knee injuries to discover that those at greatest risk were female novice skiers over the age of forty. There should have been a sign at the resort warning us off: 'Danger. Some dogs, like you, really are too old for this new trick.'

In the event, it was my MCL (medial collateral ligament) that I had torn, a lesser injury, and after a couple of weeks hobbling about in a knee brace I was back in action. In fact, when concerned acquaintances asked me what had happened, it felt quite grand to casually say I'd been 'injured on the slopes'. It gave me a certain cache, a sense of belonging, albeit quite faux, to the well-heeled, well-toned club of recreational winter athletes. And I knew that this MCL-tear moment was the closest I was ever going to come to my Alpine-skier-making-her-kids-glow-with-pride fantasy. So, I decided to enjoy the recovery period, partly by reading lots of haiku, especially Issa, who invariably had a cheering effect. Here's a winter favourite:

> *Snow melting ...*
> *the village floods*
> *with children!*

What I liked about this verse was not only the sense of danger averted, with the threat of a flood converted into a joyous gaggle of children, but the hint of spring it carried too. The snow was melting ...

It was true that living in Japan I was more attuned to the seasons than I'd ever been before. It's not as though other countries did not have seasonal changes. But in Beijing, for example, I just remember feeling hot in the summer and freezing in the winter. The constant intrusion of the seasons on the quotidian, so much part of the texture of life in Japan, had not been as noticeable there.

In Japan, unlike say, Indonesia, the seasons were climatically quite marked, but also people talked about them more than the norm. The menus in restaurants changed constantly, depending on the seasonality of the food. Flower arrangements in hotels were adjusted to remain in tune with the passage of the year. The role of the seasons in traditional art was well established. One of the rules of haiku was that the poems must have a *kigo* or seasonal reference word in them. Tea ceremony bowls and the decoration of a tearoom were always in harmony with the season. The kimonos worn at different times of the year differed not only in fabric, but also in their motifs.

So, the question arose about why the seasons seemed to have greater resonance in Japan than elsewhere. There was much writing, dare I say orientalizing, about how the Japanese race was somehow more in tune with nature than everyone else. Foreigners, like the Greek-Irish Japanologist Lafcadio Hearne (1850–1904), had bought into, and in turn, perpetuated this idea. 'It is inborn in the Japanese,' Hearne wrote in a July 1892 essay in the *Atlantic* magazine,[50] 'the soul of the race comprehends Nature infinitely better than we (Westerners) do … '

Japanese writers themselves, including Zen exponent Dr Suzuki, had long opined that 'closeness to nature' was one of the qualities that gave Japan its Japaneseness. These writings were collectively known as *nihonjinron,* and while the genre was mainly a twentieth-century phenomenon, its origins dated back to Japan's nineteenth-century encounters with an ascendant Europe. In fact, they could be seen as a response to Japan's historical quest for identity, a quest that had always been complicated by its cultural debt to China, and was further roiled by its growing knowledge of a modernizing West.

Nihonjinron has been defined as 'a popular discursive enterprise devoted to the delineation and explication of the unique qualities of the Japanese, which invariably tout the ... moral and spiritual superiority of the Japanese vis-à-vis other peoples'.[51] Its tropes included an ostensible Japanese propensity to collectivism, in which clearly defined boundaries between the self and others were ambiguous, the salience of nonverbal communication, and an exceptional relationship with nature.[52]

The self-essentialization of national traits was hardly something that the Japanese were alone in having done. All nation-building endeavours were guilty of the same. By the Meiji revolution of 1868, Japan had decided that in order to achieve power equivalence with Europe, emulation was the way forward. There was a theory that it was around this time that the archipelago acculturated 'nature' as a tool of national self-assertion. Japan's belief in its special connection to nature was therefore nothing but self-imposed orientalism, intended to elevate the East through discursive means.[53]

Yikes! So, was all my new-found seasonal sensitivity just the result of my being susceptible to the propaganda of Japanese nationalists and their fellow travellers? If I thought about it, nature was essential to poetry around the world. Wasn't the Bard forever comparing women to a 'summer's day' (which, btw, was pretty hideous in the Japanese/Indian context), and asking people to hark the nightingale and such? And then, of course, there were Chinese aesthetics, which were the fount of their Japanese counterpart. Peach trees, blossoms, moon-gazing, insect-appreciation, verse-writing; the whole shebang was Chinese, before it was Japanese.

But unlike China, Japan hadn't had a communist revolution and its aesthetes had avoided being sent down to be re-educated by shovelling manure in Inner Mongolia. Modern Japan was what China might have been if Mao Zedong had not existed. Classical traditions lived on in Japan, where they had been uprooted and smashed in China.

And yet, for all the academic training that had me primed to sniff out and pounce on even the sneakiest of orientalisms, there was something about Japan that *was* not-China, not-Europe, not anywhere but itself. I'd lived across the world, but nowhere had I seen more people stop more often to photograph flowers than in Japan. And, (I need to switch to sotto voce before writing this because it is so evidently ridiculous), *the cicadas did sound more sonorous here.*

A 'nation' was imagined into being, and the building blocks of the construction – the flotsam of national identity – became as real as the geographic borders of the nation itself.[54] In China, the sense of an unbroken 5,000-year history (total nonsense, in reality) was integral to the people's idea of who they were. In India, the ideals of secularism and plurality used to be what made us different from everyone else. In Belgium, usually warring Wallonia and Flanders were united in their firm rejection of the french fry as having anything to do with the French (it was, of course, Belgian).

In Japan, it was believed that the seasons made the country itself, and so, I think, it became true. Unlike other Asian nations, Japan had not been colonized. As a result, anti-imperialism could not become one of the defining foundations of its national identity. The Chinese were united by their humiliation in the nineteenth-century Opium Wars. Indians had the Mahatma Gandhi-led freedom struggle to bind them. Indonesia's diverse peoples all 'remembered' the egregious racism of their erstwhile Dutch colonial masters.

But Japan had been aggressor rather than victim. It could not appeal to its own victimhood to prove its essential goodness. Claiming to hear the chirping of insects in a unique way was a substitute of sort; and a beautiful, benign one at that.

I want to end this chapter with my discovery of the most gorgeous mobile phone app called '72 Seasons: A year seen through the ancient Japanese calendar'. It allowed the user to discover Japan's seventy-two micro-seasons (called *ko*), each lasting five days.[55] Using it was like a poetic pilgrimage through the ever-changing landscape of the Japanese year. I am writing these words in the season called 'white dew on grass' (approximately 7 September to 11 September). The app also gives users a corresponding haiku and a description of the food, fish and activity most closely associated with the ko. Here's what I got for 'white dew on grass':

Crisply
The carp slips
Away from the murk.

Seasonal fish: pacific Saury or sanma; seasonal vegetable: pumpkin; seasonal fruit: peach; seasonal activity: harvest moon.

A random sampling of more ko:

> 8–12 October, *Kōgan kitaru,* Wild geese return
> 7–11 November, *Tsubaki hajimete hiraku,* Camellia's bloom
> 22–26 November, *Niji kakurete miezu,* Rainbows Hide
> 1–4 January, *Yuki watarite mugi nobiru,* Wheat sprouts under snow
> 25–29 January, *Kiwamizu kōri tsumeru,* Ice thickens on streams

Research revealed that the seventy-two micro-seasons were actually based on the ancient Chinese almanac. But really, who cares? In seven years of living in China, I'd never even heard of the concept. In Japan, I have an app on my phone to I discover what's up with the flowers and rainbows every day.

4

Waterloo

It was that time of the week again. My stomach sank to my knees, but I ground my teeth (along with mixing my metaphors) and buzzed in Michiko-san, my Japanese teacher. Michiko-san was lovely. In her mid-sixties, she sported girlish bangs, always dressed neatly and was unnaturally punctual for class. How was it possible for anyone to unvaryingly time their arrival to the second? The answer, it transpired, wasn't particularly mysterious. My children discovered her hanging about in our building lobby one day, and so we learned that she usually arrived fifteen minutes early and lurked in front of the door staring at her watch until the moment the seconds-hand hit the hour before ringing the bell.

To say I preferred having a tooth cavity filled to my weekly class was only a slight exaggeration. But it should not be taken to reflect poorly on Michiko-san's teaching, as much as the subject she taught: Japanese. The language of

Japan was my linguistic Waterloo, my lexical bête noir, my syntactical antagonist.

In Jakarta, after a year-and-a-half of casual Bahasa Indonesia classes, I'd been able to chatter away with modest felicity. A decade earlier, I'd learned to get my point across in Mandarin Chinese. And Chinese, everyone agreed, was hard.

The two major differences between Chinese and most other languages were its tones and writing system. Chinese was a phonetically poor language, resulting in an abundance of homonyms distinguishable only by their tones, of which there were four in Mandarin: a high flat one, a rising question-like one, an up-and-down one and finally, a harsh downward one. The potential for confusion was infinite. '*Mai*', for example, could mean either buy or sell, depending on the tone, '*nar*' could mean there or where, and '*yanjing*' could be either eyes or spectacles.

But what Chinese lacked in range of sounds it made up for in the characters (called *hanzi*) or ideograms that formed the basis of its writing system. Instead of an alphabet that phonetically combined sounds to produce meaning, Chinese had thousands of individual characters that expressed a meaning, largely independent of phonics.

The Japanese also used Chinese characters, which they called *kanji*, as the basis for one of their scripts, which often led people who knew I spoke Mandarin to assume that I'd find Japanese a cinch. It was a poor assumption.

To begin with, I *spoke* rather than read Chinese. I knew a few characters, but infinitely less than the ones I didn't know. And even the ones I was familiar with were of scant help since they were pronounced completely differently in the two languages. Take the characters for 'character' itself as an example. They were pronounced hanzi in Mandarin Chinese and kanji in Japanese.

Chinese

Japanese

Another example: the kanji comprising the name of the Japanese Prime Minister, Abe Shinzo (安倍 晋三), were pronounced Ānbèi Jinsan in Chinese.

Worse, Japanese kanji usually had two completely different readings. Some had as many as ten. The kanji for mountain, for instance, was written the same way as the hanzi: 山. But while in Chinese the character was always pronounced *shan*, in Japanese it could be pronounced as either *yama* or *san*. Similarly, 木 meant wood/tree in both Chinese and Japanese, but although it was always *mu* in Chinese, in Japanese it could be either *moku* or *ki*. The reason for all this variability was Japan's enduring identity crisis that sprang from its simultaneous indebtedness to China and its desire to distance itself from the debt. Hence the dual readings: one that borrowed elements of the original Chinese pronunciation, called *onyomi* (for example *san* for *shan*) and the other that was 'original' Japanese, called *kunyomi* (for example, *yama*).

Moreover, some *kanji* had either several extra meanings to their hanzi counterparts or even different meanings entirely. For example, the kanji for steam train, 汽車, was the hanzi for automobile, and the kanji for the verb 'to listen', 聞 , was the hanzi for the verb 'to smell'. And so on. Dear reader, are you beginning to fantasize about fillings at the dentist? Not yet? Fear not. You'll get there soon enough.

Chinese needed characters because it didn't have an alphabet. This posed certain challenges when dealing with non-Chinese words with a phonetic universe that was broader than Mandarin's limited one. For example, it was impossible to write Pallavi in hanzi because there was no character that corresponded to the compound of sounds it entailed. Almost all foreign-origin proper nouns had to be rechristened in Chinese. America was *Mei Guo,* McDonalds *Mai Dang Lao,* the Olympics *Ao Yun Hui,* and President Trump *Telangpu.*

But Japanese not only had an alphabet, it had *two* with forty-six letters each: *hiragana* and *katakana.* I realized in my very first class with Michiko-san that Japanese did not need kanji at all. You could write down any sentence in Japanese using just hiragana; or katakana, an alphabet whose existence was even more egregious than kanji's. Katakana merely repeated all the sounds of hiragana, and its only purpose was to indicate words of foreign origin, as opposed to 'original' pristinely Japanese words. Arguably, it inscribed an ontology of race, Japanese and foreign, into the language itself.

As a foreigner, my name in Japanese was written in katakana as バ ラ ビ (Parabi), instead of in hiragana, which would have made it ばらび. Consequently, my foreignness was folded into the fabric of the language. You didn't even have to read all the letters in my name to know it was foreign. The slightest of glances would register the fact that it was written in katakana and therefore not Japanese. Katakana signalled the foreignness of what was being said, even before anything was said.

The useful thing about it was that unlike in Chinese, you could transliterate most sounds ('l' and 'v' excepted) from other languages, which accounted for all the katakana vocabulary in Japanese. These were essentially Japanified English words. Japanese for baby chair, for example, was *babychea*, spaghetti was *supagetti*, pet shop was *petto shoppu* and gasoline stand was *gasoriin sutando*.

I soon realized that the kind of pidgin that English-speaking people thought Chinese people spoke was actually *katakana* talk. It worked by giving vowel endings to English words. You could go to a restaurant in Japan and raise one finger and ask for *caki*, and you would have just intelligibly ordered a piece of cake. If you wanted your soup hot, you needed to ask for it to be *hotto*, and so on. It was a bit disconcerting talking like this. Initially, I'd felt I was being insulting, poking fun at the Japanese accent, even though katakana talk was perfectly legitimate in Japan.

My earlier point remained valid, however. Foreign sounds including *babychea*, *hotto* and the rest could have been imported with the hiragana script too. Other than highlighting the 'otherness' of certain words, katakana was redundant. Which takes me back to my original polemic on kanji. Were characters necessary at all when you had a perfectly good alphabet?

If I dared mention these thoughts publicly, even in jest, I risked causing people to run out of the room screaming, 'the horror!'. Reams have been written about the indescribable loss of richness in meaning that dispensing with kanji would entail. More reams yet exist on how the present combination of the three scripts, along with the convoluted rules governing when which one is used, allows the reader to absorb meaning in a uniquely directly manner.

There was even a theory about how the Japanese language made the brains of people unique and superior. This argument, popularized by a doctor, Tadanobu Tsunoda, was that Japanese-speaking people processed information in the right side of their brains – the side that deals with feelings rather than facts. He believed them therefore to be especially attuned to the sounds of nature, in particular the chirping of crickets, which he claimed Japanese heard as language rather than sound.[56]

It is true that the Japanese language has more than one onomatopoeia for cricket-chirping. The *matsumushi* or pine cricket goes *chin-chiro*, while the *suzumushi* or bell-ring cricket says *rin-rin-rin*. But to jump from this to Tsunoda's theories of the 'Japanese brain' was a stretch.

My suggestion of dispensing with kanji, or even katakana, is made tongue firmly in cheek. Characters do have a beauty and meaning that is impossible to fully capture in an alphabet-based language. But I did come to believe, tongue back in its place, that the Japanese language threw into relief another major contradiction characteristic of Japan: the desire for simplicity with the tendency to complicate.

In linguistic matters, the latter trumped the former, conclusively. There was seemingly nothing that the Japanese language didn't make more convoluted than necessary. Chinese had been a superbly direct language: conjugation, gender, tense were as fuss-free as a Marie Kondo-ed closet. For example, past tense was achieved by adding a '*le*' to the verb. 'I go' in past tense would be 'I go *le*'. Even with all the characters to learn, there was room in studying Chinese to move beyond the language and begin engaging with ideas. With Japanese, I felt like I'd been condemned to the end of thought. All there was space for in my brain was the different forms of verbs, and learning how to negate them.

When I queried Japanese friends about the intricacies of grammar, they tended to nod slowly and hum. Getting any clarifying response was rare. My initial reaction had been to assume that my question had triggered them into some kind of Zen meditation on language. It was also possible that they'd fallen silent out of boredom or confusion, the two emotions most commonly experienced by me in any Japanese class. Or perhaps it could have just been the fact that I was talking to them in English, a language the Japanese found notoriously hard to learn.

To be fair, Japan's English problem was but a trifle compared with my Japanese problem. I was getting older and crabbier and had less time than ever, courtesy my two boisterous boys. Blaming the language for being difficult was only an excuse for my own fallibilities as I tried and failed to learn the million ways of counting things in Japanese.

The 'one' in one person, one-year-old, one umbrella, one coffee, one ticket, one month, etc., was *different* in *every* case.[57] I begged my teacher, Michiko-san, for shortcuts and hacks. She only shook her head sadly. 'Must memorize, sorry.' For the first time in my always-the-teacher's-pet life, I began fooling around in class, trying to waste time so that the hour would hurry up and finish. I'd switch to English and deviously engage Michiko-san on topics I knew she found really interesting, like cats.

The only occasion that my Japanese teacher had ever cancelled a class was a day when she had registered to attend a seminar on feline dental hygiene. 'How do you brush your cats' teeth?' she asked me (in English) at our first session together, post-seminar. 'I don't,' I replied (in English), at which she'd been so obviously horrified that she'd flushed a deep red in embarrassment at having forced me into making this confession. She'd buried her nose in our textbook to recover, which could have taken a long time, but just then Tofu, one of my cats, had emerged from the shadows and rubbed up against her leg.

Michiko-san had been in instant ecstasy. 'Oooo, Tofu-chan,' she'd crooned. Of the many things I had grown to love about Japan – kintsugi, Zazen, safety, punctuality, etc. – a contender for the top spot was how the Japanese addressed cats and other animals with honorifics.

The most common honorific in Japan, san, was similar to the ji that Indians attach as suffixes to names, in being gender-neutral, unlike Mr or Mrs. It was, however, used more commonly than ji, with even friends referring to each other with san attached to their names. There was also *sama*, a more respectful version of san used for people of a higher social rank, guests, customers and so on. Convicted criminals got their own title, *hikoku*, which was different from the one used for undertrials, *yogisha*. Then there was *kun*, typically used by seniors for those perceived as underlings. And there was chan, an affectionate diminutive for children, a bit like Master or Miss.

There were many others (*bo, senpai, kohai*) too, but I was really taken with how the Japanese used *chan* for animals like cats. Michiko-san addressing my cat as 'Tofu-chan,' was the equivalent of her saying 'Tofu ji' or 'Miss Tofu'. (Interestingly, only dogs and cats were hailed with chan. Monkeys, goats, raccoon dogs, tigers and sundry other animals were addressed with the more adult san.)

In any event, I struggled on with my Japanese classes for well over a year, during which time I suffered the humiliation of having Michiko-*san* downgrade me from using the standard text book *Japanese for Busy People*, to the really basic *Survival Japanese*. 'I think it will be better for you,' she'd said cryptically, when suggesting the change. But at the end, all I had to show for it was the ability to ask a taxi driver to turn left/right at the next traffic light. It might not sound like much. But I could do it really politely.

Nearly anything you said in Japanese depended on the context of the formality of the conversation, as well as the relative social status of the interlocutors. For example, if you wanted to tell a friend, 'I saw our teacher, Tomoko-san', formal language would become activated even if your friend and you were at the same level socially, because the subject of the sentence, the teacher, was always of a 'higher' status. You would therefore say something like, '*Tomoko-sensei ni o me ni kakatta*', which translates as, 'My eyes respectfully fell upon teacher Tomoko.'

It was uphill all right, but I kept at it in the hope that eventually the drip-drip of vocabulary would coalesce into a mighty reservoir of knowledge. But then came a class when I tried making a sentence like, 'The cat was cute and playful.' For the conjunction 'and' I confidently used the Japanese *to* (と), which I knew to mean 'and'. It was part of my staple ordering-at-restaurants vocabulary. 'I'll take the *supagetti to caki*,' was the kind of sentence that tripped right off my tongue.

Michiko-san looked at me sorrowfully, aware that she was about to kick a woman who was already down. '*To,*' she said, 'only worked as "and" when linking two nouns.' Linking two adjectives was trickier. '*Gomenasai,*' she apologized. Linking two adjectives required changing the first adjective to an alternative verb form. However, if an adjective with a negative connotation were to be combined with one with a positive connotation, then there was yet another rule. So, you conjugated 'the room was big and cozy' differently from 'the room was big and messy'. That was it: the proverbial straw that broke the camel's back.

A few days later I wrote to Michiko-san explaining that much as I enjoyed our classes and would miss them greatly, my journalistic work was making it difficult to find the time to continue studying. The reply I received expressed regret, but understanding at my decision. I was a very clever student who had made so much progress after all, but I must, of course, prioritize my job.

Taken together, these emails were a masterpiece in mannered insincerity. Michiko-san could indeed be proud of her 'clever' student for having brought what could have been an uncomfortable rupture to an elegantly Japanese close.

5

No Foreigners Please, We Are Japanese

During the spring of our third year in Japan, mysterious billboards began sprouting alongside the blossoms all over Tokyo. They featured rows of numbered square boxes, arranged sequentially from 1 to about 40. My boys and I walked past one on our way to the local supermarket. There was another billboard in front of the park, and still another near the dentist's office.

We drove each other crazy hazarding guesses about what these were. A community lucky draw? A neighbourhood game of bingo? An effort to teach toddlers their numbers?

Then one morning, the numerals had been replaced by faces – mostly photographs of clean-cut men in near-identical dark suits and inoffensive ties. Occasionally, there was a picture of a woman, also impeccably tidy and wholesome. It transpired that this was Japanese democracy in operation. The photos were of the candidates for the 900-plus local assembly seats among Tokyo's twenty-three wards.

If I'm honest, the guessing games about the numbers I'd played with my kids were more exciting than local politics in Japan, and I would have paid no more attention had it not been for a news item in the *Japan Times*. One Yogendra Puranik had been elected as Edogawa ward councillor, becoming the first-ever Indian-born Japanese politician. This was a story I needed to follow up.

Unlike many other rich countries, Japan had resisted multiculturalism. The archipelago's foreign-born population of about 2.5 million was just 2 per cent of the total.[58] Tokyo was particularly chary of refugees. As mentioned earlier, in 2019, of the 10,375 asylum applications Japan received, it accepted forty-four.

In the great cities of the world – London, Paris, New York – taking public transport was a kaleidoscopic experience. Even in Brussels, the commute from our home to Julio's office could see me seated next to rotund Africans and lean Nordic interns, harried Vietnamese waiters and colourfully dressed Romani folks. In these cities you couldn't tell the locals from the foreigners by the colour of their skin or their clothes, as much as by their expertise in negotiating the city and its codes – perhaps from the assurance with which they rang the stop bells on buses.

But despite Japan's centrality to the world economy and its attractiveness as a rich, safe country, this was not the case in Tokyo. Everything seemed to mark out the foreignness of foreigners here, from the way they laughed (showing too many teeth), to the way they might hum aloud the song stuck in their heads. 'Otherness' was stamped into the use of katakana for writing all foreign names, regardless of whether they belonged to naturalized citizens or permanent residents.

Japan's propensity to homogeneity made Yogendra Puranik's election very intriguing. How had this visibly foreign-born man made it into the exclusive bastion of Japanese politics? I tracked down the newly minted ward counsellor's phone number and requested a meeting. Puranik sounded hoarse on the phone as he explained he didn't have a moment to spare. 'Too many interviews,' he whispered in sore-throat discomfort. The only time he could spare was on a public holiday the following week.

But Julio was travelling and my children would be home from school on that day. I explained my dilemma, expecting Puranik to say that was my problem, not his. Instead, he told me to bring the children along. 'No problem,' he wheezed. 'I love kids. They are most welcome.'

Unsuspecting Mr Puranik was not acquainted with my particular duo who were capable, on some days, of putting off humanity from any inclination towards procreation, but there was no choice. I decided to take them with me while sending up a silent thanks for the Indian Uncle. I was cognizant that in Japan, women who tried to juggle looking after small children and work outside the home had to deal with the Japanese Uncle, who, as a rule, was much less accommodating. In 2017, a city assemblywoman, Yuka

Ogata, was thrown out of an assembly session for bringing her seven-month-old to the meeting. (She was thrown out again, from another assembly session the following year, this time for speaking while sucking on a cough drop.)[59]

On the morning of our appointment, the boys and I took the metro to the Nishikasai neighbourhood in Edogawa, where Puranik lived. As we neared the eastern suburb, Indian faces began to pop up like flotsam amongst the sea of Japanese. I'd lived in Tokyo for a while by now, but this was my first time venturing into what had been dubbed by the Japanese media as Tokyo's *Little India.*

We alighted and began to navigate along quiet residential streets. With one eye on Google maps and one on our surroundings, I was slightly disappointed at how little there was to distinguish this neighbourhood from any other. This was no Brick Lane. It was 1960s-modern, clean, leafy, functional – unmistakably Tokyo. But from what I'd read, I knew that Nishikasai boasted several Indian food restaurants, three spice stores and a 600-student-strong Indian school. Almost 4,000 Indians, or about 30 per cent of the 11,153 Indians that were resident in Tokyo in 2018, lived here. They were primarily IT engineers and software programmers.[60]

By Japan's standards these were not insignificant figures. As a point of comparison, there were only 440 Indians who'd lived in Tokyo four decades ago.[61] A sharp increase in their numbers began around the turn of the millennium, when worries about the 'Y2K problem' had several Japanese companies scrambling to invite Indian engineers to work on upgrading their IT systems. In 2000, the duration of the working visa for software engineers from India was expanded from one year to three years.

Nishikasai emerged as a residential hub for these engineers because UR, a public housing group located there, began to rent to Indians without the need for a local guarantor, and more importantly, without prejudice. It was not easy at the time for foreigners to lease apartments from Japanese landlords, many of whom felt that *gaijin* could not be trusted.

In the years since, Japan's demographic woes had increased and the country faced a shortfall of about 200,000 IT engineers, a gap that was predicted to swell to 600,000 by 2030.[62] In 2018, the Japanese government announced a new visa scheme for the 'highly skilled', who would not only be allowed to renew their visas indefinitely but also to bring their families along. The response had been underwhelming, with many foreign professionals finding Japan to be less than welcoming to outsiders in terms of both language and work culture.[63]

All of this made me curious to find out what light Yogendra Puranik's life trajectory could throw on the possibility for foreigners to integrate into Japanese institutional and social structures. Puranik's home was a narrow, multi-storeyed affair, large by Japanese standards. An Indian restaurant, run by his mother, was located on the ground floor, and we entered through here, the aroma of biryani wafting about temptingly. Puranik was slim, with a receding hairline. Dressed in a turtleneck and jacket, he ushered us up to the floor above the restaurant and into a room draped in colourful Indian fabrics. Yogi, as Puranik insisted on being called, pulled up a couple of chairs for us to sit on. The boys sprawled out on the floor next to us.

Throughout our chat he stressed that it wasn't Indians who'd voted for him. Foreign nationals, even those who have been resident in Japan for years, were not permitted to vote, so Yogi's electoral success had little to do with them. He'd garnered a total of 6,477 votes in the elections, of which, he said, perhaps four or five had been from Indians who had obtained Japanese nationality.

Yogi had been born in Ambarnath, a suburb of Mumbai in western India. His father was a machinist in an ordnance factory and his mother a seamstress. Eventually, they'd moved to the nearby city of Pune, where he'd enrolled for a degree in physics at university, while studying Japanese and German in the evenings. In 1999, Yogi secured a year-long Japanese government scholarship to research educational techniques at a university in Saitama, near Tokyo. He spent the year being awed by Japanese precision, discipline and cleanliness. 'It was like, unbelievable,' he said, shaking his head as though still amazed.

In 2001, Yogi was back in Japan, having found a job as a data analyst with IBM, and he had since stayed put in the country. In 2012, following three interviews and a mountain of paperwork, he was eventually successful in getting Japanese citizenship. The process included a police inspection of his home and checks on his reputation in the locality. 'They asked my neighbours if I followed the garbage recycling rules,' he laughed.

Garbage sorting in Japan was so complicated and mistakes so frowned upon by neighbours that Yogi believed recycling training was among the most urgent needs of the foreign community in Tokyo. After all, in India most people didn't even bother to make the most basic dry and wet waste segregation before disposing their garbage, and it wasn't uncommon for people to jettison their trash in the open at roadside dumps.

But, just as the assemblyman was about to expand on this, my until-now-somewhat-decently-behaved children began squabbling. Yogi laughed indulgently. 'Lovely boys,' he murmured, revealing the soul of a true politician.

So, how did this erstwhile data analyst become involved in politics? Once I'd sorted out the boys' dispute, I put the question to him. Yogi traced his current avatar to 2005, the year he first volunteered for the Edogawa ward summer festival, helping to erect tents, run games stalls for children and clean up afterwards. He went on to become a regular volunteer at community events, but did not consider standing for elections of any kind until he was approached, in 2016, by a local assemblyman, about a plan that the ward was developing to formalize the Nishikasai neighbourhood as a Little India in Tokyo (LIT).

The plan was focused on opening more Indian restaurants in the area, building a temple and establishing a special hospital for Indians. But Yogi was unimpressed. 'What we needed was more integration, not this kind of ghettoization,' he said. 'Rather than a separate hospital, we needed more

English-speaking staff in existing hospitals and better Japanese language learning opportunities for foreigners in the ward.'[64]

Yogi made a counter proposal with an emphasis on Japanese language classes as well as 'integration training'. This brought us back to the labyrinthine garbage sorting rules that Yogi was convinced should be the centrepiece of such training, along with earthquake emergency drills. But his suggestions were brushed aside. It was then that he decided, 'If they will not change the plan, then I will have to change it.' Three years later he was spending his days standing in front of train stations and shopping malls canvassing for votes.

Yogi was aware that winning an election was going to be a tough ask in what was a notoriously foreigner-averse, arguably racist, society. The assemblyman had himself suffered so many race-related slights that he could no longer remember them all. Most commonly, he said, Japanese were reluctant to sit next to Indians on the metro. Sometimes they refused to make way for foreigners in crowded compartments, even when there was space. 'Once someone yelled at me: "You've taken our jobs".' Many landlords refuse to rent to non-Japanese, even today. At work, Yogi said that even as he climbed up the hierarchy he was kept out of crucial decision-making. His ideas were usually dismissed. 'I am forever an outsider there.'

When a Japanese friend proposed Yogi as a member of the Edogawa ward summer festival executive committee, he was initially rejected purely on the grounds of being foreign. 'It's not good for foreigners to hear about any problems with the festival, I was told,' Yogi said. But his friend countered, 'If a foreigner can help us with the festival in every way, he can also be on the committee.' Nonetheless, it took Yogi two years before he was allowed to join.

But it was many of the people he met through this voluntary community work who ultimately stepped up and campaigned for him during the ward elections. They would ride around in a specially appointed mini-van handing out flyers. Yogi himself began his campaigning day outside the local metro station, where he introduced himself to any commuter who would stop. 'Many people came up to me and told me to go home, that this election was not for foreigners,' he said. 'One guy told me that I should go and clean the public toilet before standing for elections.'

The assemblyman remained sanguine. 'There will be unpleasant incidents everywhere. At least things are getting better in Japan.' And the fact was that he had been elected to the ward assembly and was confident enough of the future to be eyeing the post of ward mayor in the next election.

Before we left, the boys and I took a few selfies as mementos. At the door, Yogi coughed into one hand and waved us goodbye with the other until we were out of sight. As we walked back to the train station, I thought about how I had been consistently, and unpleasantly, surprised by the extent to which racism permeated Japanese society in both lazy, careless ways and in more problematic, deep-seated ones.

The former included the infamous 'gaijin seat' in trains that Yogi had referred to – the seat next to a foreigner that remained stubbornly empty even on a crowded train, with some Japanese preferring to stand rather than sit next to a gaijin.[65] There was also the phenomenon of foreigners being denied tables at restaurants. Our very first attempt at a meal at a Japanese eatery, only a day after our arrival in Tokyo, had provided front-row seats to that particular experience.

We'd wandered past a sliding wooden slatted door with a fluttering *noren* curtain, the standard signifier of a Japanese restaurant. Excited about whatever gastronomic adventure awaited within, we'd slid the door open and poked our heads inside to be greeted by a flustered looking, kimono-clad woman who had hurtled towards us, arms held up to form a cross – the Japanese symbol for NO. Bewildered at this unexpected rudeness, we'd tried, in broken Japanese, to ask for a table, while the lady continued to cross her hands in front of her face and squeezed her eyes shut as though wishing us into vanishing. When she finally opened her eyes and saw us still standing there, she spoke slowly, as if to idiots. 'NO SUSHI,' she said. 'NO TEMPURA.' To her visible dismay, we'd shrugged our shoulders and said we'd eat whatever they had to give us.

In the end we were admitted, although we were mysteriously denied one of the several empty tables and made to sit at the counter instead. We ate a delicious (and expensive) meal of grilled fish and soup. As the evening wore on, the lady in the kimono turned markedly more gracious, pouring sake into our cups with dancer-like elegance. But it had been an unsettling experience.

Over the next few months, I learned that it was not all together uncommon for some restaurants, and even some hotels, to deny entry to non-Japanese. I thought this shocking, but when I brought the topic of this practice up with a group of Japanese friends, they seemed unfazed, their explanations ranging from the inadequate to the appalling.

One line of reasoning was that the restaurant staff were afraid of not being able to meet the needs of foreigners since they didn't speak English. But how did they know that the foreigners couldn't speak Japanese, I countered? Next, I was told that many foreigners didn't know how to 'behave' in Japanese settings. They might not take off their shoes before entering the tatami mat area, or they might speak loudly on their mobile phones, upsetting the harmony of the occasion for other diners. When this didn't satisfy me either, I was told consolingly that the practice of keeping foreigners out of certain establishments was not aimed at foreigners 'like me', but at the Chinese.

In a survey carried out by Japan's Justice Ministry in 2017, nearly a third of foreign residents said that they had experienced derogatory remarks because of their racial background, while about 40 per cent had suffered housing discrimination. Among the 4,252 foreigners canvassed, the majority identified as Chinese and Korean. Over 40 per cent had lived in Japan for more than a decade.

One in four job seekers said they were denied employment because of being foreign, and one in five believed they earned less than their Japanese counterparts for similar work. Putting paid to the notion that such discrimination was related to language, 95 per cent of foreigners whose job applications were rejected, and over 90 per cent of those whose housing requests were denied, were able to speak Japanese 'conversationally, professionally or fluently'.

At this point I contacted Debito Arudou, as one did when investigating racism in Japan. The author of *Embedded Racism: Japan's Visible Minorities and Racial Discrimination*, Arudou was a very vocal protestor of what he believed to be wide-ranging discriminatory practices in Japanese society. His critics painted him as a bit of a nut case. In a country like Japan, his refusal to shut up made him indisputably idiosyncratic.

Originally from the United States, Arudou has lived in Japan since 1991 and took Japanese citizenship in 2000. In 1999, he and his family were refused entry to a public bathhouse in the northern city of Otaru, on the grounds of his being foreign. When his Japanese wife asked whether this exclusion also applied to their daughters who had been born and raised in Japan, the manager said that one daughter who was 'Japanese-looking' could enter, but not the other one.

On the phone from an undisclosed location, because he claimed revealing his whereabouts could put him in danger from his many haters, Arudou pinpointed this as the moment that set him down the path of activism. He believed that in some ways, visible minorities like himself presented an even easier target of racism than north-east Asians like the Koreans. He launched into a lengthy recount of all the times he'd been stopped by the police in Japan and asked to show his identity card. The only reason for this, he claimed, was the practice of racial profiling, common amongst the Japanese police and condoned by many politicians. Arudou pointed out that the hugely popular three-time Tokyo governor, Shintaro Ishihara, had told the military in a speech in 2000 that they needed to prepare for the fact that in the event of a natural disaster, foreigners would likely riot and cause civil disorder.[66] Ishihara had also repeatedly blamed Japan's crime rate on foreigners, as had the National Police Association.[67]

It was a fact that signs stating that certain businesses – spas, hot-spring baths, hairdressers, restaurants, brothels – were only open to Japanese clientele were not exceptional in Japan. On Arudou's blog, examples of exclusionary signs were shared with distressing regularity. When I visited the website, a recent post included the refusal of entry to a golf course to Sapporo Consadole soccer player, Jay Bothroyd, on account of his not being Japanese.[68] There was also write-up of a 'Japanese Only' sign spotted at a diving and hiking tour company in Okinawa, and another at a bar in Tokyo's popular Asakusa district.

One case that gained brief press notoriety was that of a two-Michelin-star sushi restaurant in Tokyo's swanky Ginza neighbourhood that had refused to make a reservation for Mo Bangfu, a Chinese journalist who had been resident in Japan for thirty years and was fluent in Japanese. Later, the restaurant confirmed that it refused reservations to non-Japanese customers as a policy, unless a hotel concierge served as intermediary. The explanation given was that restaurant employees did not have the language proficiency to explain 'requirements' to foreign patrons.[69]

There had even been cases of 'Japanese Only' signs at Japanese-run establishments abroad. A hotel in the southern Indian city of Bengaluru, for example, was found refusing to serve Indian clientele on the grounds that their establishment was exclusively for the Japanese.[70]

Personally, I didn't encounter a 'No Foreigners Allowed' type of sign, but one of Julio's colleagues came across a note pasted outside a restaurant in Kyoto which did not mince a word: *Foreigners Visiting ban - You guys not so welcome.* I did sometimes find signs in front of business establishments that stated 'Foreigners Welcome'. These made me uncomfortable, despite their intent to reassure. I couldn't help but read them as indicative of an underlying assumption that in the absence of such a sign, foreigners would not be welcome.

It took considerable disingenuity to claim that keeping certain spaces exclusively Japanese was a benign decision taken in the interest of preserving social accord. But these were hardly the most egregious manifestations of Japanese racism. That 'honour' belonged to the regular weekend processions carried out by members of far-right organizations screaming virulently racist invective through loudspeakers.

In 2016, the Justice Ministry revealed that between April 2012 and September 2015, 1,150 rallies were held in Japan featuring hate speech, including calls for ethnic Koreans 'to get the hell out of Japan' or threatening to stamp them out like 'cockroaches'.[71] Known as *uyoku dantai,* these far-right groups were an inescapable presence in public life. The National Police Organization estimated there to be over 1,000 such organizations with about 100,000 members in total.[72]

Since we lived close to the preferred stomping grounds of ultra-nationalists – the Chinese and South Korean embassies – our Sunday mornings were regularly shattered by silver-haired septuagenarians riding around in Mad Max-style convoys, flying the rising-sun flag that was used by the

Japanese army from 1870 to 1945, screeching nasty sounding things to the background of imperial music.

Even more than the existence of these unreconstructed warmongers in an ostensibly pacifist country, what struck me – maybe because I couldn't actually understand their words – was how loud they were in a country that valued quiet. Ordinary passersby did a great job of unseeing them. Anyone caught talking on a mobile phone on a subway or crunching audibly on a rice cracker on the bus would be the object of many a tut-tut, but there was no outrage at the shenanigans of the *uyoku dantai*. People just went glaze-eyed, going about their business pretending that there was no one blocking the roads and shrieking about the glory of Japan's militaristic past.

Much of society seemed to be in denial that anything like racism even existed in Japan, there being a widespread belief that racism was about discrimination by white people against those of colour. As a non-white country, Japan was therefore exempt from the need to redress it. The notion that Japan was a uniquely homogenous, racially pure society with few 'outsiders' was deep-seated, reinforcing the ostensible irrelevance of 'racism' to public policy or discussion.

The roots of such thinking can be traced to the Meiji revolution of 1868. The new constitution promulgated in the aftermath of the revolution established a state based on the creation myth that the Emperor was a direct descendant of the 'original' Yamato clan, and that all Japanese were organically related to him. The idea of a single racial and cultural identity became central to Japan's constructed sense of itself, allowing for the fallacious reasoning that the Japanese were homogenous, ergo they could not be racist.

This was just not true. There was now scholarly consensus that the Japanese were in fact a mixture of Korean-like 'Yayoi' people who immigrated to the archipelago around 400 BC, and an indigenous population who walked over land bridges during low sea levels of ice ages some 12,000 years ago. The average Japanese, however, remained unaware of academic research into their demographic origins. Many seemed to take the legend that Japan sprang into existence fully formed in 660 BC, when the first emperor, Jimmu, the descendant of the sun goddess Amaterasu, led the 'Japanese people' to the Yamato plain in the Kyoto region, as truth-like enough to warrant little critical interrogation. Even today, Jimmu's accession is marked as National Foundation Day on 11 February.[73]

The post-Meiji development of Japanese nationalism along racial lines was partly enabled by the archipelago's natural geographical isolation and amplified by the policies of the military dictatorship of the Tokugawa shogunate that ruled Japan for almost 300 years from 1600 AD. During this time, foreigners were expelled from the country and contact with outsiders was forbidden.[74/75] Japan's seclusion only ended in 1853, when the American forces of Matthew Perry forced the country to open up to western trade through a series of what were called the 'unequal treaties'. The humiliation of these helps explain why notions of ethnic and cultural uniqueness came to underpin Japan's assertion of itself as an equal in a world dominated by western powers.[76]

But in fact Japan had never been homogenous racially or socially. The Ainu, a people who are today limited to about 12,000–15,000 on the northern island of Hokkaido, for example, certainly predated the Yayoi, possibly by thousands of years. Although their origins remained obscure, one theory was that they were a Mongoloid people who entered the Japanese islands over a land bridge from Siberia in search of a less frigid environment. Their language and culture were entirely distinct from the mainstream of Japan, but their existence did not sit well with the Jimmu myth. As a result, for much of the twentieth century they were forcefully assimilated and denied any official acknowledgment. Under international pressure, Tokyo finally recognized the Ainu as an indigenous population with a 'distinct language, religion and culture' in 2006. A bill to this effect was only passed in February 2019.[77]

Other than the Ainu, Japan also had substantial minorities of ethnic Koreans, who, along with those of Chinese origin, comprised the uyoku dantai's favourite prey. There were currently over 600,000 *zainichi*, as ethnic Koreans were known, who were either Japanese citizens or permanent residents. Some of these families could trace their roots to the post-1910 period when Japan formally annexed Korea as a colony. The number of Koreans increased hugely during the Second World War, when Japan imported forced labour to work in mines and munitions factories. By the end of the war there were almost 2 million Koreans in the country. After Japan regained its full sovereignty in 1952, the zainichi – even those who had resided in the country for decades – were stripped of their citizenship.

Many returned to Korea, but a large number stayed on despite the blatant bias against them. Over time, some zainichi managed to naturalize, but hiding their ethnic background became a means of survival. Koreans were forced to adopt Japanese names. Some chose to shelter their children from any knowledge of their original ancestry.[78]

Zainichi had remained scapegoats throughout their beleaguered history in Japan. After the 1923 Great Kanto earthquake, for example, rumours that Koreans were poisoning the wells caused Japanese vigilantes to murder thousands of them (and hundreds of Chinese).[79] Even today, zainichi were occasionally subject to panic rumours that were given an amplifying platform by social media. In 2014, for instance, mudslides in Hiroshima prefecture led to false allegations of burglaries of evacuated homes by Koreans.[80] More recently, following the 18 June 2018 earthquake in Osaka, an outpouring of anti-foreigner sentiment was rife online. The *Japan Times* reported on Twitter posts suggesting that Koreans were likely to start robbing convenience stores and ATM machines.[81]

Korean-American writer Min Jin Lee's 2017 novel, *Pachinko*, was an excellent introduction to the dilemmas of the zainichi.[82] Reading it, I learned that since ethnic Koreans were routinely denied jobs on the grounds of their 'violent' and 'emotionally unstable' character, many were forced into crime. They became closely associated with running *pachinko* parlours, popular gambling dens that were hangouts for the yakuza, the Japanese mafia.

And it was not only zainichi who were forced by prejudiced employers into affiliating with the yakuza, but also the *burakumin*, a traditionally reviled 'caste' of people who were Japan's equivalent of India's Dalits. The burakumin were not ethnically distinguishable from mainstream Japanese, but their – often unacknowledged – existence contradicted the conceit of 'unique' Japanese social homogeneity.

Between 1 million and 2 million Japanese are thought to have burakumin ancestry. Their precise numbers are unknown, since it is illegal for census takers or government offices to identify anyone thus.[83] When I first read about them, I was taken aback at how analogous they seemed to India's so-called untouchables. Burakumin were defined by a historical discourse that asserted that people engaged in 'unclean' activities involving animal carcasses and death (butchering, leatherwork, mortuary practices) were indelibly polluted and dirty. Like Dalits, burakumin too were traditionally confined to certain demarcated areas of residence, and intermarriage between them and other Japanese was shunned.

The origins of the burakumin were debated, although they probably had something to do with Buddhist opprobrium against eating meat, which was then extrapolated to the idea that handling meat was itself impure. But the burakumin as a permanent caste dated later, to the Tokugawa period

(1603–1867), when specific discriminatory policies towards them became established following the drawing up of registries that surveyed and categorized them as separate from the other four 'castes' of samurai warrior, farmer, artisan and merchant.[84] They became subject to a series of laws that restricted where they could live, what they could wear and the type of work they could engage in.

The new Meiji government banned all formal discrimination against the burakumin, and in 1889, references to buraku status were stricken from the family registers, or *koseki*. But burakumin communities remained predominantly poor and faced significant hurdles when it came to educational opportunities, marriage and employment. In a 2014 survey by the Tokyo Metropolitan Government, 26.6 per cent of respondents said they would oppose their children marrying someone of buraku lineage, while a similar 2012 survey in nearby Aichi prefecture found that a huge 48.5 per cent would protest such a marriage.[85]

And yet there was almost no public discourse on this marginalized group, with the consequence that not only was their plight rarely acknowledged, but their very existence was brushed under the carpet of supposed Japanese harmony. Over the years, I was often asked – hesitantly, because the Japanese are loath to offend – about the caste system in India, as though it was such an exotic, if ugly, beast that the person asking had no ability to comprehend it. I took to replying that it was similar to how the burakumin had developed in Japan. The responses ranged from people blushing crimson and turning away mid-splutter, to people who looked blank with a 'buraku who?' kind of look. There was embarrassment and there was ignorance, the sure signs of a dirty secret.

Once I attended a talk at the Tokyo Foreign Correspondent's Club by Iehiro Tokugawa, about why he believed the Tokugawa shogunate's achievements were under-appreciated. He waxed eloquent about his ancestors' reforms in education, sanitation and agriculture. During the Q and A, I raised my hand and asked what he thought about the era's less savoury aspects, like the hardening of discrimination against the buraku. A hostile murmur immediately rippled across the room. It was obviously felt that I had transgressed. Mr Tokugawa coughed and deflected, something along the lines that my question was not pertinent to his talk.

The bigotry faced by the burakumin was considerably less heinous than the discrimination that Dalits in India had to endure. But the stigma of buraku ancestry wasn't as easy to shed as many Japanese seemed to believe.[86] An illustrative fact was their preponderance in yakuza gangs. The mafia had never been picky about its employees, and between 60 per cent and 70 per cent of yakuza members are thought to be of buraku origin.[87]

Clearly, prejudice had a long history in Japan, and equally clearly, there were different ways of being Japanese and different experiences of being Japanese. Yet there appeared to be a societal determination to deny this diversity. Tellingly, the word for 'different' in Japanese, '*chigau*', could also carry the meaning 'you are wrong'. The extent to which homogeneity was taught in Japan became clear to me only after talking with several *kikoku shijo* – children who return to school in Japan after being partly educated abroad.

In my own school in India, there had been a few kids who'd joined in middle school after having lived overseas for a few years. They were the children of diplomats or multinational company executives and carried about them the whiff of adventure and aspiration. We'd coveted their company and hung on to their stories about life in Spain and Germany. They'd been popular without having had to try very hard. Of course, I realize this reaction was partly because India in the 1980s was a poor developing country, one where 'abroad' was associated with better, richer and more fashionable.

Japan was already rich and advanced, but I was nonetheless disturbed when I read Ruth Ozeki's 2013 novel, *A Tale for the Time Being*,[88] and its vivid passages on protagonist Nao Yasutani's torture by classmates for no sin other than standing out for being a returnee from the United States. In the novel, Nao is subject to constant verbal and emotional abuse. She is called 'Transfer Student Yasutani' instead of by her name, and classmates hold their noses when they come near her, exclaiming '*gaijin kusai*' (yucky foreigner smell). Not only do her teachers not prevent the *ijime* or bullying, they often join in. Her excellent English gives the teachers an inferiority complex so that they too want to put her in her place. Eventually, she is physically attacked by classmates and sustains serious injuries.

That kikoku shijo would be subject to ijime was simply accepted as normal; a fact of life, like autumn following summer. I read a number of academic articles on the subject with increasing horror. A sample:

'It has become common knowledge that the kikoku shijo often are more competent in English than their Japanese teachers of English and oftentimes are placed in the untenable situation of not being able to speak as it would make the teachers lose face.'[89]

'According to Osawa, her son Tatsuya experienced severe bullying after his repatriation to Japan. His peers started making fun of, or sometimes harassing him because the following factors bothered them:

1. His spoken Japanese was not grammatically correct.
2. His gesture for 'I don't know' was too American, which gave the impression he was trying to act or look cool.
3. His mannerisms, such as holding doors for girls, seemed too 'Westernized' and 'lady first'.
4. Too many English words were mixed in with his spoken Japanese.

Owing to these differences from his peers, Tatsuya's classmates would poke him in the back with umbrellas, put pencil shavings in his lunch and send him nasty messages. The constant bullying resulted in him receiving a medical diagnosis of a duodenal ulcer.'[90]

I gathered a few first-hand stories too. A couple that Julio and I were good friends with had both been kikoku shijo. The man, whom I will call Shin, had studied in Switzerland before returning to Tokyo for high school, while the woman, whom I'll call Mayumi, had been born in New York and returned to Tokyo at the start of primary school. Both told us they'd been traumatized by the bullying they experienced in school for not knowing how to act Japanese enough.

On days that fish was on the menu for lunch, Mayumi had to endure taunts if she didn't eat the head. 'In America no one ate the fish head, so I didn't like it,' she explained. She tried to dispose of the uneaten head by secreting it away in the dustbin, but her classmates would invariably 'fish' it out of the trash and present it back to her. 'They would surround me and chant "Eat it! Eat it!" until I forced myself to swallow it, even though I vomited later.' Like many other returnees, she too found that her English teachers were resentful of her fluency in the language, and so she stopped speaking it until she forgot it entirely. 'I had to relearn English from scratch in my teens,' she told us one evening at our home in Tokyo.

Shin, in the avatar we knew him, was a polished and successful professional. He was at home in the company of foreigners, but remained fiercely patriotic. As a side job he assisted one of country's leading conservative politicians with his communications strategy. A few pegs of whisky into the evening, Shin got positively teary remembering how angry he'd been at the ijime when he first moved back to Japan.

One of his clearest memories was of being hauled up in front of a school assembly and being humiliated by the principal for having been 'caught' buying a soda at a vending machine outside the school gate. Apparently, this was against the rules. 'But how was I to know that? There were so many rules, like a book-long,' he said. In the end, Shin took to skipping school rather than be subject to the steady stream of injustices that his 'foreignness' seemed to provoke. 'I became a bad boy,' he smiled sadly. This was how Shin summed up the Japanese school experience: 'It's like every student starts off with a hundred points and you'll never get more than a hundred for doing better, only get points deducted for being "worse", so the best strategy is to do nothing at all; to be the same as everyone else. It becomes ingrained.'

Yet for all of Japan's insularity, change was in the air. How significant this shift was remained open to debate, but with an influx of both tourists and foreign workers, the new normal was more obviously heterogeneous than before. Yogi, an Indian, was now an assemblyman for Edogawa. Increasingly, non-Yamato Japanese visages were representing the nation in other fields. Haitian-Japanese Naomi Osaka was the face of Japanese tennis. The Japanese rugby squad that had a star turn at the 2019 World Cup was a rainbow team, starring biracial players as well as a number of foreign-born athletes who had moved to Japan.[91]

I'd only been in Tokyo a month when the 2016 Miss Japan was announced as Priyanka Yoshikawa, a half-Indian, half-

Japanese elephant trainer. In many countries, it would be Ms Yoshikawa's felicity with large mammals that would garner attention. In Japan however, it was the fact that she was a *haafu* as people of mixed descent were referred to.

Ms Yoshikawa was born in Tokyo to an Indian father and a Japanese mother. In media interviews, she said she'd been bullied at school because of her skin colour. She'd returned to study in Japan after a few years in the United States at the age of ten. 'When I came back to Japan everyone thought I was a germ, like if they touched me they would be touching something bad.'[92]

And yet, here she was representing Japan on the world stage. Ms Yoshikawa was in fact the second consecutive haafu contestant to win the title. The 2015 pageant was won by Ariana Miyamoto, whose father was an African American from Arkansas. That neither of the haafu pageant winners was half-Caucasian seemed significant to me too. Like many other Asian countries, the Japanese had traditionally been obsessed with whiteness as a hallmark of 'beauty'. To have chosen two dark-skinned women as the most beautiful in their country seemed like tangible progress in the direction of appreciating diversity. I certainly could not imagine a half-black Miss India, for all of my home country's surface plurality.

The general reaction to Ms Yoshikawa's win in Japan was muted, without any major expressions of outrage, although on social media, comment was mixed. While many believed her to be a deserving winner, others predictably questioned the selection.

'*What's the point of holding a pageant like this now? Zero national characteristics,*' grumbled one Twitter user, while another complained: '*It's like we're saying a pure Japanese face can't be a winner.*'

But another tweet differed: '*I don't care whether she is half or pure Japanese. I actually don't want to say "pure" in Japanese. As a Japanese, the most important thing is the heart.*'

When you compared racism in Japan with its nefarious Indian counterpart, it almost felt churlish to point it out at all. Indians were the perpetrators of the ugliest kinds of racial and religious discrimination. The targets were multiple: Muslims, lower castes, inter-faith couples, north-easterners and even beef-eaters. The stereotyping of black-skinned Africans had led to fatal attacks on them. A Congolese national, for example, was bludgeoned to death in New Delhi in 2016 by three Indian men over an argument related to hiring an auto-rickshaw.[93]

In Japan, the racism was more respectable, less violent. It simmered rather than boiled over, and got mixed in with a general shyness and culture of suppression. You could be foreign and live in the posher parts of Tokyo without feeling the slightest discomfort, especially if you couldn't understand Japanese and your children didn't attend local schools. People were polite and bowed a lot. Your belongings were safe and everyone queued. The occasional negative comment you might overhear about foreigners would probably be directed at the Chinese; no skin off the 'regular' foreigner's back.

And yet, Japan's 'homogeneity' could be wearing and worrying. Uniformity was institutionally enforced by families, schools and workplaces, and the tools of enforcement could be coercive. The social cohesion that resulted had benefits, like increased trust, but there was a high price it extracted too. An overweening emphasis on harmony papered over dissent and diversity, punishing and marginalizing those that did not fit in.

The challenge for Japan today was not changing as much as acknowledging the changes that were already underway. The country may never have been a monoculture, but it was a conceit that was possible to maintain in less globalized times. Given the demographic trends and economic necessities, it was increasingly untenable. The population was predicted to fall under 100 million by 2048 (from the 127 million at present) and to about 87 million by 2060, by which time 40 per cent of Japanese would be sixty-five or older.[94]

Tokyo had responded by opening Japan's doors to the world by easing visas for blue-collar workers in designated sectors.[95] It might only be a crack, but the results were already tangible. Convenience stores across Tokyo were now commonly staffed by Nepalese and Vietnamese employees. My neighbourhood supermarket had a Spanish delivery guy. Old-age homes were filled with care workers from the Philippines. Despite the hopes of some in Japan that robots would invalidate the need for workers from abroad, it looked like Tokyo had already acknowledged that the future would include foreigners.

A more obviously diverse Japan made the idea of the nation's essence resting in its ethnic purity a trope in desperate need of an update. There was no dearth of more inclusive values and behaviours that could replace ethnicity as the thread that bound Japan together, from fluency in the language, to blissing out on sakura, to a public-minded outlook. None of these were manifestly tied to a particular race. I was put in mind of my conversation with Yogi Puranik. The Edogawa assemblyman had explained that his election had little to do with the Indian community since his voters had been almost all Japanese. 'I owe everything to my Japanese supporters, especially young people. They appreciate that I am lively and powerful, not dull and sleepy like others,' he'd said.

6

Massaging the Octopus

'**O**h, Parabi-san, I cannot explain how very difficult it is,' sighed Yumi-san, her round eyes wide with emotion in her round face as she deftly manipulated a piece of tuna from dish to mouth. We were sitting in a private dining room in a *ryokan*, or traditional inn, in the far-western prefecture of Tottori, Japan's least populated area.

In front of us a smorgasbord of delicacies shone like jewelled treats. Fresh *sashimi* glinted next to sea urchin in fragrant *dashi*. The ceramic plates that hosted these morsels fanned out in a pleasing pattern, their glaze perfectly complementing the food itself. The menu featured *wakame* and *wasabi*, *miso* and *mochi* – all the ingredients that would trip off the tongue of any self-respecting gourmand.

I was spending a week exploring Tottori and its surrounding areas on the invitation of the Japan National Tourism Organisation (JNTO), and Yumi-san was my tour guide. JNTO wanted to introduce the 'less known' parts of

Japan to an Indian audience, the Japan beyond Tokyo and Kyoto. Over the week I realized there were reasons why this region was so 'unknown.' It was vast, but difficult to get around without private transport. The hotels were tatty and very 1960s in style, although their price tags were sadly more contemporary. Many of the beaches were inundated with trash – all from China – Yumi-san assured me.

And yet, some of the vistas along the Sea of Japan sang with beauty. There were also a surprising number of high-quality museums. But the JNTO's biggest plug for the region was food: the freshest fish, the juiciest pears, the tastiest beef, I was told. Repeatedly. To drive home the point, my hosts put me on a strict *kaiseki* diet three times a day. *Kaiskei* is multi-course Japanese haute cuisine whose USP is seasonality and harmony between the various elements of the meal – taste, texture, colour and presentation. A meal usually includes a variety of appetizers, a simmered dish, a sashimi dish, a *hassun* or 'expression of the season', a grilled course and, at the end, a bowl of rice.

In other words, kaiseki was the kind of meal you got dressed up for. My guide, who was unusually garrulous for a Japanese, told me that kaiseki feasting with her charges was the best part of her job: the delectable light at the end of the dark tunnel of reciting historical trivia and chaperoning bathroom breaks.

The 'difficulties' Yumi-san was talking about referred to the culinary misadventures she inevitably suffered when taking groups of Indian travel agents around Japan on behalf of JNTO, a niche she specialized in. She liked Indian people, she insisted, but their dietary fussiness was tantamount to a series of micro-aggressions against the chefs of Japan.

'They are bejetarian of course, but they don't like tofu. This is very difficult in Japan,' Yumi-san moaned. 'And they don't like the smell of our food. Sometimes they pick up the dishes and sniff like a dog. It is very insulting. And they bring their own foods in to the restaurant. Also insulting in Japan.'

What foods, I asked? 'Like chili sauce and some pickles,' replied Yumi-san, shuddering slightly. 'Many restaurants don't appreciate it. Some have asked us not to bring the Indian groups. It is very difficult,' she repeated.

She looked at me, and her face softened. With almost maternal appreciation, she watched as I ate. 'But you are very special Indian, Parabi-san. Thank you so much for liking our food.' I was awash with guilt. The food looked stunning, artful: crab eggs, seaweed soup, fresh tofu covered in *bonito* flakes, simmered conger eel and much else. Under Yumi-san's approving gaze, I had oohed and aahed my way through course after course of the seasonal banquet. But I was hiding a terrible secret. *I wasn't all that keen on Japanese food in general and kaiseki in particular.* The admission feels blasphemous. The kind of statement that would lose me liberal friends: like admitting to not worrying much about climate change.

As an eater I was mildly adventurous. In China I'd consumed scorpions and sea cucumbers (verdict: hideous), but drawn the line at dog, donkey and rat. But the Chinese had two weapons in their gastronomic arsenal that the Japanese lacked: spices and cooking. Cooked foods bathed in spices and sauces appealed to my unsophisticated taste buds more than raw foods intended to taste mostly of themselves. For all my globetrotting, I was Indian like that.

My favourite Japanese food was probably ramen, but I'd learned not to give this answer when asked the favourite Japanese food question, because ramen was, well, Chinese. My second favourite was gyoza (pan-fried dumplings), also Chinese. And so I'd come to choose soba (buckwheat noodles), which was as Japanese as the bullet train, as my standard response. *Okonomiyaki* – yummy pancakes loaded with (cooked) goodies – were also a choice that elicited approved, as did *gindara*, black cod, glazed with miso. But for me, Japanese fare was not comfort food. It didn't warm the cockles or infiltrate daydreams. It was too cold, almost too polite. And it had too many bonito flakes.

Back at the ryokan, Yumi-san moved on to a soliloquy about her travels in Europe as a young woman. It's what made her so talkative, she said. In her early twenties, she'd spent a month in France. On returning home she'd tried talking to her parents about her adventures over dinner. In response, her mother had remarked, 'Yumi, you have become very foreign.'

'You see, Japanese are usually quiet at mealtimes,' she explained a little sadly.

Towards the end of the meal, fortified with sake, I broached the subject of a change of menu for the remainder of the trip. Such elaborate meals, albeit delicious, were proving a bit much. Would it be possible to skip the multiple courses and just go à la carte? A bowl of soup or some simple soba would more than suffice, I suggested hopefully.

Yumi-san shook her head sadly, 'I understand you, Parabi-san, but it is not possible. The meals are already in the itinerary.' But couldn't we just make a change, I persisted? It would save time and money. And it was digestively untenable to eat so much food three times a day. This seemed to touch a chord. Yumi-san excused herself to call the powers that be at JNTO headquarters back in Tokyo to discuss the 'situation'.

She returned triumphant about twenty minutes later. 'We have a solution,' she said, all teeth and smiles. 'The menu cannot be changed, but I have permission for you to order an extra à la carte dish. Whatever you want.' I looked quizzical, and she elaborated. 'Unfortunately, you will have to be served the kaiseki meal, there is no way out of that. But you can send it back without eating.'

I stared, unable to comprehend the appalling waste that was being suggested with such nonchalance. Yumi-san was sensitive to mood. 'This must be strange for you, Parabi-san,' she said quickly. 'But it is the Japanese way. We cannot change things so easily. We are not very flexible. But we are trying to help you. I hope you can understand and cooperate.'

This here, I thought, was one of Japan's big shortcomings: the need to slavishly stick to a somewhat inefficient and wasteful predetermined plan (too much expensive food three times a day) to the detriment of the ultimate goal (favourable impression article). At the end of the week-long trip, the only food piece I did write was about puffer fish and involved no kaiseki at all.[96]

Four days into nursing my overfed stomach, our travels led us to the Karato fish market in the port city of Shimonoseki. I was not much of a fish market aficionado. My hometown, Delhi, was butter chicken/daal makhani-central and mostly fish-free. But my father had worked in Bombay (now Mumbai) for a few years in the early 1990s and I'd spent a couple of summer vacations there. My dad's apartment was not too far from the Sassoon Docks, whose smell and giant rats lived on in my nightmares for years to come.

A few decades later I'd washed up in Tokyo as unenthusiastic about fishmongering and its attendant ambience as ever. The first stop on most tourist itineraries at the time was the iconic fish market of Tsukiji. Visitors, limited to a daily quota of 120, would queue up all night to catch a glimpse of the tuna auction that took place before sunrise. The market at Tsukiji was eventually relocated in 2018 (an unpopular 2020 Olympic Games-related decision), unvisited and unloved by me.

But there seemed no avoiding Karato. As Yumi-san would have put it, it was 'already in the itinerary'. We visited in the post-lunch period, very late for a fish market. The floor was slick with scales and water. The wholesalers had packed up and left for the day, leaving only stacks of wooden crates in their wake. But retailers were still hawking their wares at discounted prices. The salty smell of the ocean lay heavy; the market was at the doorstep of the Kanmon straits between the islands of Honshu and Kyushu. I cast a nervous look about, but there were no giant rats à la Bombay's Sassoon Docks.

In some ways, Karato was reminiscent of Tsukiji (or so I was told, not having visited the latter myself). But a major difference, other than size, was that Karato had a clear piscine headliner: the deadly puffer fish or *fugu*. Images of this fat, friendly looking fish were ubiquitous in Shimonoseki, decorating shop fronts and even manhole covers. But despite its almost comical appearance, the fugu secreted a powerful neurotoxin that was up to 1,200 times more poisonous than cyanide. There could be enough poison in a single pufferfish to kill thirty adult humans.

On average, about fifty people across the archipelago suffered fugu poisoning every year. To calm the nerves of would-be fugu eaters, it was usually stressed that the majority of these casualties were the result of mistakes made by amateur home cooks. Personally, I did not find this factoid tipped the balance in favour of trying the dish, but chefs who cooked at fugu-serving restaurants in Japan were required by law to have a special licence certifying that they were trained in removing all the potentially toxic parts of the fish, including its liver, kidneys and ovaries. Yet, scares still occurred. In 2018, a supermarket in Gamagori city in central Honshu failed to remove the liver from a batch of fugu before putting it on sale. In the event, the sold products were retrieved and no fatalities occurred, but considerable panic was generated.

The consensus in Japan was that fugu was delicious, prized for its subtle flavor and unique chewy texture. The fish was also low in fat and high in protein. Yumi-san assured me that there had been no cases of poisoning in Yamaguchi Prefecture, where Shimonoseki was located, for decades.

But I learned that between the late sixteenth and eighteenth centuries, the sale of fugu had been banned across the archipelago. Then in 1888, the country's first post-Meiji Restoration Prime Minister, Itou Hirobumi, stopped by a traditional restaurant in Shimonoseki and was served fugu, which the locals had not given up eating despite its illicit status. He enjoyed it so much that he lifted the prohibition.[97]

Cooking techniques have been developed and honed to remove the toxin-carrying organs of the fish, and today Japanese consume about 10,000 tonnes of fugu annually. But the best chefs leave in just enough poison so that it tingles the lips, hinting at the fragility of life. For me, appreciating cherry blossoms seemed a more alluring way of experiencing mono no aware than flirting with death while eating dinner, but perhaps I simply lacked the requisite samurai-like derring-do.

At Karato, the retail stores displayed imaginative plates of pufferfish sashimi: transparent, paper-thin strips cut into designs resembling chrysanthemum petals, peacocks tails, butterflies and even Mount Fuji. I passed on the many offers to try fugu in various forms, but I did research fugu-related haiku once I was back in Tokyo. My two favourites:

Unrequited love.
He has decided to give up.
On that night – fugu soup!
Yosa Buson (1716-1783)

And:

Well, nothing happened –
Even though yesterday I ate
Fugu soup.
Basho, of course.

Fugu and my personal gustatory shortcomings aside, food in Japan was as revered as it was for good reason; the making of it was moved by Zen precision, dedication and mindfulness. There was an emphasis on practising the same technique – be it washing rice or gutting fish – over and over and over again until the boundaries between object and subject almost become effaced.

Shokunin was one of those Japanese words, like *ikigai* and *kaizen,* beloved of global corporate gurus. It could be very irritating when people with slick suits and glib tongues smattered their sales babble with them, because in doing so they divorced these words from all meaning. But when eating out in Japan, the word shokunin attached itself firmly to the substance of what it signified: the relentless pursuit of perfection through the honing of a single craft. It was the sushi chef apprentice who trained for ten years before being allowed to cut the fish; it was the sake brewer who only dreamed of yeast.

When Katsushika Hokusai, the iconic woodblock print master of celebrated works like the Great Wave of Kanazawa, was on his deathbed, aged almost ninety, he is supposed to have said, 'If only Heaven would give me another ten years or even five, then I could become a real painter.'

I was reminded of this when I watched David Gelb's 2011 documentary about sushi chef Jiro Ono, *Jiro Dreams of Sushi*. Jiro was a shokunin personified. After decades of massaging octopus for thirty minutes before cutting it, he'd had an epiphany: it got better if massaged for an extra ten minutes. The eighty-six-year-old Jiro (at the time of filming) began to massage his octopus for forty minutes. The thing was that a shokunin was genuinely humble, aware that perfection was inevitably elusive, yet never giving up on its quest. One lifetime may be inadequate to truly master a craft, but the shokunin kept trying, and found the meaning of life in that attempt.

It was, I suppose, not only the antithesis of the affliction that seemed to have become the hashtag for our times, #Multitasking, but also of that most quintessential of Indiananities: *jugaad*. Jugaad was makeshift improvising; it was about making do and the good enough. It was about as un-Japanese as talking on the mobile phone on a commuter train.

One reason why Japanese companies found it so hard to do business with India – despite obvious synergies between the two countries – India needed technical expertise and investments to develop its infrastructure, Japan had capital to spare and know-how to share – was this jugaad-shokunin dichotomy.[98] Indian solutions were all about finding the loophole and patching the tear. In Japan this approach was anathema.

The shokunin way was not the only way in Japan. Not all cooks in Tokyo spent their waking hours fixating on perfection. Japan, I'm sure, had its share of slapdash chefs who just wanted to get off work so they could get drunk. Yet, in general, there was a level of care taken over food – its conception, preparation and presentation – that was on another plane to what obtained in any of the other countries I knew.

Restaurants in Tokyo were often tiny, with only counter seating. To foreigners they could look uncomfortable. But the point of eating out was often not to chat with one's dinner companions as much as to get ringside seats to the chef's performance. His (odds are the chef would be male) movements were balletic in their grace and hypnotic in their assurance. He seemed to know just how to coax the ingredients into the finest versions of themselves.

But the route to the masterful conducting of gastronomic symphonies was arduous. The training for any aspiring shokunin was quite brutal, and the relationship between teacher and student was not that of service provider and client as much as master and slave. The world of *shisho* (teacher) and *deshi* (disciple) was resonant in some ways of the *guru-shishya parampara* of India. It was not about paying to learn a craft from a professional as much as surrendering to a master and expressing devotion to him by complete obedience. The story of Dronacharya ordering Eklavya to cut off his thumb as *guru dakshina* in the Mahabharata would make more sense to the Japanese than most other people.

In Tokyo's kitchens, the apprentice's ability to suffer was almost more valued than his ability to cook. A deshi had to spend months, or sometimes years, before being allowed to even touch the tools of the trade like a filleting knife. In an article on Nippon.com, sushi chef Takahashi Yoshihide recalled the endless drudge of being relegated to dishwashing and cleaning the floor during his time as a deshi. He was never allowed to help with the rice or fish. Occasionally, a senior cook would strike him without warning. He remained unsure if this was because he had been too slow in getting a task done or whether the senior had just been bad tempered that day. For months Takahashi silently observed what went on behind the counter, learning slicing and filleting techniques through discrete observation rather than hands-on instruction. The night after the first time he was allowed to prepare sushi, he collapsed on to the kitchen floor sobbing in joy and relief.[99]

That so many eateries in Japan were steeped in the shokunin ethos helps to explain why there are more Michelin-starred restaurants in Tokyo than in any other city in the world, including Paris. In 2019, Tokyo boasted 230 restaurants with star ratings, while the French capital had only 118.[100]

The world's best foods – French stews, Chinese dumplings, Spanish paella – abounded in Tokyo, but my personal favourite was pizza. At the risk of being ridiculed by Italian readers, I will make the bold claim that it is to Tokyo that one must head to savour the best pizza humanity has cooked.

My family developed traditions wherever we lived. These helped to root us, however temporarily, and give the time we spent in a particular city its texture. In Tokyo, my husband and older son took *aikido* classes every Saturday morning at a *dojo* close to our home. They finished around noon, at which point my younger boy and I would cycle down to join them and we would make our way together for Saturday lunch to Pizza Strada. This temple to pizza was serendipitously located in our neighbourhood, but I suspect we would have travelled many a mile on foot to get there if it had been so required for the naked brilliance of this pizza.

We always got counter seats so we could watch the process as the pizzaiolo pinched the perimeter of the dough to create irregular air bubbles that expanded into lightly charred pockets within seconds of being placed into the fiery oven that was kept burning at a blistering 480°C to 500°C. The chef was in constant motion: scattering fistfuls of salt into the oven, adding handfuls of cedar wood chips to stoke the flames and drizzling olive oil onto the finished pizzas in calligraphic strokes. The result was a crust that had just the right amount of body, crunch and salt. We always ordered Margherita because this was a Neapolitan pizzeria and that's what it offered, to perfection. In Margherita pizza the shokunin had a challenge befitting him: a circumscribed set of ingredients (tomatoes, cheese, pizza dough, basil), a seemingly simple final product, and the need for a replicable algorithm for the many variables that affected the process.[101] I watched *Ugly Beautiful*, a Netflix documentary whose first episode was focused on pizza in the three places in the world where it was an art: Naples, New York and Tokyo. In the film there was an interview with Antonio Pace, the president of the True Neopolitan Pizza Association (Associazione Verace Pizza Napoletana).[102] The Association was founded thirty-two years ago and its purpose, according to Pace, was, 'guaranteeing the authority of pizza to the city of Naples and to spread all over the world the right way to make a Neopolitan pizza'.

Bespectacled and beleaguered, Pace talked of the manic pursuit of excellence in pizza amongst the pizzaiolos in Japan. 'They keep asking me, is it good enough? Is it perfect? And I tell them, yes, please stop now. If you make it more perfect it will be too good.'

The problem with all this perfection was not that the food tasted too good – could that ever be a problem? – but that eating out could feel like more pressure than fun (a problem that encapsulated Japanese society as a whole). Eating at a restaurant like Jiro's was almost an exam for your palette with the shokunin chef as judge. You needed to be good enough to be allowed to eat at these places.

Even at less hallowed eateries than Jiro's, eating in Japan was a minefield of etiquette. You couldn't just bite into the sushi, for example, you needed to eat it in one go without breaking the rice. Dipping the rice in soya sauce was taboo. One needed to use chopsticks to pick up the pickled ginger that accompanied sushi and use it as a brush to glaze the fish (never the rice) with a hint of soya sauce. And before any of this, there were chopstick manners to master.

Here's a 'quick' primer: Eat all of the food at the end of your chopsticks in one bite. Never raise your food above your mouth. When you're not eating, rest your chopsticks on the supplied chopstick rest or on the side of your plate. Never leave your chopsticks sticking out of your rice, as this resembles a Japanese funeral offering. Don't lick the ends of the chopsticks. Don't swirl them in soup. Don't hover your chopsticks over dishes while figuring out which ones to take from, this is considered greedy. Skim the food from the top of the dish, don't dig deep down into a shared dish with your chopsticks.[103]

For someone who was used to China, where chopstick etiquette consisted of grabbing a pair and using them to eat, keeping all of this in mind was quite exhausting.

But you could dispense with chopsticks when it came to fruit. Japanese food might not have been my favourite, but Japanese produce was. Fruit in particular was so beautiful in taste and appearance that occasionally, though not often, you could forget how expensive it was and just give in to the pure hedonism of a juicy bite.

It was common to give fruit as presents in lieu of luxury chocolates or quality champagne. The price (and taste) justified it. Specialty melons could easily cost around $200 a fruit, and a pair of Yubari King melons set a record price in 2019 when they were auctioned for 45,000 USD. A single Bijin-hime (Beautiful Princess) strawberry from the Okuda farm in Gifu prefecture could command 50,000 yen (440 USD).

My freelance journalist's earnings ensured that I remained a Bijin-hime virgin, but I spent the four months of the year that the fruit was in season in Japan with my mouth stuffed red with less elevated varieties. It was painful on the wallet but delightful for the soul.

Strawberries were arguably the most successful western import to Japan, outdoing English, and even baseball, in popularity. They first became common in the early Showa era (1926–89), but in less than a century had conquered the sweet tooth of the archipelago. In their varieties and in the rapture they evoked, they rivalled the mango in India. There were 294 varieties registered with the Ministry of Agriculture, Forestry and Fisheries at the end of 2018. The *Tochi Otome* (Tochi Maiden) for example, was a relatively small, sweet and fragrant variety, while the *Amaou* (Sweet King) from Fukouka prefecture boasted enormous berries, four to five times the average size. The most unique were the disconcertingly white strawberries of Yamanashi prefecture, called *Hatsukoi no Kaori* (Scent of First Love). These albino berries were first introduced to the market in 2006, following ten years of research and development. A box of twelve sold in supermarkets for about 1,600 yen ($14.5).

I joined a press tour to a strawberry farm in Ibaraki prefecture, Honshu island's breadbasket, to find out more about my favourite fruit. It was run by Kazutoshi Murata, a second-generation farmer, who was adamant that the high price of Japanese strawberries was justified because they were so good as to be incomparable to their 'normal' counterparts. '*Ichigo* (the Japanese word for strawberry) and strawberry are not the same, just like Wagyu and beef can't be compared,' he claimed. When asked to explain, he held out a ruby-bright fruit the size of a cricket ball and said, 'Just eat. No explanation needed.'

According to him, the care, technological know-how and precision that went into strawberry cultivation in Japan justified the price tag. The primary characteristic distinguishing ichigo from 'mere' strawberry, he said, was in its sweetness. To achieve this, carbon dioxide levels in the soil had to be kept high, at between 400–450 parts per million. This brought the sugar into the fruit in a very concentrated manner. Fertilizers including vitamin C and collagen were combined with uniquely Japanese twists, like seaweed, kombu or edible kelp.

The Murata farm had thirty-six greenhouses, each of which produced over a tonne of strawberries annually. It was a decent living, the farmer told the gathered reporters, but not an easy one. Given Japan's declining and ageing demographic, finding farm hands was difficult. Consequently, he employed about half-a-dozen young workers from Indonesia to help out. 'We learn many things about farming here,' one of them said shyly, eyes never leaving the tray of strawberries he was busy sorting. I asked, in dimly remembered Bahasa Indonseia, what he liked best about Japan. He smiled, finally making eye contact, 'Ichigo, of course.'

◆

In the early summer of 2019, I went to Kappabashi with two friends from my *taiko* (Japanese drumming) class. Kappabashi, a neighbourhood in Tokyo, was the Mecca for the kitchen aficionado. It was crammed with over 170 shops selling ceramics, chefs' knives, handcrafted chopsticks and a mind-boggling array of cooking utensils. One shop, Iidaya, had about 200 kinds of graters on offer: wasabi, ginger, radishes, all vegetables had their own specialized ones. You could also choose from 2,000 types of ladles that varied by as little as 1 cc in size to satisfy the shokunin obsessiveness of ramen chefs. Fake-food shops with hyper-realistic faux dishes for sale were thronging with buyers. These plastic reproductions of food were commonly displayed in the windows of restaurants in Japan, and the replica food industry here was worth an estimated 90 million USD.[104]

My friends and I spent a happy couple of hours browsing. I bought one of those gadgets you find in Japan that improves your life in ways you didn't know could be improved: a nut mincer. And then it was time for lunch. One of my friends suggested going to a nearby okonomiyaki restaurant that she'd heard was very good. I concurred, and we made our way there to find a hastily written note pasted on to the sliding door of its entrance: 'Very very hot! No air conditioner'.

In the event, we braved the heat, and I can testify that the okonomiyaki at the restaurant was as delicious as the manager was truthful.

The places where the heat had less to do with the lack of air conditioning and more with spices were the Indian restaurants, of which there were several. The majority of these were run by immigrants from Nepal, who had become a sizeable community in Tokyo in recent years. But 'Indian' food, or more specifically curry, had preceded the Nepalese immigrants by decades.

'Curry' was in fact as much a Japanese dish as chicken Manchurian was an Indian one. Or, to put it another way, Japanese curry was to Indian food what chicken Manchurian was to Chinese food – a vague relative.

The history of the dish in Japan dated to the 1870s, when naval officers of the British Royal navy who had picked up the curry habit in India passed it on to colleagues in Japan's imperial maritime forces. The earliest recipes for *raisu karī* (literally, rice curry) in Japanese cookbooks were lifted from the 1861 *Mrs Beeton's Book of Household Management*, whose curry ingredient lists included curry powder, flour and chopped sour apples. Since the novelty dish came from Britain, as far as the Japanese were concerned curry rice was 'Western', and it became a regular item at *yoshuku* or Western food restaurants. Even today, the Japanese navy keeps up its tradition of 'curry Fridays,' where all navy canteens offer *raisu karī* as a Friday staple.

The taste of the Japanese version of curry was sweeter and its texture more glutinous than that of its Indian ancestor, but there was one restaurant in Tokyo that prided itself in serving 'authentic India curry' – no wheat, no apple and no holds barred on the chilli: Nakamuraya. Just how this came to be involved a rip-roaring yarn featuring a revolutionary fugitive from India, a love affair, and an entrepreneurial Japanese family of bakers. It was the kind of story that was nectar to my inner bee, and within hours of it being brought to my notice by a friend (thanks, Barun), I was googling up a frenzy.

A few days later I emerged out of the metro into Shinjuku's perennially overwrought atmosphere, blinking at the brightness. Thankfully, Nakamuraya restaurant was located in the basement of a building right across the street from the exit I'd taken, and I didn't get as lost as I usually did in this part of town. I was meeting that day with a PR representative for the restaurant and another employee who would serve as interpreter. Both were dressed in smart suits. The PR man handed me a sheaf of publicity materials. But I'd already spent hours reading up on the story.

It began with a Bengali, Rash Behari Bose, who was born in 1886 in an eastern Indian village called Subaldaha. After finishing high school Bose applied for a job in the army, but was rejected, as the British, who ruled India at the time, viewed Bengalis as effete and unmasculine. By this time the young man's imagination was aflame with anti-colonial ideas acquired during the agitation against the Partition of Bengal in 1905. He worked at the Forest Research Institute in Dehradun for a while, but in 1912 became involved in an attempted assassination of the then viceroy, Lord Hardinge. As the colonial authorities closed in on him, he fled to Japan in 1915. He made his way to the city of Kobe under the assumed name of P. N. Tagore, pretending to be a relative of Nobel laureate Rabindranath Tagore, whom Bose had read was planning a trip to Japan.

From Kobe he immediately set out for Tokyo, where he befriended a number of Indians affiliated to the Gadar party, an anti-British outfit that was originally founded by Punjabi Sikhs in North America. He also met with Sun Yat-sen, the great Chinese nationalist, then also in exile in Japan. Eventually, he made the acquaintance of a number of Japanese pan-Asianists who were sympathetic to the cause of Indian independence, notably, right-wing politician Mitsuru Toyama.

Initially, Bose continued to use the pseudonym of P. N. Tagore and even gave interviews under that name. But his cover was blown when an arms shipment to his compatriots in India, arranged from Shanghai with the help of Sun Yat-sen, was intercepted in Singapore. The shipment's paper trail exposed Bose's true identity, and the British embassy in Tokyo, acting under the terms of the Anglo-Japanese Alliance, sued for his extradition.[105]

At this point, Toyama introduced Bose to the Soma family, owners of a well-known bakery called Nakamuraya.

The family allowed the Indian to hide out at the bakery for several months, during which time the Somas' eldest daughter, Toshiko, acted as his interpreter. Eventually, on Toyama's request, the two got married in 1918, a move that allowed Bose to move around Tokyo without attracting as much suspicion, and paved the way for his acquisition of Japanese citizenship in 1923. The couple had two children, a boy and a girl in quick succession, before Toshiko died from pneumonia in 1925.[106]

In subsequent years, Bose continued to lobby for the Indian national movement in Japan via extensive writings and lectures (more on this in chapter 8). But his most lasting contribution in introducing India to Japan was in debuting 'authentic' Indian curry at a new Nakamuraya café that opened shop in 1927. According to *Bose of Nakamuraya*, a biography written by Hokkaido University professor Takeshi Nakajima, Bose wanted to prove that the curry the Japanese were used to was a colonial invention. Getting his recipe on the Nakamuraya menu was therefore 'part of his anti-colonial struggle, by trying to win back India's food culture from British hands'.[107]

Nakamuraya's Indian curry proved a hit, even though it was priced eight times higher than the average *karī raisu*. Eventually, in 1939, Nakamuraya became one of the first food companies to go public on the Japanese stock exchange.

Following a bout of ill health, Bose died in 1945 at the age of fifty-eight, but in Japan his legend lives on through the curry that Nakamuraya continues to serve.

It remains the most popular item on their menu. Since 2001, the company also sells ready-to-eat packaged curries using the original Bose recipe to convenience stores. These accounted for almost half the sales value of the Nakamuraya Processed Foods division in 2016 according to the restaurant's PR rep.

By the time I finished the interview it was lunchtime and almost every table at the restaurant had a serving of Genuine Indian-style Curry, as it was billed on the menu. The curry came in a sauceboat and was accompanied by short-grain, sticky Japanese rice, but it passed the flavour test – full-bodied spice and pleasing consistency. The clientele ate under the steady gaze of a dhoti-clad Bose, whose photograph was prominently displayed near the entrance. I left feeling sated and strangely nostalgic, although I couldn't have said exactly what about.

As I walked towards the metro station, I stopped at a vending machine to buy a bottle of water and was not all together surprised to find that it also dispensed a ready-to-heat-and-eat package of Nakamuraya curry. Vending machines in Japan spoke something of the soul of the country. There was hardly a square metre of the archipelago that was unadorned by them. Even the remotest roads on desolate mountain slopes invariably featured one, often half-buried under snow, but always functional, dispensing hot corn soup at the press of a button.

According to the *Japan Times*, at the start of 2020, there were just under 5 million vending machines across the country. That's about one machine for every twenty five citizens. And although the majority of these were drinks and snacks dispensers, there were others that spat out products not typically associated with vending machines. Packaged curry for example, but also bananas and honey and cartons of milk.

I read of one in Tokushima prefecture's Awa city that dispensed curry and rice meals freshly prepared by a local farmer.[108] In the rural town of Uchiko in Ehime prefecture, there was a machine that gave out beautifully folded origami models.[109] And in the sleazier areas of Tokyo, basement-located dispensers offered the used underwear of women – although there was some controversy about whether these were in fact used or only advertised thus. It proved difficult to investigate conclusively.

In Tokyo, you could get piping hot soup, comic books, umbrellas and even sake at the right machines. Or phone chargers. Or surgical masks. Or your future. At some Shinto shrines, vending machines offered *omikuji* or random fortunes written on strips of paper for a few hundred yen. But for the most part, despite their multitudinous offerings, vending machines in Japan remained charmingly old fashioned, involving coins and buttons and a retro 1980s vibe.

According to the Vending Machine Manufacturers Association, the annual sales from these dispensers totalled over $60 billion. One had to ask what it was about Japan that made vending machines so popular. And so I did, and wrote about the answers I gleaned too.[110] The reasons, it seemed, were as diverse as the offerings of the machines themselves.

Given the teeming streets and intense work schedules that were the Japanese norm, a quick purchase was understandably appreciated. Moreover, as the country greyed – people aged sixty-five and above accounted for more than a quarter of Japan's demographic – there was a labour crunch. Manning convenience stores was increasingly difficult, and vending machines were a labour-free alternative. High real estate prices also made the machines more profitable for each square metre of scarce land than a retail store. And the fact that Japanese culture was obsessed with automation and robots helped too.

The low crime rate in Japan was another factor. Machines were almost never vandalized, so owners needed to invest little in them save an occasional tune-up. I was reminded of a seemingly unrelated incident in the Indian city of Jaipur. I'd been visiting a government-run school there to investigate how computers donated by a big IT company were transforming the learning process, when I discovered that a single broken tap was the whole school's sole drinking water source. The drip-drip of the tap all day meant that a huge amount of water drained away, wasted, which in a water-stressed city like Jaipur seemed almost criminal. When I asked why the school didn't fix the tap, the answer left me floored.

Apparently, every time they fixed it someone would scale the school walls at night and break off the metal parts of the tap to sell as scrap. It's what happened to anything with metal in the school unless it was under lock and key – manhole covers, toilet parts, everything, anything. I was hit, hard, by how all the liberal talk of the importance of public mindedness, environmentalism, even conventional morality, collapsed in the face of poverty and resource scarcity. The story of the vending machine would have been very different had I been talking of India or even China, but this was Japan. And only in its peculiarly secure environs could the machines flourish quite as they did.

One last and not much explored explanation for the popularity of these dispensers on Japanese soil was that like smartphones, vending machines provided a shield from personal interactions, something that many Japanese seem to have difficulty with. As mentioned earlier, up to a million people in Japan were classified as hikikomori or social recluses. Machines spared users the necessity of chitchat with sales people.

There could be something lonely about these machines themselves. I came across photographer Eiji Ohashi's book, *Roadside Lights*. It was a collection of images of Japan's vending machines taken in the deep night, glowing ethereally in empty landscapes where they offered the only guiding light to passersby who may never materialize. As was often the case in Japan, there was poetry to be found in the most unexpected of places – even vending machines.

7

From Japan/we want to wash/
the whole world's bottom

I've been toilet obsessed for many years; a penchant that I hasten to add is more sanitary than scatological. Long before Indian Prime Minister Narendra Modi's latrine-building spree, I'd concluded that toilets and the infrastructure surrounding them took the pulse of a society better than GDP figures or dazzling skyscrapers.

I'd written about lavatory cleaners in China, followed toilet entrepreneurs around central Java in Indonesia, and spent time pondering the inefficiency of sewage treatment plants in India.[111] The differences, stark and subtle, between the lavatorial lowdown in these countries, was socially insightful, but what all these public loos had in common was their malodorous repulsiveness. These were washrooms you'd rather not have to wash in.

Imagine then my excitement at moving to Japan. The Japanese commode was the stuff of legend. From what I'd heard, a Toto toilet (the brand that reigned supreme) could do pretty much anything short of eating dinner with you.

As soon as we'd touched down at Narita airport I'd hastened to the ladies' room, fully prepared to be washlet-wowed, and so I was. The cubicle looked ready for lift-off, the number of buttons crowding the toilet control panel rivalling those in an airplane cockpit. I'd pushed everything, activating a variety of oscillations, sounds and sprays. I'd doused and dried my rear (and front), raised and lowered the toilet seat, increased and reduced the intensity of the gush, and played chirping bird music to mask any embarrassing noises.

I'd studied the buttons and their accompanying pictures and labels with fascination. There were knobs for pressure, sound and spray. But one, titled 'wand sanitizer' in English, left me miffed. What could the 'wand' be? It didn't warrant dwelling on, but I couldn't help but dwell on it. Upon googling, I discovered (to my relief) that 'wand' referred to nothing more risqué than the nozzle that emerged from the toilet bowl to spray water.

Being confounded by a Japanese toilet was almost a rite of passage for visitors. Often the controls were not labelled in English, and the functions and icons varied by model. It could be nerve-racking trying to figure out which button to push. You might want to flush, but end up pressing the emergency call and be caught with your pants down by a Japanese SWAT team in crisis-control mode. Or you may want to gently spray your posterior, but end up vigorously sluicing your anterior.

There was a story about a hapless foreigner who wanted to adjust the bidet function and ended up with tickets to a six-hour long *Kabuki* (a classical Japanese dance drama) performance instead. The tale is likely apocryphal, but it was a fact that there were things that could be done by a Japanese toilet that many a state government might have difficulty accomplishing as efficiently.

Manufacturer Matsushita's 'smart toilet' took urine and stool analysis, and could check the user's blood pressure, temperature, and blood sugar while at it. One of its models was even equipped with electrodes that send a mild electric charge through the user's buttocks, yielding a digital measurement of body-fat ratio.

I was at pains to hide this fact or any others like it from my mother whenever she visited us in Tokyo. My mum liked her toilets unadorned and unintelligent. In Japan, she tended to return from the washroom looking as though she'd gazed into the abyss. The heated toilet seat, which to me rivalled Kyoto in full cherry blossom bloom in its delights, was her particular bête noire. She was convinced that it would electrocute her. The profusion of buttons to choose from confused her. The self-raising seat intimidated her. The whole experience left her as wobbly as a mochi.

The powers that be in Tokyo were not unaware of the effect that Japan's avant guard latrines could have on Luddite foreigners. The issue took on a particular urgency in the context of the 2020 Olympic Games that the Japanese capital was set to host (until a certain virus put paid to those plans – more on which, later).

Having lived in Beijing during the 2008 Olympics, I was used to how the international sporting event had a tendency to take toilets out of the well – closet – and onto centrestage. The hundreds of thousands of foreign athletes, fans and tourists that the world's largest sporting spectacle attracts inevitably raised the question of where – and how comfortably – these visitors would be able to powder their noses.

In Beijing, the discussion had focused on what to do about the city's plentiful but insalubrious public facilities, which often consisted of a series of pits in the floor with no flushes or running water. Ultimately, tens of millions of dollars were spent on rebuilding and upgrading toilets into what the local media dubbed 'luxurious lavatories', suitable for use by even the sniffiest of foreign athletes.[112]

In Japan, the problem was more about making the experience of using the toilet less nerve-racking for the uninitiated. To this end, Japanese manufacturers announced that they would standardize the iconography used on toilet controls. The Japan Sanitary Equipment Industry Association agreed on a range of eight symbols that signified: big flush, small flush, raise the lid, raise the seat, dry, front bidet, rear bidet and stop.[113]

The idea was to make sure that by 2020 all public toilets were refurbished to bring them in line with this standardized model, leaving tourists with scant to worry about, save to sit back on the heated seat and craft haikus in praise of the potty.

This is not just a throwaway suggestion. Long before the commode went high-tech, the toilet had occupied a special, almost lyrical place in Japanese culture. In his essay on aesthetics, 'In Praise of Shadows', Junichiro Tanazaki called the traditional Japanese toilet a 'place of spiritual repose ... the perfect place to listen to the chirping of insects, or the song of birds, to view the moon ...'[114]. It was the toilet, Tanazaki theorized, where haiku poets were likely to have come up with most of their ideas. Consider Kobayashi Issa's 1822 poem:

> *Even the outhouse*
> *Has a guardian god ...*
> *Plum blossoms.*

A couple of centuries on, Toto, the reigning heavyweight of the Japanese toilet industry,[115] began holding an annual 'Toilet Poetry Award'. Every year since 2005, the twenty best poems are *printed* on rolls of toilet paper and put on limited-edition sale.[116] A few examples of the winning entries from the 2016 competition:

> *Woshuretto*
> *kangaeta hito*
> *arigatō*

(To the person / who came up with the washlet / Thank you!)
– Meron Kame

Futa no ato
gaikokujin no
kuchi mo aki

(After the lid / the foreigner's jaw / drops in surprise.)
– Nonbiri

Nihon kara
sekai no o-shiri
araitai

(From Japan / we want to wash / the whole world's bottom.)
– Teishu Tanpaku

Potty humour aside, toilets in Japan were not a laughing matter. In folklore, *Kawaya-no-kami*, or the toilet god, was a popular deity. Traditionally, the waste from outhouses was used as fertilizer, so *Kawaya-no-kami* was associated with good harvests and fertility. The deity was also invoked to protect people from falling into the toilet pit and meeting a rather messy end.[117]

In homes, a properly appointed toilet was decorated and kept as clean as possible, since *Kawaya-no-kami* was imagined to be very beautiful. In some communities, the state of the toilet was believed to have an effect on the physical appearance of unborn children. Pregnant women asked the toilet deity to give boys a 'high nose' and dimples to girls. If the toilet was dirty, however, it was said to cause children to be born unattractive and unhappy.

Amongst the candy-floss of sakura in bloom at Kyoto's great Zen temple, Tofukuji, I'd found myself face to face with an outhouse that was considered a national treasure. Designated an 'important cultural property' since 1902, the fourteenth-century *tousu*, as restrooms in Zen temples were called, was the oldest and largest of all extant Zen toilets. I'd gazed at the row of holes in the bare earthen floor of the airy sloping-roofed structure. Outside, a sign explained how human excrement had been used for compost manure and had therefore been indispensable for maintaining an adequate supply of vegetables for the kitchens of samurai warriors and court nobles. Compost used to be a large part of any Zen temple's income.

I was brought back to the central, consequential difference between Buddhism in India, with its emphasis on renunciation, and its Japanese/Chinese variants, with their focus on work. Not only did Japanese monks work (unlike their Indian alms-seeking counterparts), they made no distinction between work and meditation. And most of the 'work' they performed was cleaning of different kinds: raking leaves, dusting the altars, scrubbing the toilets.

On a fall morning in 2018, I caught a train jam-packed with office-going commuters bleary-eyed from lack of sleep. I was headed to central Tokyo's Komyoji temple. On the way I thought about how startlingly porous the border between the secular and spiritual was in Japan. The two most ubiquitous structures across the country were convenience stores and shrines. Historic temples sheltered 7-Elevens in their shade; Family Marts were often framed by the *torii*, ceremonial entrances, of Shinto altars.

Komyoji was an unassuming two-storeyed structure only about 300 metres from the teeming entrance of Kamiyacho metro station. Yet, inside its grounds it felt 300 years distant. The morning sky was still pale, but a motley crew of about a dozen people were already gathered at the temple. There were a couple of salarymen in full suit-and-tie regalia, a fashionista sporting a silver tote, and an elderly gentleman in scuffed leather shoes. As the clock struck 7.30, they shook off jackets, put down bags and grabbed brooms, dustpans and buckets.

For the next thirty minutes they cleaned, in silence. Every inch of the temple's cemetery, veranda and yard was methodically swept and polished. All errant leaves were chased down and bagged. The fashionista spent the entirety of the half an hour on her knees with a washcloth, looking for stains that might have camouflaged themselves as part of the floor tiles. I followed the group around with a notebook in one hand and a broom in the other, managing to neither take notes nor help out with the cleaning. Finally, one of the salarymen took pity on me and unburdened me of the broom with exquisite politeness.

Whom had I been kidding with the broom anyway? I was a good-enough journalist, but a lousy cleaner. Could you blame me? I'd been brought up in a middle-class, urban home in Delhi. For most Indians this needs no further elucidation, but let me paint a picture for other readers.

I didn't come from a particularly wealthy background. I'd been brought up by a single mom who'd worked as a sales executive for a five-star hotel. And yet I'd grown into adolescence hardly ever lifting a finger in manual labour. While I studied and read, a maid had swept the house and a cook had washed the dishes. The young son of the neighbourhood press-wali (a middle-aged woman who wielded a huge coal-heated iron at a stand next to the local park) came around to polish all our brass knick-knacks once a week. And another person cleaned our toilets every morning.

The fussiness and hierarchy, the extreme specialization, were all a pernicious consequence of India's caste system. The floor-cleaning maid did not 'do' toilets. A toilet cleaning-caste lady was needed for this, although her caste was never overtly discussed. In fact, growing up, I hadn't given a thought to her caste. Or anyone else's, including mine. I was so privileged as to in effect have been caste-blind.

The end result of the manifold effects, overt and covert, of the caste system in India was the very bizarre relationship that the country shared with cleanliness. We were a people obsessed with ritual purity and personal hygiene and yet had a shocking lack of responsibility towards the cleanliness of public spaces. It was fine to piss on the streets as long as it was a considerable distance from one's own home.

The memories of my childhood were littered with images of people rolling down car windows to throw plastic bags out. They were suffused with the stench of the urine-soaked walls of Delhi. People had such a horror of dirt, of shit, that they considered it indelibly polluting to clean it themselves. And yet they ate and laughed and flirted surrounded by filth.

Back at Komyoji temple, the morning sun was finally shining strong and the merry band of cleaners put down their rags and brushes to have a cup of hot green tea, together with the presiding monk, Shoukei Matsumoto.

Matsumoto was many things: an author of a book on the art of cleaning,[118] a Young Global Leader (YGL) of the World Economic Forum and an MBA from Hyderabad's Indian School of Business (ISB). I was first introduced to him by a mutual friend a few months after moving to Japan. We'd met at a lively tavern in the downtown neighbourhood of Shimbashi.

Matsumoto was dressed in a simple navy-blue *samue*, the short kimono-style cotton jacket and loose trousers worn by Buddhist monks while performing their daily chores. He was measured in his speech and took long pauses before offering any comments. He sipped beer and took his time chewing his way through the beef dishes the restaurant specialized in. He talked about his wife and children. I remember feeling bemused by this married, meat-eating, alcohol-drinking monk. Such behaviour had not fitted in with my conceptions of monk-ness, and I'd pointed out as much.

I asked, with what I hoped was disarming naïveté, how if monks in Japan did not have to follow any special restrictions on diet or marriage, they were any different from lay members of society. Before responding, Matsumoto took another unhurried swill from his mug of beer. Then he half-smiled. 'Perhaps the only difference,' he said, 'is in these clothes we wear.' He pointed to his samue. I felt chastened, like the proverbial Zen koan disciple who asks the wrong questions.

The Japanese tended to an ambiguous relationship with religion. According to the 2013 Japanese National Character Survey, 72 per cent of respondents said they did not have any personal religious faith. Again, a 2015 Japanese General Social Survey revealed that 68.6 per cent of people did not follow any religion. And yet, according to the 2015 annual statistical research on religion by the government's Agency for Cultural Affairs, there were 188.9 million people, or 1.49 times the actual population of Japan, who declared themselves as Shinto followers (89.5 million), Buddhists (88.7 million), Christians (1.9 million) or as belonging to 'other religions' (8.9 million).[119] In short, as a popular website on Japan put it, the archipelago was the most religious atheist country in the world![120]

Most Japanese were heavy on ritual and light on theology. It was common for people without a deeply committed faith to join in religious rites like visiting shrines during festivals. The rituals participated in were not dependent on religious belief as much as on the nature of the occasion. It was fairly standard for someone to be welcomed as a baby with Shinto rites, get married in a Christian ceremony and be buried accompanied by Buddhist rituals.

Funerary rituals were the Japanese Buddhist monk's stock-in-trade. 'In Japan, when people think of Buddhism, they think of death, but what about life?' Matsumoto had asked, with a rare rhetorical flourish. On becoming a monk, he'd been quickly disillusioned as he found the temple community primarily concerned with ceremonies, rather than philosophical pursuits. And even as social conditions had rapidly changed, temples were failing to adapt to modern times, risking irrelevance.

Traditionally, temples in Japan were tended to by one priestly family, based on the principle of primogeniture. The cremated remains of neighbourhood families were buried in their grounds. Those families contributed regular donations for the temple's upkeep, which, along with the cost of graveyard plots and maintenance fees, was what kept the temples financially afloat.

But this was unsustainable in contemporary Japan, where an exodus from the countryside to the cities had left vast tracts of the nation depopulated. A growth in childless couples and people opting for secular funerals compounded the problem. Consequently, Matsumoto entered the priesthood at a time when tens of thousands of temples were in danger of closing down.

Matsumoto did not come from a temple family. His father had run a machine parts company. But the head priest at Komyoji temple did not have a male heir, and adopted Matsumoto as his successor. This background helped to explain the young monk's open outlook. He soon became convinced that a temple based entirely on revenue from grave plots and funerals was unviable. And he decided the way to fix this was to study business.

Off he went to get an MBA from ISB in Hyderabad. He was both the first Japanese and the first monk to study there, and he found the experience thought-provoking. In India, religion infused the daily lives of people in a way it no longer did in Japan. And on campus, classes in marketing, strategy and finance proved useful.

After returning to Japan, Matsumoto began to conduct temple-management seminars using the case-study business school method he'd learned at ISB. The monks who joined him studied various temples as cases and went on to design renewal plans for them. The ideas generated included ways to raise revenue and relevance by instituting meditation courses, temple stays, the supporting of volunteer activities and the hosting of music and theatre productions.

In the months following our first meeting, Matsumoto and I kept in touch.

But it had been about a year since we'd last met, when I chanced upon a review of a book he had written, in the *Guardian* newspaper.[121] The book, titled *A Monk's Guide to a Clean House and Mind,* was a slim volume about the benefits of cleaning for the mind. I immediately wrote to him to ask for a copy and he sent me a pdf within the day.

The basic premise was outlined on the first page. 'Japanese people have always regarded cleaning as more than a common chore ... It probably has to do with the notion in Japan that cleaning isn't just about removing dirt. It's also linked to "cultivating the mind".'

I read the book in a single sitting. Here are some tips my monk friend had for the would-be cleaner:

- Cleaning should be done in the morning as the first activity of the day.
- It should be done quietly, while silence envelops you.
- The toilet is an area that Zen monks put a great deal of effort into keeping clean. Adherents believe that the Bodhisattva, Ucchusma, attained enlightenment in the toilet, making it a holy space.
- People who don't respect objects don't respect people. For them, anything that is no longer needed is just rubbish.

Matsumoto invited me to join the next 'cleaning activity' he was organizing at Komyoji, which is how I found myself sharing a pot of steaming tea at the temple with the volunteer cleaning crew post-sweep. The monk introduced me and I bowed in everyone's direction, thanking them for putting up with my presence. I was curious, I said, about what motivated them to devote weekday mornings to come and sweep the temple before starting their workday.

My question had no immediate takers. Instead, everyone sipped their tea solemnly. But by now I knew to wait. A few minutes on, one of the salarymen spoke. 'Cleaning is as important as drinking water and eating food,' he said. 'I've heard that in India people often hire others to clean for them, but for us it is part of life and you should live your own life, not outsource it to someone else.'

I was taken aback by how pointed a remark this was, almost impolite by Japanese standards. But cleaning was clearly a topic that stirred passions here.

A middle-aged lady joined in. Coming to the temple helped her wake up early in the morning and face the day with focus, she said. A younger woman shyly added that cleaning with others gave her an excuse to leave the house and spend some time away from her baby in adult company. I scribbled away furiously and looked up once I was done, but no further answers were forthcoming. Finally, Matsumoto cleared his throat and spoke.

'People may ask what is the point of cleaning. It is only cleaning. Nothing more.' Everyone nodded and sipped tea. He continued. 'There is no end to cleaning. You sweep away a leaf and another one falls to take its place. That's just fine. There is no difference between the process and the goal.'

Later, after the volunteers had left, Matsumoto and I continued to sit out on the temple balcony, talking. He explained how, during his three year-long apprenticeship at a monastery in Kamakura city, he used to spend up to five hours a day in cleaning chores ranging from gardening to scrubbing out toilets. Although for monks there was no difference between cleaning and meditation, the same could not be said for lay people. 'So, I thought, why not try to change the meaning of cleaning in people's lives from something to avoid into a meditation practice?' he said.

Matsumoto knew that sitting still in meditation was not for everyone, but cleaning was relevant to all people. Through it everyone could cultivate the mind and simultaneously remove dirt, making the physical environment more pleasant. I wondered if it would ever be possible to convince my fellow Indians of the idea.

I spent the next few days pondering the India–Japan cleanliness divide, which, along with the jugaad-shokunin dichotomy, seemed to be one of the pivotal differences between my home country and my country of residence. The centrality of cleanliness in Japanese metaphysics was evident from the language itself. *Kirei*, meant clean, but also pretty, while *fuketsu*, or unclean, meant hideous. *Kitanai* (literally, dirty) meant nasty, mean and calculating. The cultural roots of this attitude were arguably located in Zen Buddhism. Until the emergence of public baths in the seventeenth century, nearly all the baths for common folk were provided by Buddhist temples. Shintoism emphasized ritual purification as well. Even today, worshippers at Shinto shrines wash their mouths and hands before entering.

But this identification of cleanliness and godliness was part of Hindu traditions and rituals too. Buddhism, after all, had Hindu ancestry. Muslims also washed before their prayers. And the phrase 'cleanliness is next to godliness' was first recorded in a sermon by the Methodist preacher, John Wesley, in 1778.

Beyond religion, a more satisfactory explanation lay in the early acculturation to cleanliness that took place in Japanese schools. The classrooms of all elementary schools in Japan were filled with rows of fresh-faced children seated behind desks. Jackets were slung on the backs of chairs. Textbooks were usually out. So far, so standard. What differentiated these from other classrooms around the world was a hook under the tables from which dangled a cleaning rag or *zokin*. Along with stationery and notebooks, this rag was an essential part of a child's school supplies, because in addition to reading, writing and maths, a major part of the educational curriculum in Japan comprised cleaning.

I decided to visit one of these schools and enlisted the help of Koyama-san, my Japanese friend from Indonesia who had once expressed concern over my being able to talk softly enough to conform in Japan. Her family had recently relocated back to Tokyo and her older son now went to a public elementary school in the affluent suburb of Kichijoji. She was able to get permission for me to spend a few hours there.

I arrived just in time for the lunch break. The two-dozen or so students in teacher Tanabe's grade-three classroom, where my friend's nine-year-old studied, packed away their books and pulled out lunch mats and chopsticks. A small group of about five children donned facemasks, hairnets and white coats. They left the room to return a few minutes later, rolling in a trolley laden with school lunches. The day's offerings included miso soup, fried chicken, a green

vegetable mix and bottles of milk. The children on duty for
the day carefully served out the lunches before eating their
own food. Afterwards, they cleaned up the leftovers and took
the trolley back to the kitchen space.

The next thirty minutes were a flurry of activity as desks
and chairs were pushed to the sides. It was time to clean.
Clutching mops and cleaning rags, the children fanned out
across hallways, staircases, classrooms and water coolers.
Some of them zipped about in a kneeling position, hands
placed on the floor over a cleaning cloth, elbows locked
straight, and hips wiggling high in the air. Others worked
earnestly, meticulously scrubbing away at stubborn stains.
A few goofed off, turning the session into a competition over
who could clean fastest. Teacher Tanabe pitched in with a
broom, occasionally calling out instructions over the bracing
marching music that was switched on.

Cleaning activities were formally mentioned in the
Japanese government's educational guidelines, but some
discretion was granted to individual schools in their
implementation. In the Kichijoji school, for example, the
children did not clean the toilets, although some Japanese
schools made that mandatory too and dispensed with janitors
altogether.

In teacher Tanabe's class the children finished their
cleaning for the day and returned their zokin to their
desk hooks. They seemed bemused at the presence of an
Indian journalist who was so interested in their lunchtime
shenanigans. I asked the class what they enjoyed most about
cleaning. A dozen hands shot up. They seemed not to have
learned the reticence of Japanese adults yet.

A bespectacled eight-year-old was particularly keen on talking and I indicated for him to answer. 'The more trash I clean, the better I feel, especially when the teacher says, "well done".' I realized my question was fodder for teacher's pets and so I asked another one. What did the children *not* like about cleaning? An equal number of hands shot up. 'It's tiring,' complained one girl. 'The water cooler area is too cold,' said another boy, somewhat mournfully. But like it or not, these children were going to clean up after themselves more or less every day for the rest of their school lives. On special occasions they would even be sent out to scrub the streets around their schools.

When I'd first broached the idea of the school visit with her, Koyama-san had told me that cleaning up classrooms and public spaces was part of daily school life even when she'd been in elementary school back in the 1980s. 'I think it helped us to really understand dirt. To become aware of the consequences of our actions,' she'd said.

For school children, daily-cleaning sessions encapsulated lessons that went beyond simple hygiene. Teacher Tanabe elaborated on these: working for others, working together and working seriously. It helped equip children with basic life skills and instilled in them a collaborative spirit. This was as much a part of education as learning multiplication tables. The result: cleaning was not seen as a punishment. It was not seen as beneath anyone's dignity. It was not seen as dirty, but as the means to be clean.

◈

My first time onboard one of Japan's iconic bullet trains was in the spring of 2017. The family and I were headed to Kyoto, a distance of 513 km that we would cover in less than 2.5 hours (138 minutes, to be precise, because, after all, this was Japan). As the train pulled up at the platform, we might as well have had 'ingénue' woodblock-printed on our foreheads. The boys squealed in excitement and I took a flurry of photographs, but the Japanese passengers milling around us were unmoved. Most stared blankly at their phones, hardly bothering to glance up.

It was evident that taking a *shinkansen* was about as exciting for them as waiting for an Uber to show up. But although familiarity might have bred indifference in them, for a bullet-virgin from India, getting on a train that fast felt miraculous. And the miracle didn't stop at the speed of the train. There was the preternatural punctuality: with about 350 trains operational on the route daily, the average annual delay time was … drumroll: thirty-six seconds.[122] Then there was the truly jaw-dropping spectacle of the cleaners who spruced up the compartments, like a mop-wielding platoon of synchronized swimmers, in the few minutes that the train rested at the station before streaking onwards.

To begin with, the cleaners lined up and bowed deeply to the train, as to a respected guest, as it pulled into the platform. Then they stood at the compartment doors holding out plastic bags for alighting passengers to drop the debris of their journeys into: assorted coffee cups, plastic bento boxes and newspapers. Once everyone had deboarded, they charged into the wagons and fanned out like unusually sanitary locusts, popping back out to bow at the incoming passengers in what felt like the time it would take me to say *konnichiwa*. In fact, the whole process had taken exactly seven minutes, a routine that was as precisely calibrated as the arrival and departure of the trains themselves.

Harvard Business School had in fact done a case study on this marvel of efficiency.[123] TESSEI, the subsidiary of Japan Railways in charge of cleaning, had developed a method that CEOs around the world could do with emulating for its economy and innovations. The TESSEI staff was divided into eleven teams, each with twenty-two people and each in charge of cleaning around twenty trains every day. The average age of the workers was fifty-two; over fifty per cent of them were women.

Their tasks were broken down into segments timed to the second: 1.5 minutes spent picking up trash, thirty seconds rotating the seats (the seats on bullet trains could be swivelled around) 180 degrees to make them all face in one direction, four minutes sweeping and cleaning, and a one-minute check before completion. Here is their standard checklist:

Minutes 0–1:30

Make sure nothing is left behind in the luggage racks on both sides of the compartment or the gaps between the seats. Turn all seats to face the direction of travel. One team member to run down the wagon's aisle sweeping out dropped trash along the way.

Minutes 1:30–4:30

On the way back up the aisle, pull down and check the blinds, and at the same time pull out the seat-back trays and wipe everything down. Seat covers to be changed if they are dirty.

Minutes 4:30–6:30

In the last two minutes, gather up all the collected trash and bag it and make sure everything on the checklist has been ticked off.

The washrooms were cleaned by specialized staff, leaving them gleaming enough to eat sushi off of, should anyone be thus inclined. But the cherry on this already well-iced cake was that once the cleaning crew was done, they lined up in front of the train cars and bowed to welcome incoming passengers on board.

Watching this salubrious spectacle unfold, I found myself remembering a flight I'd taken from Boston to New York on a snowy April night a few years earlier. The flight had been delayed by six hours; no apologies had been extended by the airline or staff. When we'd finally arrived in New York, a frazzled-looking air hostess had picked up a bag of trash left behind by a passenger on her seat and hurled it at the offending traveller, over the heads of others queuing in the aisle to deplane. 'Ma'am, take your trash with you,' she'd barked.

Back in Japan, I'd looked out of the window as the bullet train had begun to pull out of the station. The cleaning crew continued to bow in our direction all the way until it was no longer possible to see them.

After reading Matsumoto's book, I tried to take some of its lessons to heart. I began to savour the half hour I spent in the kitchen washing up after my boys had left for school in the morning. I'd look out of the window and make eye contact with the fat pigeons that often sat on the sill. I found the time became a valued segue from the chaos of chasing my boys into uniform and out of the door, to the calm focus required to write.

But if I am honest, Japanese-level cleanliness could be onerous. I found the lack of public trash cans in Tokyo particularly difficult. One reason for this litter bin lacuna was that the Japanese were encouraged to take their trash home and subject it to the elaborate recycling system rather than thoughtlessly chuck wrappers and cans in the nearest dustbin. (Another reason lay in the 1995 sarin gas attacks, which left twelve dead and more than 1,000 injured. In the aftermath, trash cans were taken out of many public areas, especially train stations, because they could potentially hold terrorist weapons.) All very good for the environment and the human conscience. But even after years of Tokyo life I did find being stuck with a wad of chewed gum and nowhere to dispose of it a little frustrating. Ditto with takeaway coffee cups.

However, there was one aspect of cleaning Japan-style that I came to enjoy without reservation: the *onsen* or hot spring baths. Onsen were a Japanese obsession. Visiting just the right one for the season was a finely honed skill. And these bubbling baths loomed large on the nation's cultural landscape. Literary giants like Yasunari Kawabata and Soseki Natsume had set (and written) some of their best-known works in hot spring towns.

Given that the Japanese archipelago was the world's most geologically active region, home to over 100 volcanoes, it had no shortage of thermal baths. But, like many things that caused little stress in other countries – making a cup of tea or sticking cut flowers in a vase – bathing in a hot spring pool could be a cultural minefield here. In onsen resorts, foreign visitors were often handed lengthy documents on bathing etiquette and some were known to turn away non-Japanese altogether, ostensibly out of fear that they would disrupt the delicate harmony of the communal bathing experience.

Being barred entry was very rare, but navigating an onsen was intimidating for newbies. To begin with, one had to enter the baths as nature intended – as bare bottomed as on the day of one's birth. Bathing suits were a strict no-no. Even towels weren't permitted, save tiny handkerchief-large squares that could be placed on the bather's head, where they remained free of any contact with the water.

Most onsen forbid entry to anyone with tattoos. (This was true even of public swimming pools. The local pool that I took my children to ordered swimmers to cover up any tattoos with a rash guard so as to avoid 'the awful feeling of other users and children'.)

買出しも行っ（おります）か、数に限り）か・こ（・
ます。

NOTICE

People who have tattoos are not allowed to enter
the pool area unless their tattoos are covered.
If you have tattoos, please wear a rash guard
over your swim suit or apply taping.
We appreciate your cooperation in eliminating
the awful feeling of other users and children
to ensure everyone's enjoyment in the pool area.
Please bring your rash guard or your tape to a pool.
(We have a limited number of rash guards for rent.)

The reason for this tattoo stricture was the association
of inked bodies with criminals or yakuza mobsters who
tattooed themselves as a sign of gang membership. In light
of the influx of visitors it was assumed the 2020 Olympic
Games would bring, the Japan Tourist Association had asked
hot spring bath operators to 'give consideration' to tattooed
foreigners wholly outside of the yakuza paradigm, but at the
time of writing the debate raged on.[124]

Onsens were also selfie-free zones. Mobile phones were
banned. So was swimming, splashing or chatter. Before
entering the pool, bathers had to first take a shower and
clean their bodies. Really clean their bodies. Like their life
depended on it. A quick soaping would be met with hostility.
Most onsen these days were sex-segregated, although mixed

bathing did exist. In either case, the eyes were to be turned inward to self-reflection, rather than on the anatomy of fellow-bathers.

For many months into my stay in Japan, I resisted visiting onsen, put off by the enforced nudity and simply not sure that a pool of hot water would be worth all the fuss. But from the first time I finally lowered myself in – at a resort in central Honshu's Nagano prefecture – I emerged a born-again onsen zealot. So much so that I suggested my family spend one of our February school half-term breaks skiing in Japan's northern-most island: Hokkaido. In fact, I detested the cold and disliked skiing, but to luxuriate in an onsen open to a snow-globe-like winter wonderland was the stuff of bucket lists.

At the resort, I breathed in white cold air as my body melted into 42-degree centigrade-induced relaxation. I took in the pine trees cloaked in snow and felt the softness of the powdery flakes as they settled on my hair. Because it's the kind of thing I do, I thought of an Issa haiku:

Children eat snow,
Soaking
In the hot spring.

All of a sudden, I was on the cusp of an epiphany. Some essential truth about the universe was about to reveal itself to my snow-and-steam-addled senses, when two excitable Thai women came splashing into the water, chattering about their day on the ski slopes. Splashing!? Chattering!? I retreated to a corner of the pool, casting passive-aggressive looks in their direction – water off their backs. A few minutes later, a young Chinese mother walked gingerly through the freezing air towards the waters with a screaming child in tow. Screaming!?

I beat a hasty retreat indoors, wearing an offended look that no one noticed, only to find a lady lounging, half-immersed in the indoor pool, flicking though photographs on her MOBILE PHONE. Traumatized by this collapse of social order, I staggered to the showers, where a blonde woman was shampooing away without a care in the world about the fact that her entire torso was covered in tattoos.

Contrary to how it felt, it wasn't the apocalypse, merely an onsen resort in peak ski season that happened to be particularly popular with foreigners. But it seemed I was going native, and glowering at overseas visitors was part of this process.

An onsen left the body as clean as a railway station in Japan (that's a metaphor that only someone living here can fathom). But it transcended the merely sanitary, levelling up what was a bath into something aesthetic. This transformation of the mundane into the artistic was a 'thing' in Japan, nowhere more obvious than in the country's manhole covers.

The longer I spent in the country the less time I spent training my eyes up at skylines and blossoms and more looking down at the roads trying to spot manholes. Across the archipelago, the lowly manhole was its own art form, with covers displaying intricate, occasionally painted, designs that revealed something of the unique history or cultural traditions of the cities whose sewers they adorned.

In Tokyo, the standard cover displayed sakura or cherry blossom petals, while in Osaka, the city castle was the dominant motif. Port cities displayed lighthouses and ocean scenes, and fishing villages featured fish. Elements of local festivals, like lanterns or certain foods, were also common. According to the Japan Society of Manhole Covers (yes, there was such a thing), which maintained an online directory of designs, there were almost 6,000 artistic manhole covers spread across the country, with trees, landscapes, flowers and birds accounting for the majority.

I did some quick research to discover that modern sewer systems, with above-ground access points called *manhoru* (manholes) dated to the late nineteenth century. But it was in the 1980s that the kind of standard drab manhole coverings with unremarkable geometric patterns transformed into the artistic works of today. At the time, several Japanese cities were slated for a sewage system overhaul, but these were met with public resistance to the cost and disruption. The idea that aesthetically appealing covers might make citizens more amenable to, and sensitized about, the importance of good sewage was floated by bureaucrats, and took hold.

Before long, municipalities were holding design competitions and vying with each other for the most appealing images. And this being Japan, the global capital of enthusiasts for obscure passions, dedicated groups of manholers began spending their free time tracking down unique designs, photographing them and even getting down on their knees to take ink impressions of covers.

In the decades since, a slew of books detailing the covers have been published. A recent example is *Manhole: Japanese Culture and History Represented by the Design*, authored by retired Tokyo Metropolitan Government official Hidetoshi Isshi, who spent over twenty years cycling across 1,700 municipalities photographing manholes. An Amazon search revealed another book called *Quilting with Manhole Covers*, a book of designs for quilters, all taken from manholes in Japan.[125]

Websites and social media fora for manholers were numerous, and there was a sewage promotion platform, Gesuido Koho Purattofomu (GKP), that had launched a series of collectible picture cards featuring manhole designs. These cards were available for free at local government facilities, like sewage plants. According to GKP, more than a million cards had been issued since they were first introduced in April 2016. The organization reckoned there were roughly 12,000 discrete manhole cover designs in the country.[126] A story in the *Japan Times* featured a travel agency in Saitama Prefecture, near Tokyo, that had developed a bus tour allowing participants to collect manhole cards.[127] Manholers had even got an annual summit going since 2014, where they got together and discussed designs.

It was easy to reduce Japan's manhole aficionados to an amusing human-interest story. But for me there was something serious, even profound, about the covers.

Mahatma Gandhi had believed that a society's commitment to true freedom and dignity lay in its approach to private and public sanitation. By this parameter, India had failed to secure either for its citizens, but Japan had succeeded. Beautiful manhole covers elevated what has always been considered the dirty, humiliating aspects of human living – refuse, sanitation, drainage – into artifacts of beauty, to be beheld, acknowledged and wondered at. This was no mean feat. I would argue that it was amongst the more significant gifts that Japan had to offer the world.

On the morning I'd spent with the volunteer cleaners at Komyoji temple, my monk friend, Matsumoto, had summed up this gift neatly. *The Monk's Guide to a Clean House and Mind* was written to demonstrate that cleaning was fun. 'You shouldn't deprive yourself of the chance to enjoy it,' he'd said, and meant it.

8

Monks, Movie Stars, Revolutionaries, Elephants

When I lived in China, Hindi movies and Buddhism had featured prominently among the stereotypes my nationality elicited. Many a garlic-breath-scented Beijing taxi driver had broken into a rendition of the 1951 song '*Awara Hoon*' as I sat on the back seat of their cabs. Others bent their heads down in a respectful posture, muttering '*Yindu! Fojiao!*' (India! Buddhism!).

Conversations with Chinese taxi drivers almost always entailed lots of chortling and spitting (on their part). In Tokyo, taxi drivers neither chortled nor spat. They usually wore white gloves and the air of haughty butlers. Small talk was rare. In four years, not a single driver offered an opinion about India, or burst into song. But despite these differences, the substance of India's image in Japan was not very different from that in China: religion and movies.

India was the birthplace of Buddhism, a faith that had gone on to become foundational to both Chinese and Japanese society. And even in the twenty-first century, it was Buddhism that made India, China and Japan intelligible to each other. We instinctively understood something of worship and belief in each other's civilizations, although we diverged in practice and temperament.

As far as I could discover, the oldest documented Indian resident in Japan was Bodhisena, a monk from Madurai, whose outsized impact on Japanese culture might be compared with that of another south Indian monk, Bodhidharma, who is credited with establishing Chan (Zen) Buddhism in China.[128]

Bodhisena, or *Bodaisenna*, as his name is pronounced in Japanese, was born in the early eighth century. His life and journeys exemplified the multi-directional flows of Buddhist influence and the complex ways in which these tied swathes of Asia into a cultural embrace. Like many South Asian Buddhist monks, Bodhisena came to believe that Manjusri (the bodhisattva of wisdom) lived on the Chinese mountain of Wutai and travelled there to pay obeisance. While in China, he met with the Japanese ambassador to the Tang court, who persuaded him to carry on to Japan on the invitation of the Emperor, Shomu (701-756), a devout Buddhist. Bodhisena voyaged to Japan via Cambodia and Champa (central and southern Vietnam) with a gaggle of theological glitterati that collectively shaped many of the contours of Japanese Buddhism and courtly culture.[129]

On board was Genbo, a bureaucrat of Emperor Shomu's court at Nara, who had spent seventeen years in China collecting over 5,000 Buddhist texts. Another shipmate, Kibi no Makibi, is linked to the development of the Japanese syllabary, as well as the katakana script that is still in use today. The influence of Sanskrit on katakana is sometimes attributed to the time Makibi spent travelling with, and learning from, Bodhisena.[130] Makibi also introduced to Japan the art of Chinese embroidery, as well as the lyre (*guzheng*), which, as the *koto*, became a standard feature of Japanese court music.

A disciple of Bodhisena from Champa, Buttetsu, rounded off the band of monastic travellers. Buttetsu went on to teach a style of dance that featured themes taken from Indian mythology, set to a musical rhythm, common in South Asia but unknown at the time in Japan. These dances became known as *rinyugaku* and were absorbed into the local artistic oeuvre.

Bodhisena's ship docked at Osaka in AD 736, and the group made their way to the capital, Nara. It was during the Nara era (AD 710–784) that Buddhism, buttressed by learnings from the Tang dynasty in China, became firmly established in Japan, overcoming initial resistance from the hitherto Shinto-devoted elite. Under Emperor Shomu, Buddhism was granted official recognition. Temples in Nara began to accumulate vast landholdings and came to wield huge political influence.[131]

Bodhisena's arrival in the capital took place within this context. Until then, Japan's knowledge of Buddhism had been entirely mediated through either Korea or China.

As an Indian, Bodhisena was immediately held in reverence and housed at Daian-ji temple, the preeminent educational and research institute for Buddhism at the time. The Indian monk taught Sanskrit and helped establish the Kegon school of Buddhism, a variant of the Chinese Huayan school. Bodhisena eventually died in AD 760 and was buried in Ryusenji-temple on the slopes of Mt Omine.

Unlike some historical Buddhist sects, the Kegon continued to flourish in the present day. Its headquarters were at Nara's Todaiji temple, a UNESCO World Heritage site. Founded in AD 738 and officially opened for worship in AD 752, Todaiji was best known for its 500-tonne, 15-metre-high sculpture of the Buddha – the largest bronze statue in the world. The gargantuan sculpture, known as the Daibutsu, was commissioned by the Emperor in hope of gaining divine favour to reverse the effects of a devastating drought that had been compounded by an outbreak of smallpox.

My family and I visited Nara 1,266 years after the opening of Todaiji, in April 2018. We had narrowly missed the blooming of the cherry blossoms, although it was still possible to see the occasional flowering tree along the hillsides. The city was smaller, but less cramped with tourists than Kyoto; wild deer strolled amidst the parks and temples. Our tour guide handed me a business card, the back of which featured a few useful phrases in Japanese. Under 'Good morning' and 'Please take me to my hotel,' was printed the Japanese for 'Help! The deer ate my map.' I chuckled at the tour company's whimsical humour, until the next day I actually witnessed a deer snatching and chomping on a tourist's map.

Useful Japanese phrases in Nara.

Deer ate my map.
>*Shikani chizuwo taberareta*

Deer bit my rear.
>*Shikani oshiriwo kamareta*

I love Nara!
>*Nara daisuki*

Any Japanese phrase you want to know?

Charming as the map-eating deer were, they were not the main attraction in town. That distinction belonged to Todaiji's Daibutsu, which we braved the crowds to visit. The statue was housed in a gargantuan wooden hall filled with selfie-taking day-trippers from Kyoto. After gawping at the statue, most visitors headed to a hole in one of the pillars that held up the edifice. According to legend, the hole was the exact size of the Daibutsu's nostril, and anyone who crawled through would gain enlightenment in their next life. The hole/nostril was only large enough for a child to tunnel through, but this didn't seem to put off any number of adult Chinese tourists, who inevitably got stuck at the hip and needed to be hauled out.

Leaving my family to wander the temple gardens, I made my way to the living quarters of Todaiji's head priest. I had arranged a meeting with Kosei Morimoto, the retired 218th temple chief and leader of the Kegon school of Buddhism. The lodgings were adjacent to the temple grounds and comprised a series of low-roofed rooms interconnected by covered walkways that overlooked classically arranged gardens. I was taken through to a reception area that faced a late-blooming weeping sakura, where the Elder Morimoto (as Kosei was respectfully know) was waiting for me, a cup of tea in his hands.

Morimoto was surprisingly sprightly, his eyes lively and darting behind half-rimmed spectacles as he talked about Bodhisena, as of an old friend. He told me how the Indian monk had been chosen by the emperor Shomu amongst all the eminent Buddhist scholars in Nara at the time to perform the 'eye opening' ceremony at the consecration of the

Daibutsu. In front of a large cosmopolitan gathering that had included ambassadors from Persia, Korea, Vietnam, China and Central Asia, Bodhisena had painted the pupils on the eyes of the Buddha statue, inviting the spirit in to animate the sculpture. 'I think in India you understand about the spirit coming into the statue?' the Elder Morimoto asked. 'It is a very difficult concept to explain to Westerners.'

And it was true. I did understand what he meant. There was much about Japan's culture that was intuitively comprehensible to an Indian. Unlike China, Japan had not suffered a communist revolution, with its attendant rupture with the past. The ubiquity of religious rituals and physical presence of shrines and temples gave it a shared lexicon with India.

In fact, the Japanese Buddhist pantheon had absorbed and adopted several Brahmanic/Hindu devas or gods (known in Japanese as *ten*) as guardian spirits or boddhisatvas. The Hindu God Shiva (Daijizaiten) for example, was associated with Avalokitesvara or Kannon, while Brahma (Bonten) was linked to Manjusri. Indra (Taishakuten) and Varuna (Raijin) were often to be found guarding temple entrances. Other common devas incorporated into Japanese Buddhism included Yama (Enmaten), Garuda (Karura), and Laxmi (Kichijoten). Saraswati (Benzaiten) was particularly popular and had hundreds of temples dedicated to her across the country.[132]

But the long journey from India (via China) to the Japanese archipelago had transformed these deities, both in their physical representations and metaphysical meanings.

For the average Japanese, the Hindu underpinnings of the deities they so often genuflected before at temples had become more or less invisible. In the case of Ganesha, this invisibility was literal, since statues of the elephant-headed deity were rarely displayed publicly. He was considered so powerful that beholding him was thought to be dangerous and his icons were secreted away.

Having returned from Nara, my head spinning with all this new information, I decided to visit Matsuchiyama Shoden, one of the oldest Ganesha temples to be found outside of India. Parts of the temple's neighbourhood, along the banks of the Sumida river in north-eastern Tokyo, were redolent of woodblock prints from Edo times. Rows of traditional shops selling kimonos and handicrafts lined the streets.

I met with Hirata Shinjyun, the *juushoku* or head priest of Matsuchiyama, in a reception room over the regulation cup of green tea. I asked if we could take a look at the temple's famous idol of Ganesha, a question that had him spasming, as though stung by a particularly vicious wasp. He held up his hands crossed in front of his face. The answer was clearly a 'no'. Once recovered from the shock of my request, he explained that he himself had never looked upon the statue. In fact, the last time it had been beheld by human eyes was following the Second World War, when it had been extracted from its underground wartime hiding place and placed in an inner sanctum that has remained shut ever since.

The priest said that the secrecy surrounding the deity added to the belief in the efficacy of its power. But there were other reasons as well. Ganesha's Japanese monikers included Kangiten, Shoten and Binayaka. As Kangiten, the deity was depicted in erotic embrace with another elephant-headed figure and was considered too sexually explicit for public display.

Kangiten was not an entirely benevolent *ten* in Japanese mythology. According to the deity's origin myth, his mother, Uma, gave birth to 1,500 evil children to her left, the first of which was Binayaka or Ganesha. On her right side she birthed 1,500 good children, the first of which was Avalokitesvara/Kannon (the Bodhisatva of compassion) in the avatar of Idaten (Skanda or Murugan in India). In order to win Binayaka over to the side of Good, Idaten reincarnated and became Kangiten's wife. The bliss generated by their union was believed to have converted Kangiten from evil to virtuous.[133]

Kangiten was therefore seen as a creator of obstacles, but an easily placated one, who could be persuaded to remove those same obstacles with the gift of a few radishes. All across Matsuchiyama, on roof eaves, staircases and pillars, carvings and paintings of *daikon* (Japanese white radish) were the main visual element. Radish was on sale as offering and the prayer hall was stacked high with the tuber.[134]

But although the Japanese Ganesha had localized taste so that the sugared ladoos he loved in India had been replaced by the vegetable crispness of daikon, he hadn't entirely lost his sweet tooth. Kangiten was also believed to calm down when given sweet rice buns, to be washed down with a cup of sake.

According to the priest, there had been well over 1,000 temples around Japan dedicated to Kangiten during the Edo period. The deity had traditionally been popular with business owners, who prayed to him to remove impediments to their success. The neighbourhood in which Matsuchiyama was located had historically been Tokyo's pleasure heartland, home to theatres, restaurants and inns. The owners of these establishments used to flock to the temple to beg Kangiten's grace. Over the centuries, the demographic of devotees had changed. Today, most were in the thirty–forty-year age group. Hirata said many women visited to ask Kangiten's favour in removing the obstacles along the path to a suitable husband.

Shrines and plaques donated by merchants and business associations dotted the walkway around the temple's main prayer hall. The priest pointed in the direction of the Sumida river, explaining that in the past an unobstructed view all the way to Mt Fuji had made this a popular vista for paintings. Now, the horizon was dominated by high-rises, amongst which the neofuturistic Tokyo Skytree reared up 634 metres into the clouds. At the temple, the paper lanterns that hung from awnings began fluttering as a gentle river breeze wafted across the grounds. The images of the intertwined radishes painted on them rocked back and forth, as though reassuring everyone that Kangiten was well fed and well disposed.

The religious linkages between India and Japan made for both fascinating and strong civilizational bonds, but in the twenty-first century they could seem a tad anachronistic. Cue: Buddhism's modern counterpart, the Indian movie, which had arguably replaced religion as the prime conveyor of India's soft power in Asia.

I had first had this epiphany when I was living in Beijing and had discovered a penchant amongst a certain demographic – the middle-aged and elderly – to burst into sepia-tinted songs from Bollywood's youth. The images stayed with me long after I left China: a toothless man taking a caged bird out for a walk singing '*Awara Hoon*'; a poker-faced maid brandished a vacuum cleaner while crooning a passable rendition of '*Piya tu ab to aa ja*' from the 1971 movie, *Caravan*.

China's love affair with Indian films and music stretched back to the period just after the Cultural Revolution (1966–76). During the 'reform and opening-up' era ushered in by Deng Xiaoping, Hindi movies were amongst the first foreign films to be shown in Chinese theatres as their socialist themes deemed suitable. Movies from India's post-Independence decade, like *Awara* and *Do Bigha Zameen,* became instant classics, acquiring a massive fan following, despite being shown in China some two decades after their India release.

The trajectory of Indian movies in Japan was quite different. Given its pro-US tilt after the Second World War, Western movies dominated the foreign film market here. And yet, however much Japan may have wanted to distance itself from its Asian-ness, it was unable to escape the regional love of melodrama. For all their surface reserve and emotional control, Japanese people revelled in technicoloured passions on screen as much as their cousins from India, China and south-east Asia. And so, while Indian movies might never have become China-like mainstream-popular in Japan, they were a niche obsession, with fervent fan groups dedicated to particular stars.

I met Hiroyoshi Takeda for the first time over lunch at an Indian restaurant in Edogawa ward, the neighbourhood favoured by Indian expats. Takeda was not a typical Japanese man. Instead of a suit and tie, he preferred t-shirts with bright caricatures of a moustachioed south Indian movie star. Rather than bowing, he danced. He didn't ride the metro, but zoomed across Tokyo in a gaudily adorned autorickshaw imported from Tamil Nadu. Not for him the hushed tones and constricted body language standard of his compatriots. Takeda talked loudly, wagging his index finger at the sky. And the smoothness with which he could toss his hair back while simultaneously removing his sunglasses was wolf-whistle worthy. In almost everything he did, Takeda consciously channelled the spirit of his shirt-hurling, cigarette-flipping, lungi-dancing hero: Tamil superstar, Rajinikanth.

I knew that in the Tamil film industry Rajinikanth was a colossus, revered so highly by his fans that they bathed cardboard cut-outs of his in milk, a practice normally reserved for the idols of Hindu gods. But despite my Tamil surname I had never seen any of his movies (I didn't speak Tamil and I preferred my movie stars a tad more subdued). Meeting with Takeda and his co-members of the Tokyo

Rajini fan club had me unusually nervous, given how ill-versed I was with the subject. And I had a strong inkling that admitting my ignorance might induce apoplexy in my interlocutors.

Joining Takeda and me for dosas that day were four other Rajinikanth aficionados, two men and two women. They ate their lunch with their hands, not a chopstick in sight, while nattering away about their favourite topic: *thalaiver*, or 'the boss', as Rajini's admirers referred to him. There were about 3,000 members of the movie star's fan club in Tokyo, they told me. Cities like Osaka and Kobe had their own associations.

I had done some digging into the origins of the Tamil actor's popularity in Japan prior to the meeting. He'd first burst onto Japanese screens in June 1998, when his film *Muthu*, called *Odoru Maharaja* (literally, The Dancing King) in Japanese, began a run that lasted twenty-three weeks and grossed 1.6 million USD. For a few months, images of Rajinikanth, his luscious co-star Meena, and for good exotic measure, an elephant, were plastered on prominent hoardings across Tokyo. Cinemas showing the movie were sold out.

I could only assume that something in the Tamilian king of kitsch's hyperbolic acting style, kinetic costume changes and exuberant dancing improbably clicked with the outwardly decorous, internally repressed Japanese audience. At the time, the bursting of the Japanese asset bubble had left both the economy, and many citizens themselves, depressed. Rajinikanth's zingy dialogues and outré panache provided laughs, escapism and a possible antidote to the bottled-up angst suffered by many cinemagoers.

In a 2010 article published in the *Hindustan Times* newspaper, Rajini fan Noriko Inagaki recalled that she first saw *Muthu* at a time when she had isolated herself from all social contact, having been downsized from her corporate job.[135] But as she watched the movie her depression lifted, and not long after, she landed another job.

Everyone had their unique explanation for Rajini's allure. One of Takeda's friends, Shinya Asanuma, recalled how he'd been gobsmacked by the actor's expressions the first time he saw him on screen. 'Oh, the way his face moved!

His expressions were just so different from us, Japanese,'
Asanuma said, almost misty eyed. Mikan, one of the women
at the table, explained her attraction to *Muthu* for its story
line, which showed 'how a little money is enough to live
peacefully.'

But the influence of *thalaiver* did not stop with *Muthu*.
In the almost two decades since they saw *Muthu*, the fans I
met with had all developed new Rajini-tinged vocations. For
instance, in 2008, Takeda and fellow fan Shinji Kashima set
up a Tokyo-based south Indian food catering business called
Masalawala. They now made a living serving up sambar,
vadas, rasam and the like in fully traditional style on banana
leaves. Mikan taught Indian movie-style dancing at a dance
school in Tokyo, while Atsuko, the other woman in the
group, had become a mehendi (henna) artist.

Takeda and Kashima had travelled to Chennai almost a
dozen times. Asanuma was just about to set off across Tamil
Nadu for a month. Takeda had even learned to speak basic
Tamil in order to feel closer to his screen idol. He showed
me his most precious possession: a picture with *thalaiver*
himself, snapped during a visit to Chennai. Rajinikanth
had never been to Japan, but if the proverbial mountain (or
Rajini, as the case may be) would not go to Mohammad,
Mohammad must go to the mountain, a concept the fans
had grasped.

And yet, despite the deep impact that some Rajinikanth
movies had obviously had on his Japanese fans' lives, the
role of Indian movies in driving the broader India–Japan
relationship was tenuous. The success of *Muthu* was never

replicated, even though several Rajinikanth starrers, including *Ejaman, Badsha, Robo* and *Arunachalam,* had been released in Japan. Hard-core followers aside, no Indian star, including *thalaiver*, had the kind of name recognition of a Hollywood heartthrob like Leonardo Di Caprio or Brad Pitt.

Takeda and his friends blamed the Tamil star's failure to break into the mainstream on bad marketing. But they also admitted that their own parents were tepid when it came to Rajini films. *Thalaiver* was simply not every Japanese moviegoer's cup of south Indian filter coffee.

As our lunch came to an end, the fans pulled out posters of Rajini and posed for pictures. Later, as they readied to ride off in their peacock- and Rajinikanth sticker-adorned autorickshaw, Takeda had a parting shot. '*Naa eppa varuveen, epdi varuven-nu yaarukkum theriyaathu. Aana, vara vendiya nerathila correct-aa varuven!*' ('No one knows when will I come and how will I come. However, when I have to come, I will come without fail!') I had to google the meaning and the source of the dialogue later. It was from *Muthu.*

Buddhism and Bollywood were the metaphorical bookends of Indo-Japanese linkages, but there was plenty of action in the middle too, notably the pan-Asianist movement of the early twentieth century. The rise of anti-colonial, nationalist sentiment in many parts of Asia helped create common intellectual cause between India, China and Japan. The goals and precise contours of pan-Asianism differed between countries and individuals, but Japan emerged as a fulcrum for the movement.

The archipelago's 'escape' from European colonialism and its victory against Russia in 1905 had given a fillip to nationalists in the region, for whom the defeat of a European power by an Asian country was a source of pride and possibilities. But even before, Indian social reformers like P. C. Mozzomdar and Swami Vivekananda had visited Japan, and impressed with what they saw had urged young Indians to learn from it.[136]

In the early years of the twentieth century, a number of leading Chinese intellectuals made Tokyo their home in exile. In 1905, the revolutionary, Sun Yat-sen, established the Tung Meng Hui (United League) in Tokyo. One of the editors of the league's newspaper, the *Min Pao*, was Zhang Binglin, a Chinese exile who published a series of essays about the relationship between China, India and Japan in a world enslaved by European colonialism.[137] He overtly expressed solidarity with Indians as fellow-victims of imperialist aggression. Asia emerged as a central organizing category in his writings, an episteme that was paralleled in the work of other intellectuals as well, including Japanese pan-Asianists like art-critic Okakura Kakuzō, known as Tenshin (1863–1913),[138] and right-wing nationalist Ôkawa Shûmei (1886–1957).

Revolutionaries like Zhang Binglin broke from the hitherto standard perception of India as the worst possible scenario for the Chinese people and the Qing empire. Zhang's erstwhile mentor, the Qing Dynasty reformer Kang

Youwei, for example, had warned against China following India's example, lest it should join in the latter's fate as a 'fallen nation'.[139]

Several Indian revolutionaries became beneficiaries of Japan's pan-Asianists, notably Rash Behari Bose of Nakamuraya chicken curry fame. Behari Bose was in fact briefly housed by Okawa Shumei and extended protection by others like Toyama Mitsuru (1855-1944), the leader of the ultra-nationalist organization, Genyosha. Behari Bose had been introduced to Toyama by Sun Yat-sen, underlining the enmeshed ties between Tokyo-based nationalists from across Asia.[140] It is likely that Behari Bose was actively supplying arms to Indian nationalists with the help of his Japanese supporters through the 1920s.[141]

Behari Bose went on to edit the *New Asia* and the *Asian Review,* Japan-based journals in support of India's independence movement. In March 1942, he helped establish the Indian Independence League, paving the way for the creation of the Indian National Army under the leadership of the 'other' Bose, Subhash Chandra.

In the Indian historical imagination, Chandra Bose is the feted freedom fighter, but in Japan it is Behari Bose whose legacy left an impact. The writings of the latter helped feed into the growing chauvinism and militarism of Japan in the 1930s, fuelled by a sense of Japan as the chosen Asian nation to spearhead a renaissance of Asia.

◆

The consequences of the links forged between India and Japan during the pan-Asian movement were complex and not always salubrious. They blended anti-colonial idealism with Japan's right-wing propaganda for the 'Greater East Asia Co-Prosperity Sphere', providing intellectual justification for the imperial army's misadventures in China, Korea and south-east Asia during the Second World War.

Asia's first Nobel laureate, the poet and philosopher Rabindranath Tagore, was wary of this tendency years before Japan's invasion of Manchuria in 1931. During his maiden voyage to Japan in 1916, he'd expressed an increasing discomfort with Japan's drift towards belligerent nationalism. At a celebrated speech at Keio University in Tokyo, he'd warned against imitating Europe's tendency to 'imbue the minds of a whole people with an abnormal vanity of its own superiority, to teach it to take pride in its moral callousness and ill-begotten wealth ... '[142]

But the Indian poet had been impressed with Japan's intimacy with nature, for which he was full of praise. 'You have known her (nature's) language of lines and music of colours, the symmetry in her irregularities, and the cadence in her freedom of movements.' Japan needed to be reminded, he said, that its strength lay in its 'genius for simplicity, love for cleanliness ... immense reserve of force in self-control.'

He acknowledged that his sentiments might seem impractical. 'Yet when standing on the outskirts of Yokohama ... I watched the sunset in your southern sea, and saw its majesty among your pine-clad hills ... the music of eternity welled up through the evening silence, and I felt that the sky and the earth and the lyrics of the dawn and the dayfall are with the poets and idealists,' he concluded.

The moment I read these words I knew I needed to stand on the spot where Tagore had heard eternity's music. But the Yokohama I was familiar with was a bustling satellite-city of Tokyo, known mostly for its China Town, shopping malls and baseball stadium.

Research revealed that Tagore had spent three months in the city's Sankeien gardens as the guest of a wealthy silk merchant and tea master, Tomitaro Hara. At the time the gardens were part of the merchant's family estate. Tagore's friend, the artist Yokoyama Taikan (1868–1958), had requested Hara to put up Tagore and his companions, with the result that they stayed at Sankeien from about mid-June to late August 1916.

It was while he lodged at the gardens that Tagore wrote the public speeches he gave in Japan, refining his attempts at developing a language to express the amalgamation of the universalism that was close to his heart with the particular Asian accents that he was also taken with.

And it was the vistas he encountered at the gardens that inspired *Stray Birds*, a collection of short, haiku-inspired poems that were amongst my favourite of his writings. I had first heard '*Stray Birds*', the poem from which the collection took its name, in Chinese translation (my Chinese teacher had been a Tagore fan, having encountered his poems in school). I read the verse in English only much later, but loved it all the more for actually understanding it:

Stray birds of summer come to my window
to sing and fly away.
And yellow leaves of autumn,
which have no songs,
flutter and fall there with a sigh.[143]

There was so much of Japan in these lines – mono no aware, melancholy, Zen. The rest of the collection was similar, filled with images of blooms, fireflies and clouds; of fleeting descriptions of seemingly ordinary moments in the natural world that unexpectedly suggested profound human truths.

The raindrop whispered to the jasmine,
'Keep me in your heart for ever.'
The Jasmine sighed, 'Alas,' and dropped to the ground.

Having discovered all this, I'd hurried to arrange a visit to the Sankeien gardens and walk in Tagore's hallowed footsteps. And so it was that I found myself shivering lightly, in anticipation and cold, as I took in the gardens on an early December morning with Toshikazu Yoshikawa, manager of the Sankeien Foundation.

The essential landscaping of the gardens had remained unchanged over the last century. Gnarled pines, delicate plum trees and majestic ginkgos formed an arboreal symphony. The grounds were strewn with temples, teahouses and historic residences, some of which Hara had transported from Kyoto and Kamakura. Pointing to a large lotus pond on the fringe of the outer garden, Yoshikawa mused that the lotuses would have been blooming through part of Tagore's stay. 'They must have had a resonance for him, as a familiar flower from India,' he said.

At a museum dedicated to Hara's art collection, one wall was hung with photographs of Tagore in Japan. The poet was often dressed in his trademark *jobba*, a long robe-like garment that was not unlike the kimono.

We walked up a bluff to survey what remained of the Shofukaku or the Pavilion of Wind-Swept Pines, the house that Tagore had lived in. The structure had been badly damaged in a 1923 earthquake and only a small section of it remained. The ocean view that Tagore had referred to in his Keio University lecture had not weathered the passing of time, as well as the gardens themselves. Concrete buildings and construction cranes crowded the horizon. And yet the breeze that blew our hair askew held a poem in it. For a moment I felt a haiku dance on my lips, but luckily for Yoshikawa-san, the moment passed and he was saved from having to be polite.

From Tagore's speeches in Japan, it was evident that he had sensed the contradictions at the heart of modern Japanese identity. Japan was both at ease and profoundly uncomfortable in its own skin; desirous of forging a different path to those of European colonialists, while admiring and imitating their agency and power. Sentiments of solidarity coexisted with those of superiority towards the rest of Asia. Japan's ontology was not clear to itself, a condition that arguably persisted today. Who am I? What should I do about it? These questions remained unanswered, in part because they were never articulated clearly, drowned in the chaos of confronting modernity, waging war, and the jingoism of nihonjinron.

The pan-Asianist chapter in the Japan-India story was disrupted, but not totally ruptured, by the Second World War. The altered shape of the post-war geostrategic landscape, coupled with Japan's wartime aggressions against its neighbouring countries, put paid to any notion of Tokyo as a member-leader of a harmonious consortium of Asian nations standing up to the West's colonial brutalities.

And yet Pan-Asianism continued to imbue the India-Japan relationship in the decades that followed, as both nations struggled to redefine and reassert themselves in the post-War, post-colonial order. India did not attend the 1951 San Francisco Peace Conference, believing the US-brokered treaty would limit Japanese sovereignty. Instead, New Delhi negotiated a separate peace with Japan in 1952, described later as ensuring Tokyo 'a proper position of honour and equality among the community of free nations'.[144] India further waived all war-related reparation claims against Japan. On this bedrock of goodwill, Tokyo gave India the first of many yen loans in 1958. In 1986, Japan became, and has since remained, India's largest aid donor.[145]

The most significant figure in the India-Japan relationship in the immediate post-War years was a Bengali Jurist, Radhabinod Pal, whom I had never heard of before moving to Tokyo. In Japan, however, his name elicited the kind of reverence that other countries reserved for the likes of Mahatma Gandhi. Biographical mini-series about the judge had been aired on Japanese TV, memorials to him were erected in Tokyo and Kyoto, and books debating his legacy were published every few years.

I first stumbled upon Judge Pal during a visit to the Yasukuni shrine in Tokyo, an expansive complex of memorials and cherry tree-dotted grounds, commemorating those who had died in the service of Imperial Japan between 1869 and 1947. I visited on a mid-spring day; gusts of wind blew blossom petals to the ground into mounds of flowery snow, making for a tranquil scene that belied the bloody accusations the shrine was at the centre of.

Yasukuni had emerged as an emblem of Japan's fraught relations with its neighbouring countries, in particular China. Amongst the 2 million people buried there were 1,068 convicted war criminals. Fourteen of these were categorized as class-A criminals, found guilty of a special category of 'crimes against peace and humanity' by the eleven-member team of justices from Allied countries that made up the 1946 Tokyo War Crimes Tribunal.

Visits to Yasukuni by senior Japanese politicians were viewed by neighbouring countries that had suffered Japanese military atrocities as provocations, tantamount to a denial of war crimes. But Japanese nationalists believed visits to be a justified exercise of sovereignty, indicating a moving on from what they considered was an overly apologetic stance to the War.

Having reported on China-Japan hostilities for years, the shrine had loomed large in my imagination and I walked about gingerly, somewhat nervous to be at the spot that had featured in so much cross-border invective. In the event, it was a pleasant morning. The blossoms were beautiful even as they waned. A series of memorials dedicated to military horses, pigeon carriers and dogs charmed camera-wielding tourists.

But the plaque that drew my attention featured a large black-and-white photograph of an Indian dressed in lawyer's robes, whom I discovered was Radhabinod Pal. A Japanese visitor gazed at the Pal memorial, silently mouthing the words written on the plaque: '*When Time shall have softened passion and prejudice ... then Justice, holding evenly her scales, will require much of past censure and praise to change places.*'

Once I was back home, I immediately delved into this latest Bengali twist (following both Boses and Tagore) in the Japan-India tale. Until the War, Pal was best known for his contributions to the Indian Income Tax Act of 1922, hardly the most riveting stuff. But his international profile came from his participation in, and eventual dissent from, the Tokyo War Crimes Tribunal. Twenty-five of Japan's top wartime leaders were convicted by the tribunal of the newly devised category of 'class A' charges. Going against the grain of Allied judgement, Pal had issued a 1,235-page dissent, in which he rejected the creation of the class-A category as *ex post facto* law. He further slammed the trials as the 'sham employment of legal process for the satisfaction of a thirst

for revenge'. And he argued that the nuclear incineration of Hiroshima and Nagasaki should also be counted as major war crimes.[146]

Although in the ensuing decades Pal tended to be valorized by historical revisionists in Japan who sought to deny the country's wartime culpability, in fact the jurist did not absolve Japan of wrongdoing. His intention was rather to highlight the flaws in the legal process of the trial. Since all the judges were appointed by the victor nations, the Indian believed the trial was biased and motivated by revenge. Pal's dissent ran to a quarter of a million words, but only a handful of cherry-picked quotes are usually used by Japanese nationalists as ballast for their agenda.[147]

The two Boses and Pal combined to cast a long, protective shadow on the India-Japan relationship. Today, the details of their stories might have been forgotten, but they have helped ensure that India is a rare Asian power with which Japan enjoys a historically uncomplicated relationship. Behind contemporary developments like the Free and Open Indo-Pacific strategy promoted by Tokyo, which India is a key part of, the ghosts of these men lurk, faint but lubricating.

One further character of heft, quite literally in this case, that it would be remiss to omit when talking of post-war India-Japan bonhomie was an elephant. In 1949, Jawaharlal Nehru, independent India's first prime minister, engaged in a deft bit of pachydermic diplomacy by dispatching an elephant named after his own daughter, Indira, to Tokyo's Ueno zoo as a gift 'to the children of Japan'. The elephant went on to become the zoo's star attraction and an enduring symbol of Indian friendliness towards Japan.

But this entire episode was occasioned by an incident that was achingly tragic and also involved former ambassadors of India: the elephants Tonki and John. A male and female pair, they had been acquired by the zoo from India in 1924. They were joined by a third elephant, Hanako, from Thailand, about a decade later.

During the Second World War, it was resolved to kill the zoo's 'most dangerous' animals to deal with the possibility of them escaping during an air attack. Consequently, in 1943, the three elephants were starved to death. There are accounts of how Tonki, who lasted the longest of the three, desperately performed tricks every time a human passed his enclosure, in the vain hope of some food.[148]

In Japan, the gruesomeness of this slaughter is often glossed over, although there are some anodyne accounts made palatable for children. For example, the enormously popular picture book *Kawaisōna Zō* (*Faithful Elephants*) was originally published in 1951 and remains in print. In general, the sad fate of Ueno's wartime elephants was largely eclipsed by the arrival of Indira, whose journey to Japan from the jungles of Mysore began in a petition submitted to the upper house of the Japanese Parliament by two precocious seventh-graders. The students were sad that they were no longer able to see an elephant at the zoo and asked whether a new one could be procured. Their petition snowballed into a public campaign. In the end the Tokyo government collected over a thousand letters from children, all addressed to the prime minister of India, pleading with him to send them a replacement elephant.

Nehru acquiesced, and Indira's arrival at Ueno on 25 September 1949 caused much excitement in Tokyo. The zoo was packed to capacity, with thousands of people trying to glimpse the new elephant. Tadamichi Koga, who was the head of the zoo at the time, later said that receiving Indira was one of the happiest moments in his life.[149] Since she could only follow commands in Kannada, her 'mother tongue', Indira's Japanese handlers, Sugaya and Shibuya, had to learn how to communicate with her from the two Indian mahouts who had accompanied the elephant from Mysore.[150] It took them two months, but they were eventually able to establish a rapport with their charge. In 1957, Indira had an 'in-person' meeting with Prime Minster Nehru and her namesake Indira Gandhi, when they visited Japan. The event was widely covered in the media.[151]

By the 1970s, the elephant's stardom had somewhat dimmed, particularly after a couple of giant pandas from China arrived at the zoo in 1972. Nonetheless, Indira remained an object of affection, and when she died in 1983, Tokyo's governor, Shunichi Suzuki, paid tribute to her. 'She gave a big dream to Japanese children and played a good role in Japan–India friendship for more than thirty years,' he said.[152]

Over the centuries, the Japan–India story had featured a motley cast of characters: travelling monks, fugitives, cooks, poets, movie stars and elephants. Attempting to tie them all neatly together for the purposes of a concluding paragraph feels somewhat disingenuous. It might be best to end this section with the letter that Jawaharlal Nehru addressed to the children of Japan when he sent them an elephant.

'Indira is a fine elephant, very well-behaved,' he wrote. 'I hope that when the children of India and the children of Japan will grow up, they will serve not only their great countries, but also the cause of peace and cooperation all over Asia and the world. So you must look upon this elephant, Indira by name, as a messenger of affection and goodwill from the children of India. The elephant is a noble animal. It is wise and patient, strong and yet, gentle. I hope all of us will also develop these qualities.'

9

To (A)be or not to (A)be?

Indian Prime Minister Narendra Modi is a divisive figure, to whom many a book has been devoted. This is not one of them. However, he does figure as a dramatis personae in the contemporary India–Japan relationship as one half of the Modi–Abe bromance. During the years I lived in Tokyo, it was rarely longer than a few months before Japanese Prime Minister Shinzo Abe and Mr Modi were photographed staring soulfully into each other's right-wing, conservative eyes somewhere in the world. When Mr Abe joined Twitter in 2014, the first world leader he followed was Mr Modi.[153]

Given their nationalist, arguably revisionist, bent, the two leaders were a good ideological fit. But the immediate impetus driving their bonhomie was a rising China, a country that both viewed with a level of discomfiture. At the concluding press conference of Mr Modi's 2018 Japan visit, which I covered, neither prime minister took any questions (they also shared a dislike of journalists). Instead, they read out prepared statements that repeated phrases like 'the rule of law' and 'democratic values': well-known code in geostrategic speak for members of the ABC (Anybody but China) club.

For Japan, long used to being top dog in Asia, the prospect of being eclipsed by China's rising star was galling. But Tokyo lacked the strategic heft to counter Beijing's muscle on its own. Under Donald Trump, the United States had become an increasingly unpredictable ally. These circumstances combined to make a partnership with India very alluring, and Mr Abe took several steps to try and cement one.

Japan pledged billions of dollars in investment and financing for Indian infrastructure. In mid-2017, seven years of rollercoaster negotiations over an India–Japan civil nuclear energy deal came to fruition when the Diet approved the pact, despite Opposition party protests.[154] At the 2018 summit, a logistics-sharing pact was announced; it would allow Japanese ships to get fuel and servicing at Indian naval bases. A raft of ministerial dialogues was instituted and a smorgasbord of MOUs signed.

But the centrepiece of all the summitry during the years I was reporting from Japan was the $12 billion loan extended by Tokyo for India's first high-speed rail corridor from Mumbai to Ahmadabad. Mr Abe inaugurated the project during a September 2017 visit to India. It became somewhat of a metaphor for the bilateral relationship in general: promising but problematic.

The platypus-snouted blue-and-white shinkansen streaking past a snow-topped Mount Fuji was a stock image of Japan. Since October 1964, when the first bullet trains collapsed the time taken to cover the 552-kilometre distance between Tokyo and the commercial center of Osaka to four hours (today it was down to two hours and twenty-two minutes), the shinkansen had emerged as the symbol of Japan's phoenix-like rise from the ashes of the Second World War to economic super-powerdom. At the time of announcing the India deal, Japan's shinkansen had carried over 10 billion passengers without a single accident or casualty and an average delay of less than one minute.

Yet, despite this admirable track record, Japan had struggled to export its bullet train know-how, even as Mr Abe had made selling the technology abroad a cornerstone of his game plan to revitalize the Japanese economy. Before signing on India, Taiwan had been Japan's only successful sale. But Taiwan was hardly a poster child for the system, given that its high-speed line had suffered heavy losses since opening in 2007.

In fact, profitability was a notoriously hard ask for high-speed train networks. In Japan, some routes, notably the Tokyo-Osaka one, were moneymaking, but to achieve this required high volumes of passengers and highly priced tickets. It cost around 130 USD for a one-way ticket from Tokyo to Osaka on a bullet train. And over 350 shinkansen operated on this line daily, ferrying about 163 million passengers a year. The region served was demographically dense, home to over half of Japan's population. These conditions were not easy to replicate, and other high-speed lines in Japan had struggled.

It was a tall order to expect the Mumbai-Ahmadabad route to meet these criteria. Unsurprisingly, the project came in for its fair share of criticism in India on the grounds of expense, safety and misplaced priorities. It had its detractors in Japan too, given India's less than stellar record on land acquisition for infrastructure projects and the tendency for estimated costs to balloon. In the event, many of the concerns proved legitimate. At the time of writing, a budget shortfall of some 500 billion yen (4.56 billion USD) had been discovered and the inauguration of the project pushed back by five years to 2028, from an originally scheduled 2023, following a site-acquisition delay.[155]

But, as with many strategic decisions, the India high-speed rail investment was not about trains and profit as much as about China. To Japan's chagrin, Beijing's infrastructure dominance had extended to that most Japanese of preserves: the bullet train. Over the last decade, China had created a 22,000 km high-speed rail network, dwarfing Japan's in size and speed of development. It boasted the world's fastest train, the Shanghai Maglev, which reached speeds of 430 km per hour. And China's technology was also cheaper, making it an attractive proposition for the cost-conscious developing and middle-income countries of Asia.

In 2015, China pipped Japan to the post at the last minute by securing a high-speed rail project in Indonesia that had been considered by Tokyo to be in the bag. One reason Beijing unexpectedly won out was because China offered to finance the line without any recourse to Indonesia's government coffers.[156] China had also beaten Tokyo to becoming Thailand's choice of partner for its first bullet train line. The two countries were facing off in bids to win contracts for other south-east Asian high-speed projects, including one between Singapore and Kuala Lumpur.[157]

The battle to export bullet trains was a manifestation of the broader rivalry between China and Japan for influence over Asia. The India deal needed to be viewed in this context, but it was nonetheless a hard-won victory for Japan. The 12 billion USD loan at 0.1 per cent interest was to be paid back over fifty years. Japan was also to supplement the financing with a generous package of technical assistance and training.

Involvement in a major Indian infrastructure project was not without precedent for Japan, the Delhi Metro being a case in point. From 2002, when it first started operations, the Indian capital's metro had expanded to 389 km of track (as of December 2019) and become an iconic part of the contemporary cityscape. Japan had provided support for the project through development loans and technical assistance from the outset.[158]

Yet I remained sceptical about the plausibility of India's bullet train. As I made my way to meet with Tomoyuki Nakano, the director of the International Engineering Affairs of Japan's Railway Bureau, a few days before Mr Abe's 2017 India visit, I remembered how during my college days I had once taken a train from Delhi to the city of Cochin in the south. It was a 2,800 km journey with a scheduled travel time of about forty-five hours. My train ended up being an entire twenty-four hours late, so that it pulled up at the platform in Cochin at the same time as the train that had departed Delhi the day after I'd left. I walked through the characterless corridors of the Railway Bureau's office building thinking of Mumbai's commuter trains, where upwards of 2,000 people died in accidents annually. The idea of transplanting a *shinkansen t*o India felt wrong-headed.

When I put my concerns to Mr Nakano, he listened quite solemnly before countering with the fact that Japan had first developed its high-speed lines in the 1960s when it had also been a poor country, requiring loans from the World Bank. Yes, some tweaks to the Japanese technology would be necessary for the project, taking into account climatic differences between Japan and India, he said. The possibility of electrical black-outs and the far larger quantities of dust in the air and on the tracks would also need to be factored in. But overall, he was confident of ironing these out in consultation with Indian counterparts.

In many ways, the project was set to be a bellwether of how the Japan-India relationship might fare going forward. If it succeeded it would pave the way for more Japanese investment in critical Indian infrastructure, boosting trust and facilitating cooperation in third countries as well. But if it failed, it could indicate other snags in any potential Tokyo–New Delhi éntente. As the jugaad-shokunin dichotomy indicated, Japan and India were cultural misfits in many ways. The difference in the cultural relationship to punctuality was a glaring example. In Japan, being on time was akin to religion, whereas in India time was fungible.

But Mr Nakano was sanguine. 'When we had Indians coming here (to Tokyo) for training in the past, I noticed some of them were quite late. But after two weeks in Japan they became very punctual,' he concluded. I loved it. #TwoWeeksInTokyo was a great hashtag. I imagined it as the solution to all of India's problems. Habitually late? Nothing #TwoWeeksInTokyo can't fix. Feeling slipshod and lazy? #TwoWeeksInTokyo for you. In need of discipline? All you really need is #TwoWeeksInTokyo.

In the years following the inauguration of the Mumbai-Ahmadabad bullet corridor, the project languished in the manner of many an infrastructure deal in India (although to be fair, high-speed rail projects were in trouble all across south-east Asia). Its less-than-efficient progress was symptomatic of larger issues in the India–Japan business story, which looked like a no-brainer on paper, but struggled to take off in practice.

At the end of 2018, there were 1,369 Japanese companies and over 4,800 Japanese corporate offices active in India. Japanese investment in India totaled 4.7 billion USD in 2016-17, sharply up from the 2.6 billion USD of the previous year. Japan was amongst the largest foreign investors in India.

And yet the bilateral economic relationship remained underwhelming, not only in relation to its potential but also when compared with the ties that each nation shared with their common bête noir: China. According to Japan External Trade Organization (JETRO) data, China received

116 billion USD in Japanese investments between 1996 and 2015, about five times more than the 24 billion USD that India had. Japan-India two-way trade (17.63 billion USD in 2018-19) was also a fraction of the mighty, 350 billion USD Sino–Japan trade relationship. Even Sino-Indian trade was worth substantially more, at 92.68 billion USD (for 2018-19).[159] In fact, the share of India–Japan trade in Japan's trade basket was barely 1 per cent and only a little over 2 per cent of India's total global trade.

The gap between theoretical perfection and practical distance could not wholly be explained by the usual suspects that plagued foreign investors in Indian ventures, Japan's bullet train deal included. Corruption, inadequate infrastructure, complex tax regulations and land-acquisition problems were certainly significant challenges, but they did not constitute the whole, troubled, picture.

Tomofumi Nishizawa, manager of JETRO's Overseas Research Department, had spent five years at his organization's India office between 2011 and 2015. I met with him one afternoon at his offices in the swish ARK Hills commercial complex in downtown Tokyo. He was despairing of the attitude of Japanese businesses in India, which he said lay somewhere between naïve and obtuse. As a result, it took a Japanese company much longer than its Korean or Chinese counterparts to learn how best to localize their products for the Indian market.

He elaborated with the example of air conditioners. The Japanese tended to think the most important element was the quality of the air conditioner so that it was able to last without the need for repairs for years. But in India it was cheap to have an air conditioner repaired and technicians were abundant. The consumer was therefore more focused on cost than durability.

Mr Nishizawa felt that one company that had cottoned on to India's particularities was the Japanese manufacturer Daikin, which had eventually switched from importing expensive parts from Japan to sourcing locally. Daikin India had a turnover of 3,250 crore INR in 2016-17, and in late 2017 had opened a second manufacturing facility in Rajasthan.[160]

But the greatest challenge, according to Nishizawa, was cultural: an outdated and negative image of India. The JETRO official was unexpectedly candid, leaning forward conspiratorially as he revealed that employees picked for jobs in India often acted as though they had drawn the short straw. The larger corporations may realize India's potential, but small and medium enterprises were the 'worst' culprits of this attitude. 'Maybe our attitude can be called racist,' he said. 'It is very difficult to change it.'

In the final analysis, Japanese corporations were strongly risk averse, which made it difficult for them to cope in the freewheeling, jugaad-proud environment of India, where impromptu decision making was a necessary skill in the business arsenal. 'We [the Japanese] are not the global norm, but we act like we are. Unless we become more flexible and adapt better to other ways, we will not succeed,' Nishizawa concluded. Clearly, favourable political optics were insufficient for Japan–India business ties to gain serious traction.

Moreover, both Mr Modi and Mr Abe found their foreign agendas hamstrung by domestic troubles. In December 2019, Mr Abe indefinitely postponed a scheduled visit to India after violent protests broke out over the controversial Citizenship Amendment Bill in the state of Assam.[161] But the focus here is not on the many ills of Mr Modi's tenure at India's helm. It is on Japan, and consequently on Mr Abe, who bestrode the Japanese political landscape like a colossus in salaryman clothing for the best part of a decade. On November 2019, he became the longest serving prime minister of the country, overtaking Mr Taro Katsura's three-term run between 1901 and 1913, with an all-time record of 2,886 days in office.

Mr Abe's lineage was so robust as to endow his rise to the political summit almost with a sense of inevitability. His maternal grandfather, Nobusuke Kishi, was prime minister from 1957 to 1960, while his paternal grandfather, Kan Abe, was a member of the House of Representatives. His father, Shintaro Abe, had served as foreign minister. Another former prime minister, Sato Eisaku (1964–72), was his great uncle.

Mr Abe served at the head of government in two different spells: a sprint between July 2006 and September 2007, and a marathon between 2012 and August 2020. During his second act, he brought stability to what had been a fractured polity, honing the image of a strong leader readying Japan for a newly muscular role on the world stage. He had steered the economy out of deflation and decline, if not into growth, then at least into a less turbulent holding pattern. He had presided over an increase in the country's military capabilities and attempted to expand Japan's strategic options beyond its traditional reliance on the United States.

And yet his legacy was unlikely to be as long lasting as his time in office. It was difficult to live in Japan and avoid the feeling that the only reason Mr Abe remained in power was because of a weak and uninspiring Opposition – in other words, because of the TINA (there is no alternative) factor that voters around the world were all too familiar with.

Just over a year after I moved to Tokyo, in September 2017, Shinzo Abe declared snap elections to be held a month later, on October 22. The polls would be more than a year ahead of schedule. Coming from a country where anyone in power clung to it till the bitter end, the idea of precipitating a vote when there was no crisis was bizarre enough, but the really disconcerting phenomenon was what followed, ie., not much.

Having just spent four years in Indonesia, with its India-style election jamborees featuring noisy political rallies, outspoken trade unionists and a free and assertive press, Japan's electioneering was so bland it cried out for some masala. With one week to go for the elections, lead stories in the newspaper were as follows: G20 finance chiefs upbeat on world economy; Shift towards renewable energy picking up steam; Japan's 'way of the sword' baffling to foreigners; and Japan zoo mourns death of anime-loving celebrity penguin.

Whenever I asked my Japanese friends whom they planned to vote for, their embarrassed silences would eventually dissolve into a cough, from which it was just possible to discern 'the LDP', Mr Abe's Liberal Democratic Party. Not that any of them actually liked the man, but there was no viable Opposition, and ultimately few felt that the choice of prime minister made a significant difference to their lives.

There was a baffling chasm between what the electorate seemed to want and what their would-be elected representatives seemed interested in representing. This was illustrated most clearly by Mr Abe's most cherished political goal: the amendment of Article 9 of the Constitution, the clause that restricted Japan's ability to maintain a military deterrent. The article in question explicitly stated the decision to 'forever renounce war as a sovereign right' and to eschew the maintenance of military forces. It essentially enshrined a pacifist stance into the codes governing Japan, facilitated by a security alliance with the US that committed the latter to defending the archipelago in the event of an attack.

But for nationalists like Mr Abe, Article 9 was a humiliating reminder of Japan's Second World War defeat and the subsequent imposition of a US-drafted constitution. Moreover, in a regional security environment shaped by North Korea's nuclear and missile programmes and an assertive China on the prowl, Article 9 was seen by them as an unreasonable limitation of Japan's ability to project power and defend itself.

Article 9 had in fact been reinterpreted (without formal amendment) several times over the decades. Since 1954, Japan had maintained a self-defence force (SDF), which had long morphed into an impressive military in much but name. It was about 250,000-strong and trained to use some of the most cutting-edge defence equipment in all of Asia.[162] In 2015, Mr Abe revised the SDF law to permit 'collective self-defence', giving the green light for Japan to come to the military aid of allies under attack. In April 2019, for the first time, Japan even contributed two soldiers to an American-led peacekeeping mission, rather than a UN one, in Egypt's Sinai peninsula.

Oddly, given Mr Abe's electoral popularity, none of these changes was popular. The 2015 law revision had led to a huge public outcry.[163] And opinion polls regularly demonstrated that the majority of Japanese remained opposed to the prime minister's goal of Constitutional amendment.[164]

Technically, all Mr Abe wanted was a formal recognition of the de facto reality of the SDF by inscribing it in the Constitution. But the symbolism of it was suspect, particularly given the prime minister and the LDP's history of downplaying Japanese war crimes. A few examples: In a 1995 resolution in the House of Representatives, 221 members of the LDP had emphasized that the Pacific War had been a war to 'liberate' Asia from colonialism. In 1997, a group of young LDP politicians promoting revisionist history, *Nihon no Zento to Rekishi Kyōiku wo Kangaeru Wakate Giin no Kai* (Group of Young Diet Members for Consideration of Japan's Future and History Education), was established. Mr Abe was a founding member and executive secretary of the group. Later, during his first tenure as prime minister, he publicly shared his belief that 'comfort women', as the largely Chinese and Korean sex slaves of the Imperial Japanese Army during the war were referred to, had not in fact been coerced into sex work.[165]

The point here is not to debate the merits of Mr Abe's proposed Constitutional revision. It is to highlight the deeper flaws in Japan's democracy, which tended towards being formal rather than substantial. People voted in regular elections between an array of political parties, yet the LDP had almost never been out power since it was established in 1955. The only exceptions were brief periods between 1993 and 1994, and again from 2009 to 2012.

In contrast, one of the most common words in the Indian political lexicon was 'anti incumbency,' or the tendency to vote ruling politicians out of power. India, in fact, has the highest rate of anti-incumbency in the world, with incumbents from the ruling party having a less than fifty-fifty shot at returning to Parliament.[166]/[167]

But in Japan, I remained unable to locate the wellsprings of love for the LDP that its constancy in power suggested. Instead, a substantial share of the votes that the party garnered were simply votes by default, cast by citizens on auto-mode, because that's what they'd always done. The sense of disconnect between politicians and the electorate generated a kind of unreality, where the general public seemed more exercised about the death of a penguin at the zoo than in determining the leadership of their country.

Julio and I often marvelled at how we found the Chinese and Japanese political landscapes at almost diametric odds. In China an authoritarian government ruled over a politically engaged populace, while in Japan a democratic government presided over a politically passive populace. It was ironic.

Even though the average Chinese person could not express herself freely in the manner typical of more liberal polities, via street demonstrations or the media, she loved a piece of political gossip. People remained chary of 'off limit' topics like the Tiananmen Square killings, but it had been impossible to say '*Ni hao*' without someone telling me their opinion about the state of world affairs (abysmal), democracy (too chaotic) corruption (everywhere), and even telecom policy (more competition needed). In Japan I was likelier to have more luck engaging someone in conversation about cat dental hygiene than electoral preferences.

To be fair, there was a minor frisson of excitement preceding the 2017 election in the form of popular Tokyo Governor Yuriko Koike, who suddenly cobbled together a brand-new political party, Party of Hope, in combination with the remnants of Japan's erstwhile primary Opposition, the Democratic Party (DP). The DP had imploded with less than a month to go for the elections, its members forming new ingredients in the alphabet soup that was Japanese politics. Many joined Ms Koike, while more left-leaning ones established the CDP or Constitutional Democratic Party of Japan.

But despite the Koike googly, the Opposition was in almost cartoonish disarray, and on 22 October Mr Abe emerged triumphant again. The Japanese electorate sighed at the inevitability of it all and turned their attention to more pressing matters, like the colour of the autumn leaves.

Notwithstanding the lacklustre Opposition, it wasn't all smooth sailing for the Japanese prime minister. Through his tenure, Mr Abe was embroiled in a series of corruption charges that came to light with the regularity of the change of seasons. For an Indian like me, used to truly operatic governmental scandals, Japanese-style corruption could come across as a tad feeble. The charges facing the PM and his government included the sanctioning of a veterinary school licence, the alleged bribing of constituents with crabs and melons and the guest list for a cherry blossom viewing party. But these were not as inconsequential as they might seem. The evidence pointed to cronyisim and dishonesty being deep-seated in Japanese institutions.

In 2018, Mr Abe was in the hotseat over two charges. One had to do with facilitating a veterinary school licence for a friend of his, the first such school to get a new license in more than fifty years. The second was related to the prime minister's possible involvement in a heavily discounted sale of state-owned land to a kindergarten operator, Moritomo Gakuen. The operator, who had established ties to Mr Abe's wife, made an alleged profit of 7.5 million USD over the land deal. The Moritomo incident had first emerged in early 2017, but resurfaced after a revelation that official documents related to the sale had been doctored, with references to

Mr Abe and his wife, Akie Abe, scrubbed out. Ms Abe was originally listed as the honorary principal for the school planned on the land in question, although she stepped down after the controversy broke. In the veterinary school matter, although Mr Abe repeatedly denied using any influence to help his friend, an official document emerged that suggested otherwise.[168]

But the prime minister denied all charges. In the Moritomo case, he parried matters by claiming that the unaltered documents may have mentioned his name but did not constitute evidence of either his or his wife's involvement with the land sale.

A year on, in late 2019, the Abe government faced more accusations. It began in October with the resignation of two newly appointed cabinet ministers in quick succession.[169] The first to go was Trade Minister Isshu Sugawara, who stepped down just a month after taking over the key post, following a report by the *Shukan Bunshun* magazine that claimed he had gifted expensive melons, oranges and crabs to voters. He was also accused of offering 20,000 yen (185 USD) as condolence money to a supporter to help him defray the costs of a funeral of one of his family members.[170]

Less than a week later, it was Justice Minister Katsuyuki Kawai's turn after another report in the same magazine alleged that his campaign staff had sent potatoes, corn, mangoes and other presents to constituents. The prime minister accepted the resignations and apologized to 'the people' for the errors in his judgement in appointing the alleged offenders. 'As the person who appointed him, I bear

responsibility for this, for which I apologize to the nation,'
Mr Abe told reporters shortly after accepting Mr Kawai's
resignation.[171]

But he bore no such responsibility in the matter of
allegations against himself that emerged a few weeks
later, about his having rewarded his own supporters with
invitations to a cherry blossom-viewing party that cost the
public exchequer 55 million yen (504,000 USD). The matter
got murkier as it appeared that figures from the world of
organized crime had been among the attendees and that
crucial documents, including the guest list for the party, had
been suspiciously shredded on the very day the Opposition
asked to see them.[172]

In the immediate aftermath of every scandal, Mr Abe saw
his popularity ratings dip. But he was always able to shake
off the consequences within a few weeks, winning elections
and in 2019 securing another three-year term as Liberal
Democratic Party (LDP) leader.

Given the baroque levels of corruption that afflicted
India, Indonesia and China, the charges against Mr Abe and
his fellow politicians could be spun as demonstrating how
little leeway there was in Japan for transgressing laws. Was
inviting a few friends to a cherry blossom party that bad?
Was giving supporters a few mangoes and melons really
heinous?

If these 'gifts' had been the whole iceberg of corruption
in Japan, I'd probably answer in the negative. But there was
widespread acknowledgement that they were merely the
tip. In Japan there was a tendency to miss the woods for

the trees by focusing on minor rules while ignoring larger transgressions.

Even corporate heavyweights, for all their tom-tomming of their superior quality and processes, were not as 'clean' as their image abroad suggested. Kobe Steel, Japan's third-largest steelmaker, for example, was indicted in 2018 after it admitted to having fabricated the strength and quality data of products sold to hundreds of clients.[173] A few years earlier, Toshiba Corp, a nuclear power plant and semiconductor heavyweight, was found to have misled investors by filing false financial statements.[174] Top executives at camera and medical equipment firm Olympus were also found to have been falsifying accounts for years, possibly decades, concealing losses amounting to 1.7 billion USD.[175] Consequently, in 2017 a Tokyo court fined six former top-executives of the company, including the ex-chairman, Tsuyoshi Kikukawa, 529 million USD.[176]

Jeff Kingston, a professor at Temple University Japan in Tokyo and former columnist at the *Japan Times,* was a vocal critic of the Japanese prime minister. I'd first met Kingston in Jakarta, when he'd visited to research a book on nationalist movements across Asia. After I moved to Tokyo, we became friends and met up every few months, usually over a bowl of soba. He was interviewed so frequently by journalists on all things Japan-related that he'd developed a habit of speaking in sound bytes, even in social contexts. 'The Iron Triangle of the LDP, bureaucrats and big business still runs the show, where backscratching and corruption are extensive but rarely prosecuted,' he told me one afternoon, as he slurped on tofu skin noodles. When I emailed him to get his reaction regarding the fruit bribery scandal, he'd replied: 'Melons and mangoes are pricey in Japan, but having to resign over doling them out to supporters cultivates an undeserved image of probity.'

Kingston was caustic but correct. Politics in Japan was rife with nepotism. Some 30 per cent of the members of the Diet were *nisei* or second-generation parliamentarians with 'inherited' seats. Among LDP MPs, about 40 per cent were *nisei*. And only three of the 30 post-war prime ministers of Japan had not had some kind of political lineage. Most, like Mr Abe, were the children or grandchildren of former PMs and ministers.[177] Japan's democracy was based on a hereditary politics of privilege that was legitimized and reinforced by electoral politics.

Japan wasn't unique in its 'democratic fiefdoms', but its politics were more sclerotic than dynamic. The obsession of the country's political elite with the past and its disconnect with the general electorate placed it in a disadvantageous position to achieve the flexibility and innovation that the twenty-first century world called for, and which authoritarian China often seemed able to display.

In August 2020 after a tumultuous few months (more in the next chapter), Shinzo Abe abruptly resigned a year ahead of schedule, citing ill health. His term as leader of the Liberal Democratic Party was supposed to have run until September 2021.

Assessments of his legacy vary, depending on the subjectivities of the analyst. Mr Abe certainly enjoyed great power and status while in office. He was unafflicted by the forgettability that was the chief characteristic of the revolving door of five prime ministers, lasting only about a year each, that had preceded him. And yet, I believe he will only get a pass in the history books, though not with distinction. 'A' for longevity, but a 'C', at most, for everything else.

When he had returned to power in 2012, Mr Abe had made a set of economic reforms to stimulate the economy his priority. Popularly dubbed Abenomics, the three pillars of this plan included monetary easing, fiscal spending and deregulation to promote private investment. Fast-forward to the beginning of 2020 and the Japanese economy remained limp, even prior to the upheavals to come later in the year. The country's corporations had proved unable to transform themselves into twenty-first century technology leaders. And although Japan had benefited from periods of economic growth and low unemployment under Mr Abe, the country was still mired in a slow-growth, high-debt deflationary trap.

The prime minister's plans to revive the economy had included an effort to bring more women into the workforce, an attempt nicknamed 'Womenomics'. But in the World Economic Forum's annual Global Gender Gap Report 2020, Japan dropped to 121st place, the lowest among advanced economies, down ten rungs from the previous year.

Globally, Japan suffered from a negative image when it came to gender empowerment. The stereotype of a land of misogynist men and meek, long-suffering women was an entrenched one. Even Indians often tutted and shook their heads sadly when they learned that I lived in Tokyo. 'Terrible situation for women there,' they would say. 'So sad.'

In some ways this was absurd. To begin with, women in Japan were safe. Unlike in say, India, they occupied public spaces with confidence. They dressed as they liked. They drank what they liked. They tended to be more sexually liberated than the global norm. They controlled the purse strings of the household, doling out pocket money, called *okozukai*, to their husbands.[178]

Even the idea that Japanese women stayed at home, unwelcome by the workforce, needed to be tempered. Women in Japan in fact exceeded the rate of labour force participation of women (defined as the fraction of the population either working or searching for work) in the United States. In 2016, Japan's prime-age female labour force participation rate was at 76.3 per cent, higher than US's 74.3 per cent.[179]

The problem was that greater participation in the workforce did not automatically lead to greater empowerment. Far more Japanese women worked in part-time and non-regular jobs than men. Women also occupied a much smaller share of executive positions in Japan than in other countries. In Japan, women held only 8 per cent of management jobs, according to a July 2020 survey by market research firm Teikoku Databank.[180] The corresponding figures were 51.8 per cent in the US and 37.3 per cent in France.[181]

There was, furthermore, an egregious absence of women in politics. According to the Geneva-based Inter-Parliamentary Union, Japan was ranked lowest among the advanced economies of the Group of 20 nations in terms of the percentage of female politicians. Women accounted for just 10.2 per cent of the 463 seats in the Lower House.[182]

A cabinet reshuffle in October 2018 left Mr Abe's nineteen-member cabinet with a sole woman, Satsuki Katayama, in charge of regional revitalization and female empowerment. When asked how he justified such a gender-skewed cabinet, the prime minister had been sexistly glib. 'She (Katayama) is incredibly feisty. I know there is only one woman in this cabinet, but she has the presence of two or three women,' he'd said.

Ms Katayama had also been forced to buy a new dress shortly before a ceremony at the Imperial Palace to announce the new ministers, after a Cabinet Office official turned up his nose at her initially chosen outfit because the jackets and dresses were of different colours, adding that a long dress and jacket of the same colour was 'the norm', reportedly suggesting silver.[183]

That the patriarchy had deep roots in Japan was indisputable. Its tentacles were spread widely, from the world of Sumo wrestling to the country's universities. Two incidents stuck out.

In April 2018, the mayor of Maizuru, a city in south-central Japan, had a stroke and collapsed while making a speech inside the ring at a local sumo tournament. Two women, one of whom was a nurse, rushed to his assistance.

But instead of appreciating their efforts, an agitated referee asked them to immediately leave the ring, because they were female.

Sumo, I learned, was not just a match between hefty wrestlers but was deeply intertwined with Shinto religious rites. It was believed that the spirits of *kami* or Shinto deities moved through the wrestlers when they sparred. Elaborate purifying rituals, including the sprinkling of salt were part of the performance. Women were not welcome in any of this, being deemed impure because of menstruation and childbirth, an aversion that is part of many Hindu, Buddhist and Shinto practices. They are, therefore, prohibited from entering the sumo *dohyo* (ring), a sacred space that would supposedly be 'polluted' by their presence.

Television channels and social media were abuzz following the incident, with one Twitter user suggesting, 'if this is the response to someone who tried to save a life, we had better sprinkle salt on the head of the sumo association'. The Japan Sumo Association (JSA) eventually issued an apology and judged the referee's response as inappropriate, given the life-threatening nature of the situation. However, its general attitude to women and the sport was unchanged. Only a day later, when the mayor of Takarazuka city, Tomoko Nakagawa, applied to give a speech from within the *dohyo* of a sumo tournament, she was turned down.

'I'm a female mayor but I am a human being,' she said, according to Japanese media, 'but because I am a woman, despite being mayor, I cannot make a speech in the ring. It is regrettable and mortifying.'[184] And two days on, schoolgirls hoping to participate in a children's spring sumo tour in Gunma prefecture were barred by the JSA, ostensibly on grounds of 'girls' safety'.

For an Indian, the exclusion of women on religious grounds, however spurious, was somewhat par for the course. But the revelation a few months later that a leading medical school in Tokyo had been systematically rigging its entrance exams against women applicants for more than a decade was shocking, even by Japan's unedifying standards of sexism. In August 2018, Tokyo Medical University admitted to having regularly subtracted points from the test scores of every woman who took the entrance tests. Officials even worked from a manual that laid out precisely how the scores were to be manipulated in order to keep the number of women students at the university down to around 30 per cent of the total. The rationale: too many women doctors would cause problems down the line, including staffing shortages when they stopped work or took time off to raise children.

Less than 22 per cent of doctors in Japan were women, according to a 2018 survey conducted by the Ministry of Health, Labour, and Welfare, the lowest among all OECD countries.[185] At the decision-making levels in doctors' associations and academic bodies, the percentage of women plummeted to 2 to 3 per cent.

The reasons why women in Japan struggled in the workplace were manifold. Discrimination dogged them from their early years. As the Medical University case demonstrated, they had to work harder and prove themselves more able than their male competition. Many of these challenges were universal, stemming from the persistence of patriarchal norms that viewed the 'home' as the proper place for a woman.

But there was one obstacle that was particularly acute in Japan: the general habit of overwork that penalized flexibility and rewarded time spent at the workplace. An almost sacred reverence for hard work was built into the company culture in Japan. For employees, stoic endurance was considered a virtue, while leaving the office before one's superiors was frowned upon. When someone did go home before their seniors did, they took their leave with the phrase, *osaki ni shitsureishimasu*, which translates as 'apologies for leaving before you'.

It bordered on the impossible to balance the demands of raising children with work norms like these. A friend, a former employee of Mitsubishi who now stayed at home looking after her two boys, told me about when she went to her boss to explain the fact that the long hours at work were proving impossible to reconcile with the needs of her children. He'd nodded sympathetically and said he understood, leading her momentarily to imagine the various solutions to the problem that he might propose. Instead, he suggested she quit. She did.

Japan might have been one of the safest countries in the world in terms of violent crime, but it had a disproportionate number of deaths from one deadly killer: work. Death by overwork had its own word in Japanese – *karoshi*, a term first coined in the 1970s, but one that still dominated the headlines.

Among the first stories I reported on was the case of a December 2015 suicide by Matsuri Takahashi, a twenty-four-year-old employee of Dentsu, one of Japan's most established advertising firms.[186] Takahashi had been working in the digital accounts division of Dentusu for about eight months when she'd jumped off the top floor of a company dormitory, having allegedly survived on about ten hours of sleep a week, for several weeks. Japan's statutory working hours are eight hours a day for a maximum of forty hours a week.

A government white paper revealed that ninety-three people had committed or attempted suicide because of overwork in 2015. A further ninety-six deaths from brain and cardiac illnesses were also designated as karoshi-related that year. Following the Takahashi suicide, a number of government and corporate initiatives to combat karoshi were rolled out. A campaign dubbed Premium Friday that encouraged companies to allow employees an early finish on the last Friday of every month was announced. Legislation limiting overtime to an average of sixty hours a month over the course of the calendar year was devised.

These moves failed. Employees refused to leave early on Fridays. According to Labour Ministry figures, 190 cases of karoshi were confirmed in 2017. These included suicides as well as deaths due to other illnesses linked to working too much. In 90 per cent of the cases, the individuals had clocked eighty hours or more in overtime in a month.

There was more to the practice of staying long hours at the office than either the demands of the boss or even virtue-signalling. Employees often had nowhere else to go. With cramped homes and long commutes as the norm, offices served as quiet spaces or 'dens' for many people. An Indian friend from university in Delhi who had lived in Japan for over two decades, worked for a large accounting firm where an employee-death was designated as karoshi after an investigation by the Ministry of Health, Labour and Welfare. Subsequently, all staff were ordered to go home at a reasonable time in the evening, with lights forcibly turned off at 10 p.m. My friend was put in charge of ensuring compliance with the new rule for his team. His instructions were to stay at work until every team member had left for the day. Ironically, he found himself having to work later and later into the night as recalcitrant colleagues refused to go home despite his urgings. People begged him to be allowed to stay, swearing they would not work but merely use the office as a place to catch up on reading or study.

I began to understand this behaviour only after visiting a Japanese friend's home for the first time. We'd spent months in Tokyo without being invited over to anyone's residence. Friends always took us out to restaurants. Play dates with children were organized outdoors, in parks. I was cognizant of real estate prices in Japan and that most apartments were cramped. But I was nonetheless unprepared for my first non-expat home visit.

Julio had a dear Japanese friend, whom I will call Yuji, from his days as an undergraduate at university in England. He had spent a month travelling around Japan with this friend in the late 1990s. They had subsequently lost touch. Before moving to Tokyo, Julio had tried to track down Yuji on social media but hadn't had any luck. He was therefore over the moon when one day he unexpectedly had an email from Yuji waiting in his inbox. In a manner that inspired faith in cosmic design, Yuji, who had grown up to become a mid-level manager for a Japanese auto major with operations in Europe, had been browsing an EU website to look for a relevant regulation, when he discovered that Julio had recently joined the delegation in Japan.

Reunited after almost two decades, Julio and his friend made up for lost time meeting up at various watering holes every few weeks, until one day we received in invitation to visit Yuji's home and meet his family. It took us an hour by train from central Tokyo, where we lived, to travel to Yuji's suburb. Yuji himself made this journey twice a day, since his office was located downtown. From the station it was a short walk to Yuji's building complex, which turned out to be a depressingly good example of 1960s-style brutalist architecture. It was an enormous box-like cement structure with long, sparse corridors interspersed with hovel-sized apartments. We were welcomed by Yuji, his delightful wife and two lively children into what was essentially a studio apartment, comprising a single, medium-sized room, a bathroom and a tiny kitchen.

'Is this it?' whispered one of my brats loudly, while I tried to shush him. 'Where are the beds?' asked the other, as Julio stamped on his foot in warning. We sat down on the floor (as was Japanese custom) around a table laden with strawberries and other fruit. I assumed the beds were futon mattresses hidden away in cupboards and brought out at night to sleep on, after the table was moved out of the way. The room was stuffed full of toys, books and sundry other items. Our friends repeatedly alluded to the smallness of the space, even as we smiled and assured them that it was lovely. For dinner they took us out to a restaurant. And then we had to make the long commute back to town.

My boys had gotten over their first reaction to Yuji's home within minutes, bonding with the other children and cracking up at shared jokes. But Julio and I took a little longer to digest the fact that his friend, who had been educated in the UK and had a good job at a world-renowned company, lived in what felt to us like straitened circumstances.

Yuji's wife told me that her husband stayed out drinking with colleagues most nights and only returned late, after the rest of the family had gone to bed. But she confessed it worked best like that. On evenings that Yuji returned home early, he only got in the way of the children's evening study and bedtime routines. Over the years we became very close to the couple and even holidayed together in the summer. As he opened up, Yuji told me he felt awkward going home early on weekday evenings. He had no space to wind down and felt like an intruder in his own home.

Rather than just a lack of women in the workforce, the larger problem for Japan, it seemed to me, was its punishing work culture that made any semblance of work-life balance impossible for men or women. A culture of overwork certainly kept women out of the economy and did little to encourage Japan's woefully low birth rate. As a result, many Japanese were choosing not to have children or even to get married. And overwork did not make employees more productive, only more stressed out. In 2018, Japan's GDP per hour worked was 47 USD,[187] the lowest, other than South Korea's, amongst the G7 group of most advanced economies. What was needed therefore was a systemic overhaul of Japan's work practices. Working less but smarter would benefit men, women, and families.

Under current circumstances I would rather be the average Japanese housewife than a typical salaryman. A life of long commutes, suffering insufferable bosses, bowing and scraping to clients and being forced to ingest vast quantities of alcohol most nights was just not appealing.

The year 2020 began innocently, its numerically symmetrical bookends holding within them the anticipation of the summer Olympic Games that would ensure Mr Abe closed out his term triumphantly, having signalled Japan's renaissance on the global stage. For me personally, it promised to be a year of movement. After four years in Tokyo, we were scheduled to relocate that summer, this time to Spain. The plan was to spend our last few months travelling feverishly, making sure we made it to every part of the Japanese archipelago that remained unticked-off on our bucket list. But even as the family and I began negotiating the destination for our next trip – the boys wanted to go skiing, I wanted temples covered in snow – a term began to emerge from the headlines of newspapers with which, unlike most people, I was well acquainted: coronavirus.

10

Coronavirus

In the spring of 2003, I'd been teaching English writing at the Beijing Broadcasting Institute, a university located in what was then the hinterlands of the Chinese capital. In March, foreign newspapers had begun reporting on an atypical pneumonia, a large number of cases of which were being reported in south China. The disease was called SARS, an abbreviation for severe acute respiratory syndrome. But there had been scant mention of it in the local newspapers. As late as 3 April, then Chinese health minister, Zhang Wenkang, gave a televised press conference assuring everyone that Beijing had only a small handful of SARS cases. But it was soon clear that a cover-up to hide the true extent of the deadly virus had been underway for months.

I ended up weathering SARS quarantine in the trenches of the university, and it became the first big story I reported on for the Indian media from abroad. Consequently, when I wrote *Smoke and Mirrors*, my debut book about my years in

China, I titled the third chapter, 'Coronavirus,' the class of viruses that SARS belonged to.

Fast-forwarding nearly two decades to January 2020, I found myself reaching for a copy of that book, to refresh my memory as news of a novel coronavirus in China wafted into the headlines. I wrote an opinion piece for *The Hindu* newspaper in late January comparing the Chinese government's response to the new virus favourably to their response of 2003, despite the fact that China seemed to be getting more international flak this time round. When my piece was published, COVID-19, as the novel coronavirus went on to be named, had infected just over 63,000 people, of which 1,300 had died, almost all in China.

February got underway and I remained sanguine. A few friends brought up COVID at dinner parties; worry lines flitting across their foreheads. I had lived, indeed flourished, through SARS. And I was an Indian. Viruses did not terrify me. I had grown up with an intimate experience of them and their bacterial cousins. They had sickened me in myriad ways, but so what? To be Indian meant to be assaulted on a daily basis by malaria, dengue fever, chikunguniya, amoebiasis, typhoid, jaundice, tuberculosis. But none of these risks defined us. And so I tended towards dismissing the terror of infection as a first-world problem.

During the SARS epidemic, when panicked expats had fled China, I'd been somewhat scornful of their lily-livers. When my Chinese students had become aware of the government cover-up, many of them too had 'overreacted', in my smug opinion, breaking college quarantine to hunker down in their hometowns. As events played out, I'd felt vindicated. By the summer of 2003, the SARS coronavirus had gone away, leaving only the slightest of traces on global memory.

And so, as I sat in the drawing rooms of my Japanese friends in the first flush of COVID-awareness, I was patronizing in my assessment of the worries of others, fancying myself experienced in the ways of viruses, including those of a corona disposition. How foolish we can be; how dangerously close to hubris without knowing it.

Through February, Japan's chief exposure to the virus appeared to be seaborne. At the beginning of the month, the *Diamond Princess*, a cruise ship with 3,700 passengers and crew onboard, docked in Yokohama in a state of alarm after it came to light that a passenger, who had disembarked a few days earlier in Hong Kong, had tested positive for the novel infection. A two-week long series of missteps and botched communication ensued.[188]

To begin with, it took the Japanese authorities more than seventy-two hours to impose a lockdown on the passengers after they were first notified of the initial case connected to the ship, with the result that for a day after the quarantine began, hundreds of passengers continued gathering for cruise activities and eating together. Moreover, throughout the two weeks, the 1000-plus crew members were confined in tight quarters below deck. Eighty-five of them were eventually found to have been infected. Sick crew members slept in cabins with roommates who remained active servicing the ship, undercutting the quarantine. Staff often wore the same pair of gloves to deliver food to dozens of cabins at a time and had face-to-face contact with passengers while dropping and picking up food and linen.

Ultimately, eight people died and more than 700 were infected in the *Diamond Princess* COVID-19 outbreak, including some government officials who boarded the ship to supervise the quarantine. It transpired that bureaucrats with little experience in managing infectious diseases were included amongst those tasked with testing and curtailing the virus. According to some reports, there were instances of officials failing to wear full protective gear. Most of the roughly ninety health ministry employees who visited the ship during the quarantine initially returned to their normal work duties immediately after.

Despite boasting one of the world's largest economies and cutting-edge technological know-how, Japan's authorities were also unable to provide sufficient medical resources for testing. Many quarantined passengers complained of problems in getting medical attention even after showing symptoms. While in China, a purpose-built hospital for virus patients had been constructed in a week's time, Japan was unable to find any alternative facility to house the cruise ship passengers, despite the knowledge that the infection was spreading onboard. Consequently, potentially exposed passengers were left on the ship during the testing process rather than taken ashore and isolated, despite contrary guidelines.

As the quarantine continued, Japan's usual orderliness was supplanted by chaos aboard what was dubbed the 'floating petri dish'. Some countries, like the United States, took citizens off the cruise liner and repatriated them before the two-week quarantine period in Japan was up, as long as they underwent another, ostensibly 'properly-supervised' quarantine period after their return. But in Japan, close to 1,000 passengers who tested negative walked free on 19 February, even though experts were warning that some of them could have been exposed and would develop symptoms only later. The Japanese health minister eventually revealed that twenty-three passengers had been released from the ship without taking a valid recent test and had travelled by public transport after disembarking.

The *Diamond Princess* was the first big outbreak of COVID-19 outside of the Chinese epicenter. For the audience of the news story, following its narrative arc was akin to watching a reality TV show, allowing for a range of emotions from schadenfreude to horror, to a there-but-for-the-grace-of-God-go-I sense of relief. But, in fact, the luxury ship was a portent of the battle that would soon be waged around the world. It was but a trailer for the delayed responses, ill-conceived plans, bungled implementation and misinformation that characterized the handling of the COVID-19 pandemic across the globe.

By March, the coronavirus was increasingly less novel as it made homes in the countries of Europe and further west and then back east, binding the world as one in its infectious embrace. Nowhere was immune to the tumult. However, the uniform outcome – a botched public health response – did hide some divergences in the causes.

In many Western countries, the greatest failure was arrogance born of a sense of invulnerability, a misguided notion that the disease was 'other', of faraway places where people ate the unreliable. At the offices of the European Union Delegation in Tokyo, where my husband worked, employees were told to disregard local customs like wearing masks, because these were purportedly a foolish placebo, without medical effect. Japan might have had the last laugh at such an attitude were the matter at stake not so deadly.

Moreover, as the *Diamond Princess* saga demonstrated, its fortuitous culture of mask-wearing aside, Japan had its own shortcomings. The mishandling of the ship's quarantine was emblematic of Tokyo's inability to deal flexibly with a hectic, changing environment, in part because of an overreliance on algorithm-following bureaucracy and the accompanying tendency to be less than transparent in a crisis. The country might have functioned like a finely tuned piece of machinery when things were going according to plan. But an unexpected googly, in this case the infected ship, saw Japan's usual efficiency devolve into a tragedy of errors.

By the end of February, schools in Japan were closed as a precaution, even as the country remained open to the Chinese tourists (with the exception of those from Hubei and Zhejiang provinces) that the service and retail economy were so reliant on. Through March, COVID-19 morphed from a localized outbreak in Wuhan into a global pandemic. But in Japan, Shinzo Abe remained ostrich-like in his denial of the virus's seriousness, particularly in his insistence that the Tokyo summer Olympic Games remained on schedule.[189]

It's difficult not to feel some sympathy for the government. The Games had cost the organizers more than 25 billion USD. For Mr Abe, they were to have been his swan song, securing his personal legacy and demonstrating to the world his success in revitalizing the country after the devastation of the 2011 Tohoku earthquake.

But his Olympics-propelled refusal to accept the gravity of COVID-19 left many dangerously complacent about the spread of the disease in Japan. Springtime meant that people were out and about in droves, shaking off the winter as they inhaled the newly blossoming flowers and prepared for the annual sakura-viewing festivities. Even Akie Abe, the first lady, was photographed attending a blossom party in contravention of the government's own, admittedly pallid, social distancing advice.[190]

One casual victim of Abe's insouciance was Jaipur-based businessman Kamal Vijayvargiya. An exporter of tea and herbal products, he flew to Tokyo on 18 March, expecting to stay in town for around four days meeting with prospective buyers. Vijayvargiya had been lulled by Tokyo's assurance that the Olympic Games would go ahead as planned. 'I took it as a green signal to travel,' he told me later. In the event, the day after his arrival in Japan, India closed its borders, leaving him stranded in the Japanese capital for months at the mercy of an elderly client who offered him a sofa to sleep on.

Many analysts remarked upon the 'coincidence' between Mr Abe finally announcing the postponement of the Olympics on 24 March and the sudden spike in officially acknowledged COVID figures in the Japanese capital immediately afterwards. The very day after the cancellation, Tokyo's mayor asked residents to stay at home during the weekends, a glaringly belated directive, given that a large number of other countries had already instituted lockdowns. Mr Abe eventually declared an emergency on 7 April.

As a result, malls and centres of entertainment were asked to close, corporations were encouraged to have employees work from home and people requested to self-isolate. Unlike in other countries, all of these measures were suggestions rather than orders. I realized that an emergency in the Land of the Rising Sun was a different cup of matcha to its draconian counterparts elsewhere. The difference lay in the fact that the Japanese authorities lacked legal means of coercion, like fines, to give penal-heft to their COVID-fighting restrictions.

Historical memories of civil rights abuses during the Second World War had imbued the country's US-drafted post-War Constitution, which enshrined civil liberties and denuded the power of the state. Constitutionally therefore, while political leaders could request people and businesses to comply with social distancing guidelines, enforcement relied on peer pressure and a culture of conformism.

Amongst the deadliest of the options available to the government was the naming and shaming of businesses that refused to submit. In any 'normal' country this would have rendered the authorities almost laughably impotent, but in Japan a voluntary lockdown was not an oxymoron as much as a superpower. A public health crisis played to Japanese society's strengths where hygiene, social reticence, mask-wearing and civic discipline were long-established norms.

The face mask went on to become the most visible symbol of the global response to COVID-19. But in Japan it was a trend that long preceded the virus and had a history that traversed a century's worth of past pandemics, natural disasters, air pollution, new kinds of flora, allergies and technology. A massive outbreak of influenza in the early years of the twentieth century first inaugurated the custom of covering the face with scarves. Then the Great Kanto Earthquake of 1923 triggered a massive fire that filled the sky of the capital with smoke and ash for weeks. Face masks became a standard sight on the streets of Tokyo and neighbouring Yokohama.

In the 1950s, Japan's rapid post-War industrialization caused rampant air pollution and a concomitant spread of the pollen-rich Japanese cedar tree, which flourished due to rising ambient levels of carbon dioxide. Large parts of the population developed allergic reactions to the pollen emitted by these trees. In 2003, the SARS scare once again caused a spike in mask-wearing, helped by a technological innovation that popularized a new type of non-woven material for masks.

The antecedents of face mask-wearing were multiple, but their unified result was that Japan emerged as one of the safest places from which to weather COVID-19's assault. Even at the height of that first state of emergency, Tokyo rarely had more than a couple of hundred cases a day, against the tens of thousands in many other parts of the world.

We weren't wholly confined to our apartments and were able to take walks and go out shopping at will. At my neighbourhood grocery store, only a limited number of people were allowed in at a time and the queues could be long. But everyone endured, if not with humour, then with civility and the requisite physical distance. Toilet paper was the worst casualty of hoarding (less onerous to an Indian than most others), as was butter. The lockdown had made bakers of the world, and Japan was no exception. The smell of rising bread infused social media feeds. I, who had thus far managed life as an oven-virgin, was now regularly distributing homemade chocolate brownies to the neighbours. I also did jigsaw puzzles and wrote coronavirus-spoof lyrics set to popular songs like the 'Sounds of Silence'. I felt cushioned by the patience and caution that was so emblematic of the country I lived in. Japan made finding the silver linings to the COVID cloud easy.

Some peculiarities suddenly became more intelligible. For instance, I had long pondered why many of the Japanese friends we invited to our home spent an inordinate amount of time in the toilet, right after arrival. I could hear much gurgling, spitting and the running of water taps as I waited for them to emerge. They were, in fact, washing hands to the length of two happy birthdays and also gargling, a habit every mother in Japan ingrained in her child: wash your hands thoroughly and gargle. Post-COVID, these habits no longer felt like 'idiosyncrasies' as much as wisdom.

Unfortunately, Japanese leaders seem to have been immune to this wisdom. As April got underway and the emergency entered into force, an anxious citizenry awaited concrete details of the government's plan to tackle the crisis. Their bated breath was rewarded with the announcement that two cloth face masks would be posted to every household in the country. The 'Abenomask', a pun on the prime minister's signature Abenomics economic policy, was widely pilloried as an ineffectual waste of taxpayers' money. Once the masks began to be delivered, there were further complaints of the products being stained, damaged or contaminated with human hair and dust. A large number had to be recalled.[191]

When ours arrived in the mail, my boys tried them on but found them so thick as to be impossible to breathe through. We tried to donate our unused ones, but no one would have them. Eventually they were used to mop up an orange-juice spill in the kitchen.

Other than dispatching his unloved Abenomasks, Mr Abe's pandemic redressal arsenal included an address to the nation in the form of a public relations video meant to persuade the country about the small pleasures of staying at home. It featured the PM cuddling his dog in his spacious apartment, winding down with a large, presumably warm, beverage and watching TV.[192]

But the majority of Japanese lived in cramped accommodation, and like others around the world, were struggling to balance childcare with making a living, all amid an uncertain economic environment. At a time when the governor of Osaka city was pleading for raincoat donations because doctors had resorted to wearing trash bags as protective gear, Mr Abe's video struck some as a tad tone deaf. 'You look so elegant at a time when many people feel they are being strangled slowly (with the virus). Why don't you go and see hospitals that have been the battleground?' asked one tweet.

And Mr Abe had plenty of company amongst the country's leadership in signalling just how cosseted they were from the consequences of the policies they were in charge of formulating. Soon it was the turn of Ichiro Matsui, the mayor of Osaka, to be out of touch. Speaking to reporters, he suggested that women stay at home and send men in their stead to do the grocery shopping during the pandemic. So far so emancipated, but then he elaborated on his reasoning. Men were more focused and less likely to dawdle in shops, Mr Matsui explained. Women, 'take a long time as they browse around and hesitate about this and that', he continued, seemingly oblivious to just how deep a hole he was digging himself into, while 'men can snap up things they are told (to buy) and go, so I think it's good that they go shopping, avoiding human contact'.[193]

As matters played out, Japan's tryst with COVID was less deadly than that of many of its first world counterparts. Even without a total lockdown, the country avoided an explosion of cases and maintained a relatively low mortality rate. At the end of April, the number of deaths per million people in Japan stood at 2.85, against 164.5 in the United States and 490 in Spain. Much ink has been used opining on the reasons for this, but in fact we just don't know. It probably resulted from a combination of cultural norms, luck and some other factor we will discover in the future.

But while Japan fared relatively well when it came to the COVID mortality rate, the pandemic shone a less-than-agreeable light on the 'cutting-edge' image of Japan, as the country was revealed to be startlingly anachronistic.

I had become aware of how analogue Japan was within the first few weeks of having moved to Tokyo. My credit card often proved useless because of the strictly cash-only nature of many transactions. Making online payments had involved physical trips to the bank every time a new payee had to be added. I was asked, on more than one occasion, to fax a request for an interview I was chasing down. When in 2018, Yoshitaka Sakurada, the deputy head of the government's cyber security panel made headlines by admitting to never having used a computer in his professional life, it confirmed just how much of a fish-out-of-digital-water Japan could seem in the twenty-first century.[194]

In normal times, it was just possible to rose-wash the requirement to fax in information requests to government offices as endearingly quaint. But in the world of COVID-19, the deleterious impact of Japan's failure to embrace digital transformation was amplified.

In the days following the declaration of the state of emergency, people were told to stay at home and work remotely, but most companies were ill equipped to facilitate telework. In a March survey conducted by IT research group ITR, 45 per cent of corporations said that they had no systems in place to allow staff to work from home.[195] Only

28 per cent said they were ready to make the switch. Some employees did not have laptops at home (even though a third of Japanese households had fax machines). Others found it difficult to do without the constant supervision and approval of superiors, given the strict hierarchies of the workplace.

But it was the *hanko*, or personalized carved seal, that emerged as the greatest obstacle to social distancing.[196] Most official documents in Japan still required the physical stamp of a company hanko, which was expected to remain in the office. So the most common reason for people not following work-from-home edicts was the need to go in to stamp documentation. The government's emergency declaration-target was to reduce office attendance by 70 per cent. But on 8 April, the day after the emergency was announced, Yahoo data showed only a 26 per cent drop in users' movements.

Telemedicine was another area where the pandemic exposed big problems. For years the government had failed to approve measures like remote medical exams for first-time patients, in part due to opposition from lobbies like the Japan Medical Association. COVID-19 finally prodded the authorities to lift some of these restrictions, but an array of hurdles remained. A large number of Japanese clinics didn't even accept credit card payments, the most basic building block of telemedicine, and about 65 per cent of patient health records were still kept in hard copy.[197]

For me personally, probably because I was a mother of school-going children, the most shocking digital lacunae were in education. My children attended a private, international school, and the switch to online learning had been largely seamless. The boys spent their school days' at home, splitting their time between in-person, zoom-enabled classes and self-study assignments posted to an online classroom daily, which were promptly marked and returned with feedback from teachers.

It wasn't ideal. There were times when I caught my offspring playing video games instead of solving fractions, and they raced through some of their lessons with careless speed. But the resultant extra time proved rich in other ways. My older son made soufflés. The younger one, Nico, developed a fascination with black holes. By the time school started up again in June, Nico no longer wanted to be a YouTuber, but an astrophysicist. It was enough to make one feel less-than-visceral hatred towards the school closure.

This was patently not the case for parents with children in Japanese schools. My friend Koyama-san, whose son went to the school I'd visited to observe cleaning activities, was distraught. She sent me long messages every other day describing the almost medieval manner in which the school was responding to the crisis. Their chosen method was to supply families with hard copies of maths and Japanese language work sheets by *post*. Parents were also provided an answer-key and expected to correct the work themselves, after which they were instructed to send the worksheets back to the school – by *post*. Teachers occasionally telephoned parents to check in on how they were coping, but had no direct contact with the children themselves. It was almost a blessing that they didn't require work to be written using quills and ink.

Throughout the closure, Koyama-san's son's school remained unable to figure out how to set up an online learning system that would allow teachers to post videos or enable any two-way communication between students and teachers. 'It's really not that hard, but I think the problem is that they [the school administrators] only follow the commands of the government's education board and cannot take any initiative themselves,' fumed my friend in one message.

Furuya-san, another friend whose children attended the alma mater of the current emperor of Japan, told me that it took this most hallowed of schools six weeks to do any online activity at all. When they finally went digital, it was to organize a single social chat for the class, during which mothers (not fathers) were expected to remain on standby, in the same room.

By early June, the emergency measures in Tokyo were gradually eased and our school began to allow children in for a few hours of in-person classes daily. I also cautiously resumed meeting with select friends in well-ventilated spaces. The virulence of COVID had left me chastened, and I was much less dismissive about the pandemic's seriousness than I'd been a few months earlier. Nevertheless, I tended to zone out when the conversation focused on the minutiae of the elaborate rituals some of my friends had developed around disinfecting individual vegetables and the grocery bags they came in. I simply wasn't capable of obsessing about the virus twenty-four hours a day. I had lived in countries where deadly air- and water-borne diseases were rampant;

where simply breathing the air was dangerous, given the levels of pollution. In Tokyo, a city with 30 million residents in its catchment area, 200 cases of COVID a day had me less worried than I'd been about diarrhoea deaths in young children in India, for years.[198] The difference, of course, was that money and privilege were no bulwark against COVID, or at least were less effective as a bulwark than they were against diarrhoea. An awareness of the privilege of COVID-preoccupation dampened my fear of it.

Besides, I had other things on my mind too. Four years – the term of Julio's posting in Tokyo – had somehow snuck up on us, and we had to say our adieus to Japan. Come August, we were moving to Spain. The pandemic denied me the protracted farewells that had helped the digesting of departures in the past. My bucket list for travel remained incomplete. There were no tears-and-sake-soaked gatherings of friends from the different branches of our Japan journey. There were no Olympic Games, the attending of which was to have bookended our stay in Tokyo.

I usually spent the last month in a country knitting together the diverse experiences I'd had there into a tapestry that gave cohesive shape to my memories. But this proved difficult, a consequence of the byzantine logistics of moving in a pandemic. There were shifting quarantine regulations, a drought of flights and uncertain shipping dates. Julio and I spent days figuring out how to transport the cats out of Tokyo. COVID leant an air of the absurd to our preparations, since the irreducible uncertainty it had unleashed made a mockery of the very idea of preparation.

And so, in the middle of writing up a list of our belongings for insurance purposes, I decided to work on another kind of list. People often asked me what I liked most about Japan. It was the kind of question that I inevitably got asked about every country I'd lived in – as trite and confounding as being asked what one's favourite colour was. I rarely bothered to formulate an honest answer, but this time I grabbed a pencil and began scribbling.

This stream of consciousness is what I came up with:

'Sakura, gyoza, aural peace, my dentist (who knew root canals could be such a pleasure?), an awareness of others, focus, miso. Toilets.

That toilets in Japan were objets d'art has already been established. But their true awesomeness lay not in their gadgetry so much as in their cleanliness and easy availability. As a woman on the move, a decent toilet was manna. We had smaller bladders than men, we had monthly periods, and those of us who had given birth had urinary tracts that were as capricious in the timing of their needs as the annual blooming of the cherry blossoms. The simple fact of being able to use a toilet with confidence in public spaces – parks, metro stations, highway pit stops – enhanced the quality of life enough to make toilets my number one favourite thing about Japan.

As our departure neared, I spent more time reading about Spain and dusting off my memories of travelling there; it was raucous, as un-Japanese an adjective as could be. I began learning Spanish online in preparation. My teacher told me Spaniards used *por favour*, 'please' sparingly. Using it too much could sound sarcastic. I thought about how my life was one long episode in culture shock.

I took long walks around our neighbourhood, adrift on the emotions sparked by the sights that had been the wallpaper to my Tokyo life. I said goodbye to the magnolia trees that lined our street. I surreptitiously photographed the construction workers across from our apartment block on their smoke break, their heads wrapped in bandanas, their bell-shaped *tabi* pants splattered with paint. I mooched about the local 7-Eleven, which I had always favoured over its rival Family Mart. I passed by people pushing dogs in prams and kindergarten teachers taking their impossibly cute wards on walks to the neighbourhood park. Inside the park, I looked at the signs that read, 'Please cherish all living beings.' I used the park toilet. Later, I cycled past the temple where I had spent so many mornings in Zazen meditation. It was blanketed by the susurration of cicadas in their death throes.

A few days before our departure I met with two of my closest Japanese friends, who braved their COVID-worries to meet me for lunch. These were women with whom I had been learning *taiko*, Japanese drumming, for the past three years. Our friendship had spilled out of the taiko dojo into long walks in the autumn and spring to take in flowers and leaves.

I shared my fears about my impending relocation. The move to Spain was different to the other moves I had made, for it would put me on unequal terrain to my husband for the first time. Instead of being joined in our wide-eyed explorations of a new country together, I would be the outsider in my husband's territory. What would that shift in power relations mean for our marriage, I wondered aloud? And how would I manage living within walking distance from my mother-in-law?

My friends appeared gently startled by my musings – understandable, given that they were more personal in nature than was the norm in our friendship. The initial reaction from them was one of sympathetic silence, which seemed enough, because Japan had taught me that friendship lay in listening as much as in words. But then one of them spoke. It had been her experience, she said softly, that it was best to expect very little, for then disappointment was less likely and contentment more plausible. There was something so old fashioned about this sentiment, so against the grain of the contemporary culture of excess and focus on ever more personal 'happiness'. It had a quality of emotion that I associated more generally with Japan: of the power of the moderate, of the complexity of the simple and the capaciousness of the just enough.

When I went home that afternoon I looked up my copy of Rabindranath Tagore's 'Spirit of Japan' speech in Tokyo, which he'd given to students at Keio University during his 1916 visit.[199] He began by saying: 'My stay here has been so short that one may think I have not earned my right to speak to you about anything concerning your country. I feel sure that I shall be told that I am idealizing certain aspects, while leaving others unnoticed.'

How true this was of me and everyone else, who had washed up somewhere and dared to write about it a few years later. To write a nation, to explain it, was always foolhardy. A more honest claim was one that admitted to bewilderment and delight, intuition and hunches, to vignettes and snatches of coherence, but resisted assertions of authority. This book was ultimately probably as much about me as observer, my circumstances and predilections, as it was about Japan. It was best to read it as a haiku – a subjective suggestion of a mood, a tantalizing glimpse, a truth yes, but only one of many.

I knew I couldn't bid farewell to Japan without one last meeting, and so it was that the doorbell rang one afternoon to reveal Michiko-san, my erstwhile Japanese teacher and cat dental hygiene enthusiast. When I'd extended the invite for tea, she had accepted with alacrity. For the occasion she had worn a kimono, signalling the importance she gave the meeting. I found myself unconsciously adopting ceremonial gestures while pouring her a cup of green tea. It didn't feel ridiculous, but apt. 'How is your Japanese?' she asked politely at one point. I smiled and muttered an indecipherable response, which she accepted graciously without pressing me further. We passed the hour talking in large part about Caramel and Tofu-chan and their moods and appetites. When she left, even my older son, an unsentimental, irascible pre-teen, looked a tad forlorn. With this goodbye our departure felt sealed and final.

On our last night in Japan, I found it hard to fall asleep. The apartment was bereft of furniture, its life drained and packed into boxes. I had a sole book on the floor next to my mattress and I turned to it to help me fall asleep. It was a slim volume of haiku, and I will leave you with a couple, for it's always best to let the poets have the last say.

Except for a woodpecker
tapping at a post,
the house is silent.
–Matsuo Basho

I got drunk
then wept in my sleep
dreaming of wild cherry blossoms.
– Masaoka Shiki

Notes

1. 'India has the lowest mobile data cost in the world: report', *telecomlead.com*, https://www.telecomlead.com/latest-news/india-offers-cheapest-mobile-data-plan-in-the-world-report-89450

2. Alec Ash, 'Beggars are cashless and loos recognise users in China's hi-tech boom', *The Times*, 03 June 2018, https://www.thetimes.co.uk/article/beggars-are-cashless-and-loos-recognise-users-in-chinas-hi-tech-boom-99m2jq87b

3. According to JNTO (Japan National Tourism Organization), 8.38 million Chinese, and about 134,000 Indians, visited Japan in 2018.

4. Most classical writings in Japan about Mt Fuji refer to it as '*sangoku ichi yama*' or 'the most splendid mountain in the three worlds': India, China and Japan. The import of this phrase is equivalent to calling Mt Fuji the 'best' mountain in the world. See, for example: 'A Glimpse of Mt. Fuji in Legend and Cult' by Royall Tyler, 'A Glimpse of Mt. Fuji

259

in Legend and Cult', The Journal of the Association of Teachers of Japanese 16 (1981): 140

5. C. Diep, 'Convenience store numbers in Japan 2010-2019', *statista.com*, https://www.statista.com/statistics/810901/japan-convenience-store-numbers/

6. Pamela Engel, 'How Japan's Murder Rate Got To Be So Incredibly Low', *Business Insider India*, 12 April 2014, https://www.businessinsider.in/How-Japans-Murder-Rate-Got-To-Be-So-Incredibly-Low/articleshow/33628667.cms

7. 'Crime at New Low in Japan' 12 January 2021 https://www.nippon.com/en/japan-data/h00898/
For contrast, in Mexico, a country with an equivalent population, 33,341 murders were reported in 2018. See: Eli Meixler, 'Cartel-Ravaged Mexico Sets a New Record for Murders', *Time*, 22 January 2019, https://time.com/5509216/mexico-murder-rate-sets-record-2018/
In the Philippines, there were 6,866 murders in 2018. See: Emmanuel Tupas, 'PNP: Total crime volume down in 2018', *Philstar.com*, 26 February 2019, https://www.philstar.com/nation/2019/02/26/1896714/pnp-total-crime-volume-down-2018

8. 'Apology after Japanese train departs 20 seconds early', *BBC*, https://www.bbc.com/news/world-asia-42009839

9. Selena Hoy, 'Why Japanese Kids Can Walk to School Alone', *The Atlantic*, 3 October 2015, https://www.theatlantic.com/technology/archive/2015/10/why-japanese-kids-can-walk-to-school-alone/408475/

10. Mizuho Aoki, 'Lost: Struggling to cope with millions of unclaimed items in Tokyo', *The Japan Times*, 27 May 2017,

https://www.japantimes.co.jp/life/2017/05/27/lifestyle/
lost-struggling-cope-millions-unclaimed-items-tokyo/

11. Ibid.

12. 'Why Japan's Lost and Found System Works So Well',
Bloomberg, 2 October 2020, https://www.bloomberg.com/
news/articles/2020-02-10/why-japan-s-lost-and-found-
system-works-so-well

13. Pallavi Aiyar, *Punjabi Parmesan* (India: Penguin India,
2014)

14. '"KOBAN," the Japanese policing system spreading
across the globe', *Keishicho*: Tokyo Metropolitan Police
Department, https://www.keishicho.metro.tokyo.jp/
multilingual/english/about_us/activity/koban.html

15. Hirotaka Fujibayashi, 'Rethinking Japan's refugee and
asylum policy', *East Asia Forum*, 19 January 2021, https://
www.eastasiaforum.org/2021/01/19/rethinking-japans-
refugee-and-asylum-policy/

16. Phillip Connor, 'India is a top source and destination for
world's migrants', *Pew Research Center*, 3 March 2017,
https://www.pewresearch.org/fact-tank/2017/03/03/india-
is-a-top-source-and-destination-for-worlds-migrants/

17. Pallavi Aiyar, 'Opening Up the border to immigrants',
The Hindu, 10 November 2018, https://www.thehindu.
com/news/international/opening-up-the-borders-to-
immigrants/article25464006.ece

18. 'Survey Findings Suggest Japan Has More than 1 Million
"Hikikomori"', *nippon.com*, https://www.nippon.com/en/
japan-data/h00463/survey-findings-suggest-japan-has-
more-than-1-million-hikikomori.html

19. Pallavi Aiyar, 'Working overtime to death in Japan', *The Hindu*, 19 February 2017, https://www.thehindu.com/news/international/Working-overtime-to-death-in-Japan/article17327183.ece

20. There is an entire genre of writing that tries to explain Japanese uniqueness, called Nihonjinron. It includes theories that claim the Japanese race is different from others because of the nation's sui generis climate, linguistic characteristics and geographical isolation.

21. 'Shinjuku Station is Enormous! Daily Passengers Equivalent to Population of Yokohama', *nippon.com*, https://www.nippon.com/en/features/h00273/shinjuku-station-is-enormous!-daily-passengers-equivalent-to-population-of-yokohama.html

22. D.T. Suzuki, *Zen and Japanese Culture* (Tuttle Publishing, 1988), p. 12

23. Ibid., p. 1

24. Pallavi Aiyar, 'Believers at the Wall', *Outlook*, 14 April 2021, https://www.outlookindia.com/magazine/story/believers-at-the-wall/239956

25. D.T. Suzuki, *Zen and Japanese Culture* (Tuttle Publishing, 1988), p. 4

26. Pallavi Aiyar, *Smoke and Mirrors*, (India: Harper Collins India, 2008)

27. Georges Duthuit, *Chinese Mysticism and Modern Painting* (Paris: Chroniques du jour, 1936)

28. Roger J Davies, *Japanese Culture: The Religious and Philosophical Foundations* (Tuttle Publishing, 2016), p. 97

29. The folding fan is popularly thought to have originated in Japan around AD 670. In the Chinese official historical record of the Song Dynasty (960–1279) it is written that *the Japanese monk Chonen gifted folding fans to the emperor of China in 988*, which makes the Japanese folding fan a rare original invention of Japan. 'Origin of the folding fan', *SOAS University of London*, https://www.soas.ac.uk/gallery/traditionsrevised/origin-of-the-folding-fan.html

30. When tea ceremony first came to Japan in the ninth century AD, it was very China-influenced. Held in the palatial homes of *daimyo* (feudal lords) it featured expensive utensils of jade, gold and celadon imported from China.

31. D.T. Suzuki, *Zen and Japanese Culture* (Tuttle Publishing, 1988), p. 23.

32. The word Zen comes from the Chinese *Ch'an*, which in turn derives from the Sanskrit *dhyana*. The founder of the Ch'an school was an Indian monk, Bodhidharma, who according to legend spent nine years gazing at the wall of a cave near the famous Shaolin temple in central China. In one version of the story, he fell asleep seven years into this wall-gazing marathon. Upon waking, he became so enraged with himself that he cut off his eyelids to prevent any future napping. As his leaf-like eyelids hit the floor they sprouted miraculously into tea plants. Instinctively, Bodhidharma reached over and plucked a few leaves from the bushes to chew on and suddenly found himself refreshed. With a clear and focused mind, he was able to resume his meditation, and thereafter tea was used as a stimulant to help monks stay alert.

Matt Stefon, 'Bodhidharma', *Britannica*, https://www. britannica.com/biography/Bodhidharma

33. Alex Kerr, *Another Kyoto*, (Seka Bunkai Publishing, 2016), pp. 98-99.

34. Roger Davies, *Japanese Culture: The Religious and Philosophical Foundations*, (Tuttle, Publishing, 2016)

35. Suzuki, *Zen and Japanese Culture*, pp. 26-27.

36. Alex Kerr, *Another Kyoto* (Sekai bunka Publishing, 2016) p. 93.

37. Junichiro Tanazaki, *In praise of Shadows*, trans. Thomas J Harper and Edward G Seidensticker (Tuttle Publishing, 1977)

38. Ibid., p. 25.

39. It was only in 2020 that our Tokyo supermarket finally began charging for plastic bags.

40. Zoë Schlanger, 'Japan's single-use plastic problem on display at the G20 Summit', *Quartz*, 28 June 2019, https://qz.com/1655248/japans-single-use-plastic-problem-on-display-at-the-g20-summit

41. 'Messy 'manshons' less visible than junk houses, but just as filthy', *JapanToday*, 7 May 2016, https://japantoday.com/category/features/kuchikomi/messy-manshons-less-visible-than-junk-houses-but-just-as-filthy.

Amy Chavez, 'Japan has a reputation for cleanliness – just don't look in our closets', *Japan Times*, 25 November 2018, www.japantimes.co.jp/community/2018/11/25/our-lives/japan-reputation-cleanliness-just-dont-look-closets/#.XWssL1CLkxc

42. Pallavi Aiyar, 'A Touch of Recycling, Japanese Style', *The Hindu,* 18 March 2017, https://www.thehindu.com/ news/international/a-touch-of-recycling-japanese-style/ article17528941.ece

43. Pallavi Aiyar, 'The Plight of Japan's Social Recluses', *The Hindu,* 25 August 2019, https://www.thehindu.com/ news/international/the-plight-of-japans-social-recluses/ article29244298.ece

44. John Elflein, 'Rate of suicide Canada by age group 2019', *statista.com,* https://www.statista.com/statistics/437701/ rate-of-suicide-canada-by-age-group/;

    'Suicides in the UK: 2018 registrations', *Office for National Statistics Website,* https://www.ons.gov.uk/ peoplepopulationandcommunity/birthsdeathsand marriages/deaths/bulletins/suicidesintheunitedking dom/2018registrations

45. Pallavi Aiyar, 'A Japanese ceramic repair technique teaches us to embrace our scars', *Nikkei Asian Review,* 1 December 2016, https://asia.nikkei.com/NAR/Articles/A-Japanese- ceramic-repair-technique-teaches-us-to-embrace-our-scars

46. Alex Kerr, *Lost Japan: Last Glimpse of Beautiful Japan,* (Penguin Books, 2015), pp. 88-90.

47. Yoshida Kenkō, *Essays in Idleness: the Tsurezuregusa of Kenko,* trans. Donald Keene (Tuttle Publishing, 2018)

48. Prior to the Second World War, Kyoto Imperial University became the hub for a group academics known as the 'Kyoto School'. The story goes that two amongst this cohort, the philosopher Kitaro Nishida and the economist Hajime Kawakami, often walked the path along the creek

by the Silver Pavilion. While walking they came up with some of their most influential ideas. Hence, the name: The Philosopher's Path.

49. Pico Iyer, *Autumn Light: Season of Fire and Farewells* (Vintage Books, 2020).

50. Lafcadio Hearn, 'In a Japanese Garden', *The Atlantic Magazine* (1892) https://www.theatlantic.com/magazine/archive/1892/07/in-a-japanese-garden/376180

51. Robert H. Sharf, 'The Zen of Japanese Nationalism', *History of Religions* 33 (1993), pp. 1–43.

52. Florian Coulmas, 'Japan's endless search for identity', *The Japan Times*, 24 June 2001, https://www.japantimes.co.jp/culture/2001/06/24/books/book-reviews/japans-endless-search-for-identity/#.XXmcPiWLkxc

53. Alexander MacNeil, 'From Nature to Nation: Shizen and The Japanese National Imaginary', *Contingent Horizons* 3 (2017), https://contingenthorizons.wordpress.com/2017/02/25/from-nature-to-nation-shizen-and-the-japanese-national-imaginary/

54. Benedict Anderson, *Imagined Communities: Reflections on the Origin and Spread of Nationalism* (Verso Books, 1983)

55. '72 Seasons', *Kurashikata.com*, http://www.kurashikata.com/72seasons/

56. Tadanobu Tsunada, *The Japanese Brain: Uniqueness and Universality*, (Taishukan Pub. Co., 1985).
    See also: Masaomi Ise, 'The Japanese Language Brain', August 2002, Japan on the Globe. http://www2s.biglobe.ne.jp/nippon/file/jog240e.html
    For a criticism of this theory, see Peter Dale, 'The Voice of Cicadas: Linguistic Uniqueness, Tsunoda Tananobu's

Theory of the Japanese Brain, and Some Classical Perspectives', *ELECTRONIC ANTIQUITY*, November 1993, vol. 1 No. 6.

57. Caitlin Sacasas, 'Japanese Numbers: Counting in Japanese from 1-100+', *fluentin3months.com*, https://www.fluentin3months.com/japanese-numbers/

58. Yutaka Okada, 'Japan's foreign population hitting a record high', *Mizuho Economic Outlook & Analysis*, https://www.mizuho-ir.co.jp/publication/mhri/research/pdf/eo/MEA180913.pdf

59. Justin McCurry, 'Japanese politician in baby row thrown out again – for sucking cough drop', *The Guardian*, 1 October 2018, https://www.theguardian.com/world/2018/oct/01/japanese-politician-thrown-out-of-meeting-for-sucking-cough-drop-yuka-ogata-breastfeeding-row

60. Tsukuru Ikeda, 'Tokyo's Nishikasai a second home for Indians in Japan', *The Statesman*, 20 May 2018, https://www.thestatesman.com/world/tokyos-nishikasai-second-home-indians-japan-1502638470.html

61. Tokyo metropolitan government statistics.

62. 'Foreign IT workers seen as solution to industry shortage', *The Japan Times*, 30 June 2017, https://www.japantimes.co.jp/news/2017/06/30/national/foreign-workers-seen-solution-industry-shortage/

63. Panos Mourdoukoutas, 'Japan Tries to Recruit IT Engineers from India, But it Won't', *Forbes*, 30 June 2017, https://www.forbes.com/sites/panosmourdoukoutas/2017/06/30/japan-tries-to-recruit-it-engineers-from-india-but-it-wont-work/

64. Pallavi Aiyar, 'Foreign-born candidate shows Tokyo, all politics are local', *Nikkei Asian Review*, 29 May 2019, https://asia.nikkei.com/Editor-s-Picks/Tea-Leaves/Foreign-born-candidate-shows-Tokyo-all-politics-are-local

65. Baye McNeil, 'The empty seat on a crowded Japanese train: 10 years on, the 'gaijin seat' still grates', *The Japan Times*, 17 October 2018, https://www.japantimes.co.jp/community/2018/10/17/our-lives/empty-seat-crowded-japanese-train-10-years-gaijin-seat-still-grates/

66. In his infamous speech, Ishihara in fact used the term '*sangokujin*', which in the aftermath of the Second World War, had become unmoored from its original reference to India, China and Japan as the three great Buddhist civilizations and transformed into a racial epithet for Koreans (from the north and south) and Taiwanese. 'Mr. Ishihara's insensitivity', *The Japan Times,* 15 April 2000, https://www.japantimes.co.jp/opinion/2000/04/15/editorials/mr-ishiharas-insensitivity/

67. Jonathan Watts, 'Governor sparks Tokyo race row'. *The Guardian*, 12 April 2000. https://www.theguardian.com/world/2000/apr/13/jonathanwatts. See also: Howard W. French, 'Disdainful of Foreigners, the Japanese Blame Them for Crime', *New York Times*, 30 September 1999.

68. Debito Arudou, 'Sapporo Consadole player and former England Team soccer striker Jay Bothroyd refused entry to Hokkaido Classic golf course for being "not Japanese"', *Debito.org,* 30 May 2018, http://www.debito.org/?p=15013; also: Paul Withers, 'Former England striker turned away from golf club in Japan 'because he is foreign', *Express*, 30 May 2018, https://www.express.co.uk/news/uk/967171/

england-football-player-jay-bothroyd-cardiff-japan-golf-course-racism-twitter

69. 'Michelin-star sushi house rejects foreign bookings', *news. com.au*, 6 May 2015, https://www.news.com.au/lifestyle/ food/restaurants-bars/michelinstar-sushi-house-rejects-foreign-bookings/news-story/218ef7c689794fb5d78a3754 9ef459ea

70. Afsha Khan, Tapasya Mitra Mazumder, "Only Japanese, no Indian people, ma'am", *Bangalore Mirror*, 24 June 2014, https://bangaloremirror.indiatimes.com/bangalore/cover-story/uno-in-hotel-bars-langford-cross-road-japanese-nationals-nic-u-iqbal-japanese-food-bruhat-bangalore-mahanagara-palike-/articleshow/37097278.cms

71. Tomohiri Osaki, 'Japan's first-ever hate speech probe finds rallies are fewer but still a problem', *The Japan Times*, 30 May 2016, https://www.japantimes.co.jp/news/2016/03/30/ national/japans-first-ever-hate-speech-probe-finds-rallies-are-fewer-but-still-a-problem/#.XYvxViWLkxc

72. 'Uyoku Dantai: Japan's Growing Far-Right Movement', *Vice.com*, https://www.vice.com/en_us/article/3b7b7b/ uyoku-dentai-japans-growing-far-right-movement

73. In 2001, the Japanese Emperor, Akihito, publicly acknowledged in a speech that he had Korean ancestors. This was covered widely in the Korean press, but almost entirely unreported by the Japanese media (with the exception of the *Asahi Shimbun*). Jonathan Watts, 'The Emperor's New Roots', *The Guardian*, 28 December 2001, https://www.theguardian.com/world/2001/dec/28/japan. worlddispatch

74. The exception was trade with China and the Dutch through the port of Nagasaki.

75. A.L. Sadler, *Shogun: The Life of Tokugawa Ieyasu* (Tuttle Publishing, 2009 first published, 1977).

76. Michael Auslin, *Negotiating with Imperialism: The Unequal Treaties and the Culture of Japanese Diplomacy* (Cambridge: Harvard University Press, 2006)

77. Emiko Jozuka, 'Japan's "vanishing" Ainu will finally be recognized as indigenous people', CNN, 22 April 2019 https://www.cnn.com/2019/04/20/asia/japan-ainu-indigenous-peoples-bill-intl/index.html

78. Philip Brasor, 'Japan's resident Koreans endure a climate of hate', *The Japan Times*, 7 May 2016, https://www.japantimes.co.jp/news/2016/05/07/national/media-national/japans-resident-koreans-endure-climate-hate/#.XZ_KniWLkxc

79. Mina Pollmann, 'Japan's Xenophobia Problem', *The Diplomat*, 24 July 2015, https://thediplomat.com/2015/07/japans-xenophobia-problem/.
See also: 'JCP urges Tokyo governor to send eulogy to memorial for Koreans massacred in 1923 earthquake', *Japan Press Weekly*, 30 August 2017, http://www.japan-press.co.jp/s/news/?id=10903

80. Philip Brasor, 'Social media aids rehashing of historical hate', *The Japan Times*, 13 September 2014, https://www.japantimes.co.jp/news/2014/09/13/national/media-national/social-media-aids-rehashing-historical-hate/

81. Tomohiro Osaki, 'Different disaster, same story: Osaka quake prompts online hate speech targeting foreigners',

The Japan Times, 19 June 2018, https://www.japantimes.
co.jp/news/2018/06/19/national/different-disaster-story-
osaka-quake-prompts-online-hate-speech-targeting-
foreigners/#.XZ_RGSWLkxc

82. Min Jin Lee, *Pachinko* (New York: Grand Central
Publishing, 2017)

83. 'Japan's hidden caste of untouchables', BBC, 23 Oct 2015.
Source: https://www.bbc.com/news/world-asia-34615972.
See also: Katelyn Coyle, 'A History of the Untouchables:
The Buraku and the Dalit,' *Agora* 15, no. 15 (2006), https://
digitalshowcase.lynchburg.edu/agora/vol15/iss2006/15

84. Leslie D. Alldritt, 'The *Burakumin*: The Complicity of
Japanese Buddhism in Oppression and an Opportunity for
Liberation', *Journal of Buddhist Ethics* 7 (2000), https://web.
archive.org/web/20051125094650/http://jbe.gold.ac.uk/7/
alldritt001.html

85. Tomohiro Osaki, 'New law to fight bias against
"burakumin" seen falling short', *The Japan Times*,
19 December, 2016, https://www.japantimes.co.jp/
news/2016/12/19/reference/new-toothless-law-fight-bias-
burakumin-seen-falling-short/#.XaPOmSWLkxc.
See also: Alex K.T. Martin, 'Embracing a buraku
heritage: Examining changing attitudes toward a social
minority', *The Japan Times*, 16 February 2019, https://
www.japantimes.co.jp/news/2019/02/16/national/social-
issues/embracing-buraku-heritage-examining-changing-
attitudes-toward-social-minority/#.XaPSsSWLkxc

86. See website of the Buraku Liberation League: http://www.
bll.gr.jp/en/index.html

87. David Kaplan and Alec Dubro, *Yakuza: The Explosive Account of Japan's Criminal Underworld* (Boston: Addison-Wesley Publishing Co., 1986)

88. Ruth Ozeki, *A Tale for the Time Being* (Edinburgh: Canongate Books Ltd, 2013)

89. Donna T Fujimoto, 'Kikoku Shijo, (Japanese Returnees): Trends and Awarenesses', International University of Japan, 1997, Working Papers, vol. 8. Source: https://www.iuj.ac.jp/language/pdf/research/LP-8-1.pdf

90. Osawa, C, *Tatta Hitotsu no Aoi Sora: Kaigai Kikokushijo wa Gendai no Sutego ka?* (Tokyo: Bungei Shunju Publishing, 1986)

91. Stephen Wade, 'Japan's rugby team shows off the changing face of the nation', *JapanToday*, 14 October 2019, https://japantoday.com/category/rugby-world-cup-2019/japan%27s-rugby-team-shows-off-changing-face-of-the-nation

92. 'Miss Japan won by half Indian Priyanka Yoshikawa', *BBC*, 8 September 2016, https://www.bbc.com/news/world-asia-37283518

93. Pallavi Aiyar, 'Indian fury at foreign racist attacks hides shameful truth', *Nikkei Asian Review*, 6 April 2017, https://asia.nikkei.com/Opinion/Indian-fury-at-foreign-racist-attacks-hides-shameful-truth2

94. Population Projections for Japan (2017): 2016 to 2065, National Institute of Population and Social Security Research. Source: https://fpcj.jp/wp/wp-content/uploads/2017/04/1db9de3ea4ade06c3023d3ba54dd980f.pdf

95. 'Japan eases immigration rules for workers', *BBC*, 8 December 2018, https://www.bbc.com/news/world-asia-46492216, Also: Mit Suru Obe, 'Five things to know about Japan's revised immigration law', *Nikkei Asia*, 1 April 2019, https://asia.nikkei.com/Spotlight/Japan-immigration/Five-things-to-know-about-Japan-s-revised-immigration-law

96. Pallavi Aiyar, 'The Poison of Choice in Japan', *The Hindu*, 16 March 2019, https://www.thehindu.com/news/international/the-poison-of-choice-for-many-japanese/article26555489.ece

97. Joseph Coleman, 'Possibility of Death Contributes to Allure Of Eating Puffer Fish', *The Washington Post*, 4 February 2001, https://www.washingtonpost.com/archive/politics/2001/02/04/possibility-of-death-contributes-to-allure-of-eating-puffer-fish/64d3e6b4-e4e1-49e3-9f30-26637060d529/

98. Pallavi Aiyar, 'Far Short of the Potential', *The Hindu*, 15 March 2018, https://www.thehindu.com/opinion/op-ed/far-short-of-the-potential/article23247078.ece

99. Aoyama Reijiro, 'Japan's Craftsmanship Goes Global: A Japanese Sushi Chef, a Bartender and a Hair Stylist Abroad', *nippon.com*, 28 March 2019. Source: https://www.nippon.com/en/japan-topics/g00660/japan%E2%80%99s-craftsmanship-goes-global-a-japanese-sushi-chef-a-bartender-and-a-hair-stylist-a.html

100. Ryusei Takahashi, 'Tokyo holds on to coveted spot as city with most stars in 2019 Michelin Guide', *The Japan Times*, 27 November 2018, https://www.japantimes.co.jp/

life/2018/11/27/food/tokyo-holds-coveted-spot-city-stars-2019-michelin-guide/#.XcijhL-Lkxc. See also: https://guide.michelin.co.jp/

101. Craig Mod, 'Tokyo Neapolitan: The New Wave of Japanese Pizza', *Eater*, 21 February 2017, https://www.eater.com/2017/2/21/14670944/best-pizza-tokyo-guide

102. Source: https://www.pizzanapoletana.org/en/

103. Emiko, '10 Golden Rules for Japanese Chopstick Manners', *Japan Talk*, https://www.japan-talk.com/jt/new/10-golden-rules-for-japanese-chopstick-manners

104. Justin McCurry, 'Looks good enough to eat: inside the home of Japan's fake food industry', *The Guardian*, 3 March 2018, https://www.theguardian.com/world/2018/mar/03/looks-good-enough-to-eat-inside-the-home-of-japans-fake-food-industry and Jay Reed and Abby Narishkin, 'How hyper-realistic plastic food became a $90 million industry in Japan', *Business Insider India*, 16 January 2019, https://www.businessinsider.com/how-fake-food-became-90-million-dollar-industry-japan-2019-1

105. Stephen Earle, *Heaven's Wind: The Life and Teachings of Nakamura Tempu-A Mind-Body Integration Pioneer*, (North Atlantic Books, 2017).

106. Ramachandra Guha, 'The other Bose: The Bengali revolutionary who patented a curry in Tokyo', *The Telegraph*, 13 June 2015, https://www.telegraphindia.com/opinion/the-other-bose/cid/1441267

107. Takeshi Nakajima, *Bose of Nakamuraya: An Indian Revolutionary in Japan* (Promilla & Co. Publishers, 2009)

108. Source: https://www.youtube.com/embed/O_
CSLU28hCI?fbclid=IwAR25rQi_IuTcguCzWxyZmUsaY-
BWrhdOegsFkX1ZMEJRnLmyOjX_cWxF_sw

109. Lisa Wallin, 'Two New Vending Machines: High-tech
Cashless Versus Old-school Origami', *Tokyo Weekender*,
20 April 2017, https://www.tokyoweekender.com/2017/04/
two-new-vending-machines-high-tech-cashless-versus-
old-school-origami/

110. Pallavi Aiyar, 'Japan's Vending Marvels', *The Mint*,
6 April 2018, https://www.livemint.com/Leisure/
PEnTFuPI1MfLutDSEnB4pN/Japans-vending-marvels.html

111. Pallavi Aiyar, 'In the men's room, China leaves India
standing', Asia Times Online, 5 December 2005. See also:
Pallavi Aiyar, 'Indonesia's Toilet Trojans', *The Hindu*,
2 December 2013, https://www.thehindu.com/opinion/
op-ed/indonesias-toilet-trojans/article5411221.ece

112. In fact, the influx of foreigners that accompanied the 1964
Tokyo Olympics was partly responsible for hastening the
transition from traditional squat toilets to the comfortable
lavatories of today's Japan.

113. Justin McCurry, 'Japan to end tourists' toilet trouble with
standardised buttons', *The Guardian*, 18 January 2017,
https://www.theguardian.com/world/2017/jan/18/japan-
to-end-tourists-toilet-trouble-with-standardised-buttons-
olympics

114. Jun'ichirō Tanazaki, *In Praise of Shadows* (Tuttle
Publishing, 1977), p. 10.

115. As of 2018, Toto had sold over 40 million washlets (as its commodes are called) worldwide and boasted over 60 percent of the Japanese toilet market share.

116. Mark Schreiber, 'Toto rolls out droll toilet humor with a whiff of class', *The Japan Times,* 13 March 2017, https://www.japantimes.co.jp/life/2017/03/13/language/poetic-praise-for-japanese-toilets/#.Xdzjm7-Lkxc. See also: https://jp.toto.com/senryu/

117. Anna Fifield, 'How Japan's toilet obsession produced some of the world's best bathrooms', *The Washington Post,* 15 December 2015, https://www.washingtonpost.com/news/worldviews/wp/2015/12/15/how-japans-toilet-obsession-produced-some-of-the-worlds-best-bathrooms/

118. Shoukei Matsumoto, *A Monk's Guide to a Clean House and Mind,* (Penguin Books, 2018).

119. Noriko Iwai, 'Measuring religion in Japan: ISM, NHK and JGSS', *Pew Research Center,* https://www.pewresearch.org/wp-content/uploads/sites/7/2017/11/Religion20171117.pdf

120. Matthew Coslett, 'Japan: The Most Religious Atheist Country', *Gaijinpot Blog,* 8 February 2015, https://blog.gaijinpot.com/japan-religious-atheist-country/

121. John Grace, 'A Monk's Guide to a Clean House and Mind by Shoukei Matsumoto – digested read', *The Guardian,* 7 January 2018, https://www.theguardian.com/books/2018/jan/07/a-monks-guide-to-a-clean-house-and-mind-by-shoukei-matsumoto-digested-read

122. Norio Tomii, 'How the punctuality of the Shinkansen has been achieved', 2010, https://www.witpress.com/Secure/elibrary/papers/CR10/CR10011FU1.pdf

123. Ethan Bernstein and Ryan W Buell. 'Trouble at Tessei', Harvard Business School Case 615-044, January 2015 (revised, October 2015).

124. 'Hot-spring resorts debate allowing tattooed tourists ahead of Rugby World Cup', *The Japan Times*, 7 July 2019, https://www.japantimes.co.jp/news/2019/07/07/national/ hot-spring-resorts-debate-allowing-tattooed-tourists-ahead-rugby-world-cup/

125. Shirley MacGregor, *Quilting with Manhole Covers - A Treasure Trove of Unique Designs from the Streets of Japan* (Carriage Trade Press, 1999)

126. Mizuho Aoki, 'Lifting the lid on Japan's growing crowd of manhole cover spotters', *The Japan Times*, 28 August 2016, https://www.japantimes.co.jp/news/2016/08/28/national/ lifting-the-lid-on-japans-growing-crowd-of-manhole-cover-spotters/#.XhfACeuLn6Y

127. 'Collectible manhole cards detailing Japan's intricate designs top 1 million issued', *The Japan Times*, 7 October 2017, https://www.japantimes.co.jp/news/2017/10/07/ national/number-manhole-cards-handed-collectors-18-months-exceeds-1-million/#.Xhe_s-uLn6Y

128. Historical sources regarding Bodhidharma are practically non-existent. Two very brief contemporary accounts disagree on his nationality (one identifies him as Persian, the other as south Indian).

129. Upendra Thakur, *India and Japan, a Study in Interaction during 5th Cent.-14th Cent. A.D.* (Abhinav Publications, 1992)

130. Hisho Saito and Elizabeth Lee, *A History of Japan* (Wentworth Press, 2016)

131. Tsukamoto Zenryū and Hirano Umeyo, 'Buddhism in the Asuka-Nara Period', *The Eastern Buddhist* 7 (1974) pp. 19-36.

132. Benoy K Behl, *Hindu Deities Worshipped in Japan* (The Hindu Group, 2019)

133. James Sanford, 'Literary Aspects of Japan's dual-Ganesa cult', in *Studies of an Asian God*, Ed. Robert L Brown, SUNY Press, 1991.

134. Source: http://www.matsuchiyama.jp/english.html

135. Noriko Inagaki, 'More Rajni please, we are Japanese', *Hindustan Times*, 10 October 2010, https://www.hindustantimes.com/entertainment/more-rajni-please-we-are-japanese/story-2K7DFCcDc7IxA6KrZFgsZN.html

136. *'I cannot write what I have in my mind about the Japanese in one short letter. Only I want that numbers of our young men should pay a visit to Japan and China every year . . . In my opinion, if all our rich and educated men once go and see Japan, their eyes will be opened. There, in Japan, you find a fine assimilation of knowledge, and not its indigestion, as we have here. They have taken everything from the Europeans, but they remain Japanese all the same, and have not turned European; while in our country, the terrible mania of becoming Westernised has seized upon us like a plague.'*
The Complete Works of Swami Vivekananda/vol. 5/'Conversations and Dialogues' (Calcutta: Advaita Ashrama, 2001).

137. Andrew B Liu, 'On the comparisons of India and China in the works of Kang Youwei and Zhang Taiyan', paper presented at the Fall 2007 Graduate Seminar on Modern Chinese Literature, Colombia University, New York, USA.

138. 'The Ideals of the East with special reference to the art of Japan, (Tōyō no risō, 1903), Awakening of the East' (1901-02) is famous for its opening paragraph, in which the author sees a spiritual unity throughout Asia, which distinguishes it from the West: '*Asia is one. The Himalayas divide, only to accentuate two mighty civilisations, the Chinese with its communism of Confucius, and the Indian with its individualism of the Vedas. But not even the snowy barriers can interrupt for one moment that broad expanse of love for the Ultimate and Universal, which is the common thought-inheritance of every Asiatic race, enabling them to produce all the great religions of the world, and distinguishing them from those maritime peoples of the Mediterranean and the Baltic, who love to dwell on the Particular, and to search out the means, not the end, of life.*'

139. 'A letter to Liang Qichao and other students on [the fact that] the Fall of India [as an independent country] was due to the Independence of Its Provinces'. Kang wrote this letter to Liang, his closest student and associate, who was also a famous intellectual, when Kang was in Darjeeling in May 1902. India was seen as country whose internal weakness, exploited by invaders, had forced it into a state of subjugation that was morally and psychologically shameful, as well as politically and economically catastrophic.

140. On 1 August1942, Rash Behari wrote about his early interactions with Sun Yat-sen: '*From my personal contact with Dr J-sen, I know how firmly he believed that Asia could never be free unless the British was destroyed root and*

branch. It was also his firm belief that the British Empire could never be destroyed so long as India was under the British yoke.' Rashbehari Bose, *His Struggle for India's Independence*, ed. Radhanath Rath, Sabitri Prasanna Chatterjee (Calcutta: Biplabi Mahanayak Rashbehari Basu Smarak Samiti, 1963), p. 185.

141. Sven Saaler and Christopher W.A. Szpilman, ed., *Pan Asianism: A Documentary History 1850–1926* (Rowan and Littlefield, 2011), pp. 234-235.

142. Rabindranath Tagore, 'The Spirit of Japan: A Lecture' delivered to the students of the private colleges of Tokyo and the members of the Indo-Japanese Association at the Keio Gijuku University, Tokyo, Japan, (Indo-Japanese Association, 1916).

143. Rabindranath Tagore, *Stray Birds* (Wilder Publications, 2008)

144. From PM Manmohan Singh's 2005 speech in Japan.

145. Ministry of Foreign Affairs, Japan. Source: https://www.mofa.go.jp/region/asia-paci/india/relation/relation.html

146. Norimitsu Onishi, 'Decades After War Trials, Japan Still Honors a Dissenting Judge', *New York Times,* 31 August 2007

147. Nakajima Takeshi, 'The Tokyo Tribunal, Justice Pal and the Revisionist Distortion of History', *The Asia-Pacific Journal* 9, no. 3 (2011), https://apjjf.org/2011/9/44/Nakajima-Takeshi/3627/article.html

148. Frederick S. Litten, 'Starving the Elephants: The Slaughter of Animals in Wartime Tokyo's Ueno Zoo', *The Asia-Pacific Journal* 7, no. 3 (2009), https://apjjf.org/-Frederick-S.-Litten/3225/article.html

149 'An elephant named Indira', *The Tropicalist*, https://www. thetropicalist.press/2017/05/an-elephant-named-indira/

150. M. Itoh, *Japanese Wartime Zoo Policy: The Silent Victims of World War II* (Palgrave MacMillan, 2010)

151. 'Nehru arrives in Japan on goodwill visit', *Stars and Stripes*, 12 August 1976 https://www.stripes.com/news/nehru-arrives-in-japan-on-goodwill-visit-1.41661

152. 'Indira, a female elephant presented to Japan by the...', UPI, https://www.upi.com/Archives/1983/08/11/Indira-a-female-elephant-presented-to-Japan-by-the/9968429422400/

153. 'Abe, Modi become Twitter pals', *The Japan Times*, 22 May 2014, https://www.japantimes.co.jp/news/2014/05/22/national/online-connection-links-indian-japanese-leaders/#.XkS3D-uLmt8

154. Pallavi Aiyar, 'The arc to Tokyo', *The Hindu*, 10 June 2017, https://www.thehindu.com/opinion/op-ed/the-arc-to-tokyo/article18951487.ece

155. 'India's railway project with Japan faces $4.5 bil. budget shortfall', *Kyodo News*, 8 February 2020, https://english.kyodonews.net/news/2020/02/297b586def24-indias-railway-project-with-japan-faces-45-bil-budget-shortfall.html

156. In mid-2020, the Indonesian government expressed interest in the possibility of integrating a separate Japanese-led medium-speed train project into the Chinese-led high-speed rail link, in the hope of spurring progress on the latter after delays in construction and ballooning costs. Koya Jibiki, 'Indonesia woos Japan as China-led high-

speed-rail project stalls', *Nikkei Asia*, 8 June 2020, https://asia.nikkei.com/Business/Transportation/Indonesia-woos-Japan-as-China-led-high-speed-rail-project-stalls

157. Shang Su-Wu, 'Is Japan's rail diplomacy on the right track in S.E. Asia?', *The Japan Times*, 12 February 2020, https://www.japantimes.co.jp/news/2019/10/28/business/japans-rail-diplomacy-right-track-s-e-asia/#.XkXvYeuLn6Y

158. Oriental Consultants, a Japanese consultancy firm focused on public transport construction management, worked with the Delhi metro team on the safety and efficiency of the construction sites. Mitsubishi Electric supplied the propulsion system for the rolling stocks and Mitsui & Co. was partnered for rail procurement.

159 Figures for 2018-19; KJM Varma, 'India-China trade dips by nearly \$3 billion in 2019', *Mint*, 14 January 2020, https://www.livemint.com/news/india/india-china-trade-dips-by-nearly-3-billion-in-2019-11579011500398.html

160. 'Daikin India aims to be a Rs 5,000-crore firm in FY20, looks for 20% growth', *The Economic Times*, 14 April 2019, Press Trust of India. https://economictimes.indiatimes.com/industry/cons-products/durables/daikin-india-aims-to-be-a-rs-5000-crore-firm-in-fy20-looks-for-20-growth/articleshow/68875720.cms?from=mdr

161. Amiti Sen, 'CAB effect: Japanese PM puts off India visit', *The Hindu Business Line*, 13 December 2019, https://www.thehindubusinessline.com/news/world/japans-pm-shinzo-abe-says-he-is-still-planning-to-visit-india-next-week/article30294451.ece

162. These included fourth-generation battle tanks, licence-built Apache attack helicopters and modern reconnaissance drones. The SDF had also begun the development of a seaborne strike force. The F-35-laden helicopter carrier Izumo was in fact being converted into an aircraft carrier.

163. Tomohiro Osaki, 'Thousands protest Abe, security bills at Diet rally', *The Japan Times*, 30 August 2015, https://www.japantimes.co.jp/news/2015/08/30/national/thousands-protest-abe-security-bills-diet-rally/

164. 'Poll shows 56% of Japanese oppose amending Constitution under Abe government', *The Japan Times*, 24 July 2019, https://www.japantimes.co.jp/news/2019/07/24/national/politics-diplomacy/56-japanese-oppose-amending-constitution-abe-government-poll-shows/#.Xlc1ZxczbR1

165. Jared Genser and Michelle Brignone, 'Shinzo Abe and the Japanese Constitution', *The Diplomat*, 20 July 2015, https://thediplomat.com/2015/07/shinzo-abe-and-the-japanese-constitution/. See also: Tomomi Yamaguchi, 'The "Japan Is Great!" Boom, Historical Revisionism, and the Government', *Asia Pacific Journal* 15, no. 3 (2017)

166. Ruchir Sharma, *Democracy on The Road: A 25 Year journey Through India* (Penguin, 2019)

167. The current government of Narendra Modi, however, appears to be bucking this decades-long trend towards anti-incumbency. See: Richard Rossow, 'The quiet decline of anti-incumbency', *Gateway House*, 24 February 2015, https://www.gatewayhouse.in/the-quiet-decline-of-anti-incumbency/

168. 'Abe faces 3 big questions over vet school scandal', *Nikkei Asia*, 19 July 2017, https://asia.nikkei.com/Politics/Abe-faces-3-big-questions-over-vet-school-scandal

   See also: Shoko Oda, 'Everything You Need to Know About the School Scandal Haunting Abe', *Bloomberg*, 12 March 2018, https://www.bloomberg.com/news/articles/2018-03-12/the-school-scandal-haunting-japan-prime-minister-abe-quicktake

   Pallavi Aiyar, 'Shinzō Abe's difficult year', *The Hindu*, 24 April 2018, https://www.thehindu.com/opinion/op-ed/shinz-abes-difficult-year/article23650516.ece

169. Pallavi Aiyar, 'When Ministers quit for bribing voters with melons and mangoes', *The Hindu*, 10 November 2019, https://www.thehindu.com/news/international/when-ministers-quit-for-bribing-voters-with-melons-and-mangoes/article29932342.ece

170. Isshu Sugawara, 'Minister quits after gifting melons and crabs to constituents', *BBC*, 25 October 2019 https://www.bbc.com/news/world-asia-50178408

171. 'Second minister in a week resigns from Japan cabinet', *Reuters*, 31 October 2019, https://www.reuters.com/article/us-japan-politics-kawai/second-minister-in-a-week-resigns-from-japan-cabinet-idUSKBN1X92RL

172. 'Japan's cherry blossom scandal starts to drag down Prime Minister Shinzo Abe's support', *The Straits Times*, 2 December 2019, https://www.straitstimes.com/asia/east-asia/japans-cherry-blossom-scandal-starts-to-drag-down-prime-minister-shinzo-abes-support

173. 'Japan's Kobe Steel indicted over quality scandal', *BBC*, 20 July 2018, https://www.bbc.com/news/business-44895564

174. Makiko Yamazaki, 'Toshiba shareholders sue in Tokyo for $2.45 million after stock plunge', *Reuters*, 7 December 2015, https://www.reuters.com/article/us-toshiba-accounting-idUSKBN0TQ0D020151207

175. 'Olympus scandal: Former bosses to pay $529m over fraud', *BBC*, 28 April 2017, https://www.bbc.com/news/business-39741921

176. 'Olympus scandal: Former bosses to pay $529m over fraud', *BBC*, 28 April 2017, https://www.bbc.com/news/business-39741921

177. Cesare M. Scartozzi, 'Hereditary Politics in Japan: A Family Business', *The Diplomat,* 9 February 2017, https://thediplomat.com/2017/02/hereditary-politics-in-japan-a-family-business/

178. 'Pocket money for Japan's salarymen continues to shrink', *Nikkei Asia*, 3 July 2017, https://asia.nikkei.com/Economy/Pocket-money-for-Japan-s-salarymen-continues-to-shrink

179. Source: https://www.brookings.edu/research/lessons-from-the-rise-of-womens-labor-force-participation-in-japan/

180. Tatsuhiro Yuki, 'Japan women hold 8% of manager jobs, far from 2020 goal of 30%', *Nikkei Asian Review,* 19 August 2020

181. Daichi Mishima, 'Japan sees record number of women working, but challenges remain', *Nikkei Asia*, 30 July 2019, https://asia.nikkei.com/Economy/Japan-sees-record-number-of-women-working-but-challenges-remain

182. Eric Johnston, 'Japan ranks at bottom of G20, and in lowest quarter globally, for percentage of female MPs', *The Japan Times*, 6 March 2019, https://www.japantimes.co.jp/news/2019/03/06/national/japan-ranks-bottom-g20-lowest-quarter-globally-percentage-female-mps/

183. Justin McCurry, 'Shinzo Abe reshuffle leaves just one woman in Japanese cabinet', *The Guardian*, 3 October 2018, https://www.theguardian.com/world/2018/oct/03/shinzo-abe-reshuffle-leaves-just-one-woman-in-japanese-cabinet-satsuki-katayama

184. Pallavi Aiyar, 'Men remain the lords of Sumo ring', *The Hindu*, 21 April 2018, https://www.thehindu.com/news/international/men-remain-the-lords-of-sumo-rings/article23630258.ece

185. 'Clear Gender Gap for Japan's Doctors', *nippon.com*, 18 March 2020, https://www.nippon.com/en/japan-data/h00652/clear-gender-gap-for-japan%E2%80%99s-doctors.html

186. Pallavi Aiyar, 'Working Overtime to Death in Japan', *The Hindu*, 19 February 2017, https://www.thehindu.com/news/international/Working-overtime-to-death-in-Japan/article17327183.ece

187. 'Labor productivity per hour in Japan 2000-2018', *statista.com*, 13 October 2020, https://www.statista.com/statistics/878174/japan-labor-productivity-per-hour/

188. Lauren Smiley, '27 Days in Tokyo Bay: What Happened on the Diamond Princess,' *Wired*, 30 April 2020, https://www.wired.com/story/diamond-princess-coronavirus-covid-19-tokyo-bay/

189. Rupakjyoti Borah, 'Why Japan Hesitated Before Postponing the 2020 Olympics', *The Diplomat*, 27 March 2020, https://thediplomat.com/2020/03/why-japan-hesitated-before-postponing-the-2020-olympics/

190. 'Abe denies wife attended cherry blossom party in defiance of coronavirus calls to abstain', *Japan Times*, 27 March 2020, https://www.japantimes.co.jp/news/2020/03/27/national/politics-diplomacy/abe-denies-wife-attended-cherry-blossom-party-defiance-coronavirus-calls-abstain/

191. Lucy Dayman, 'Small, Stained and, Actually, Expensive: Why "Abenomask" Is An Epic Fail', *Tokyo Weekender*, 27 April 2020, https://www.tokyoweekender.com/2020/04/why-abenomask-is-a-failure/

192. Emiko Jozuka, 'Japan leader Shinzo Abe's video at home with pet dog prompts social media backlash', *CNN*, 13 April 2020 https://edition.cnn.com/2020/04/13/asia/japan-coronavirus-pm-video-backlash-dp-intl-hnk-scli/index.html

193. 'Osaka mayor sets Twitter abuzz with claim that women dawdle at shops', *The Japan Times*, 24 April 2020, https://www.japantimes.co.jp/news/2020/04/24/national/osaka-mayor-ichiro-matsui-women-shopping/

194. 'Japan's cyber-security minister has "never used a computer"', *BBC*, 15 November 2018, https://www.bbc.com/news/technology-46222026

195. Leo Lewis, 'How coronavirus exposed Japan's low-tech blind spot', Financial Times, 15 April 2020, https://www.ft.com/content/7992a88a-7dde-11ea-82f6-150830b3b99a

196. Isabel Reynolds, 'Coronavirus Is Forcing Japan to Rethink Its Custom of Stamping Documents by Hand', *Time*, 28 April 2020, https://time.com/5828326/japan-coronavirus-hanko-office-traditions/

197. Mitsuru Obe, 'Screen-shunning doctors open up to telehealth in pandemic era', *Nikkei Asian Review*, 7 April 2020, https://asia.nikkei.com/Spotlight/Coronavirus/Screen-shunning-doctors-open-up-to-telehealth-in-pandemic-era

198. More than half a million children died of diarrhea every year globally. Source: https://ourworldindata.org/childhood-diarrheal-diseases

199. Rabindranath Tagore, 'The Spirit of Japan: A Lecture' delivered to the students of the private colleges of Tokyo and the members of the Indo-Japanese Association at the Keio Gijuku University, Tokyo, Japan (Indo-Japanese Association, Tokyo, 1916).

Acknowledgements

Many thanks for many reasons, and in no particular order, to:

Shekhar Aiyar, Gitanjali Aiyar, Julio Arias, Swaminathan Aiyar, Kiran Ganguli, Jean-Pierre Lehmann, Moko Igarashi, Jeff Kingston, Beth Thomas, Sohini Basak, Udayan Mitra, Miko Yamanouchi, James Kondo, Preeti Kothari, Vivek Kothari, Yumiko Watanabe, Yoko Renner, Wakako Ch'en, Miyuki Hayashi Suyari, Obiageli Onyekpe, Zubin Atre, Arisa Koyama, Maho Furuya, Shun Nagao, Shokei Matsumoto, Sol Ramos, Santosh, Barun Mitra, Junichi Yano, Kumi Fujisawa, Anna Jassem, Brajeshwar Banerjee, Vikram Shahani, Michiko Takaishi, Gwen Robinson, Muanpuii Saiawi , Mukund Padmanabhan, Ishaan, Nico.

About the Author

Pallavi Aiyar is an award-winning foreign correspondent who has reported from across China, Europe, Indonesia and Japan. She is the author of several books of fiction and non-fiction, including the bestselling China memoir, *Smoke and Mirrors.* She currently lives in Spain with her family – human and feline.

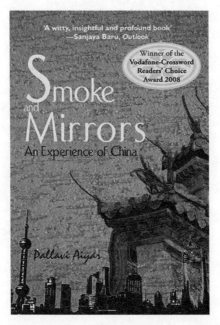